Robert
ALDRICH

a guide to
references and resources

A
Reference
Publication
in
Film

Ronald Gottesman

Editor

Robert
ALDRICH

---

a guide to
references and resources

ALAIN SILVER

ELIZABETH WARD

G.K.HALL&CO.
70 LINCOLN STREET, BOSTON, MASS.

Distributed in the United Kingdom and Europe
by George Prior Associated Publishers Ltd.,
37-41 Bedford Row, London WC1R 4JH, England
ISBN (U.K.)   0-86043-232-7

Library of Congress Cataloging in Publication Data

Silver, Alain, 1947-
    Robert Aldrich : a guide to references and sources.

    (A Reference publication in film)
    Based on Silver's master's thesis, UCLA, 1973.
    Includes indexes.
    1. Aldrich, Robert, 1918-   --Bibliography.
I. Ward, Elizabeth, joint author. II. Title.
III. Series.
Z8025.49.S56   [PN1998.A3]   016.79143'0233'0924
ISBN 0-8161-7993-X   79-4676

This publication is printed on permanent/durable acid-free paper
MANUFACTURED IN THE UNITED STATES OF AMERICA

Contents

Preface

The basis for this reference guide was "Robert Aldrich: A Critical Study," a Master of Theater Arts thesis by Alain Joel Silver, completed at the University of California, Los Angeles, in 1973. The research was conducted at UCLA and at the Maragaret Herrick Library of The Academy of Motion Picture Arts and Sciences. The thesis contains extensive critical analyses of each film and is available for reading at the UCLA Research Library and Theater Arts Library, and also through University Microfilms.*

For this reference guide, additional research was conducted at the Margaret Herrick Library and the Charles K. Feldman Library at the American Film Institute, Center for Advanced Film Studies.

Archival sources and special collections specifically on Robert Aldrich have not been located in the western United States. We consulted Linda Harris Mehr, the bibliographer of *Motion Pictures, Television, and Radio: A Union Catalogue of Manuscripts and Special Collections in the Western United States* (Boston: G.K. Hall, 1977) — a project of the Film and Television Study Center.** Ms. Mehr informed us that her extensive field research has not uncovered any special collections especially pertinent to Robert Aldrich at the present time in the western United States. Unfortunately, there is no similar inventory of collections for the remainder of the United States.

Copies of the screenplays and stills from any motion picture, including Robert Aldrich's films, are closely guarded but often uncatalogued, as library procedures for motion picture materials have not been standardized. Therefore, as with the lack of published information concerning archival and special collections, it is difficult to ascertain which screenplays and other materials are available without visiting each library. Indeed, to make use of any part of a library's motion picture collection requires a personal visit because interlibrary loans of original materials are quite rare and copyright restrictions prohibit screenplays being copied in any manner. Following are the addresses of the major motion picture collections and libraries in the United States.

* Address: 300 North Zeeb Road, Ann Arbor, MI 48106.
**Address: P.O. Box 38775, Los Angeles, CA 90038.

Margaret Herrick Library
Academy of Motion Picture Arts and Sciences
8949 Wilshire Blvd.
Beverly Hills, CA 90211

Charles K. Feldman Library
American Film Institute, Center for
  Advanced Film Studies
501 Doheny Rd.
Beverly Hills, CA 90210

Theater Arts Library
University Research Library
University of California, Los Angeles
405 Hilgard Ave.
Los Angeles, CA 90024

Department of Special Collections
Doheny Library
University of Southern California
University Park
Los Angeles, CA 90007

George Eastman House
Library
900 East Avenue
Rochester, NY 14607

Museum of Modern Art
Department of Film
11 W. 53rd. St.
New York, NY 10019

Library and Museum of the Performing Arts
Theater Collection
New York Public Library
Lincoln Center
111 Amsterdam Ave.
New York, NY 10023

Library of Congress
Motion Picture Division
Washington, DC 20541

Wisconsin Center for Theater Research
University of Wisconsin
1166 Van Hise Hall
1220 Linden Drive
Madison, WI 53706

ACKNOWLEDGMENTS

Thanks, first of all, to Robert Aldrich for an interview, a coke, and for making the films. Thanks also to his company's associates, in particular to William Aldrich, for reference materials and loan of film prints, and to Joan Bennett; to Pattie Zimerman of Lorimar Productions; to Pierre Sauvage for a preview copy of his interview with Aldrich; to Elmer and Christiane Silver, Paul and Roberta Ward for reading parts of the manuscript; to Anne Schlosser, Bonnie Baty, Terry Roach, Bonnie Rothbart, Stacy Endres, Debra Bergman, Carol Cullen, Mary Olivarez, Cheryl Behnke, and Sam Gill for patient library research assistance; to Ian Cameron and James Ursini for bibliographic information; to Blake Lucas for refreshing our memory of *The Last Sunset;* to David Bradley and Nick Peterson for other titles; to Susan Pile . for material on *No Knife;* to Janey Place, Richard Symington, The American Cinema, and The Film Screening Cooperative for help in screening prints; and finally, to *Film Comment* for permission to reprint the interview.

Biography

Robert Aldrich was born on August 9, 1918, in Cranston, Rhode Island, the son of Edward and Lora Lawson Aldrich. The Aldriches are a prominent banking family with business and political ties. His aunt Abby was Mrs. John D. Rockefeller; his paternal grandfather, Nelson W. Aldrich, had been a United States Senator; his uncle Richard was a member of Congress; and his uncle Winthrop was Ambassador to Great Britain.

Aldrich's memories of his education center on football: he played tackle at the Moses Brown School in Providence and was later on the varsity team of the University of Virginia, where he majored in economics, ostensibly to prepare for a banking career. Although he spent four years at the University he did not complete his Bachelor's degree. But he had been head of the campus dance society, booking such orchestras as the Dorsey Brothers and Glenn Miller. Ultimately he decided that show business was a more interesting area of endeavor than banking. In 1940 an uncle with Hollywood connections got Aldrich a six month trial job as production clerk at RKO studios for twenty-five dollars a week. He did the usual production office "go-fer" work: delivering messages, answering telephones, getting coffee, eventually moving up to filing actors' time cards, call sheets, and production reports. Like most "go-fers" he worked for little pay, hoping for someone important to notice and promote him. Soon he became a third assistant director, a job not unlike a clerk in duties: but it was the first rung on a well-defined ladder of production positions which led to promotion to second assistant and eventually first assistant director.

Joan of Paris (1942), starring Michele Morgan in her American debut and directed by Robert Stevenson, was Aldrich's first job as second assistant director. For the next two years he worked on RKO films directed by Irving Reis, Richard Wallace, Edward Dmytryk, Leslie Goodwins and John H. Auer. He quickly learned that the director is the "creative hub" of motion pictures and that "if you have ambition, and you don't want to be a producer or a writer, then you want to be a director."[1] Although few directors have emerged from the ranks of assistant directors, Aldrich had such an ambition. He also claims that luck played a part; an old football injury released him from duty after three days in the Motion Picture Unit of the Air Force in

World War II, and the lack of manpower in the studios made a young, energetic and eager second assistant like Aldrich stand out on the set.

He was promoted to first assistant on the Edgar Kennedy and the Leon Errol comedy shorts being produced at RKO and then took the risk of leaving the studio system to do freelance work on feature films in 1944. Immediately after leaving RKO, he began work as first assistant director for Jean Renoir on the *The Southerner* (1945). From 1945 to 1948 Aldrich was under contract to Enterprise Studios, serving variously as a unit production manager, studio manager, and assistant screenwriter. Simultaneously, he worked as first assistant director on numerous United Artists productions. In 1949 he began working independently in various capacities in both motion picture and television production.

These years exposed Aldrich to the methods of directors, producers, and screenwriters whom he considered "the best."[2] He credits learning diplomacy with actors from Lewis Milestone and Joseph Losey (for whom Aldrich played a bit as ringside fan in *The Big Night*), concentration from William Wellman, authenticity and precision of set and costumes from Jean Renoir, and the importance of energy and enthusiasm from Charles Chaplin. Aldrich worked with these men and with screenwriters such as Dalton Trumbo, Hugo Butler, Ring Lardner, Jules Dassin, Robert Rossen and Abraham Polonsky (also as director) just prior to the major HUAC investigations and the blacklist. Many were making their last films before leaving the country or prematurely retiring. Later, as a director, Aldrich wrote *World For Ransom* with Butler, who had to remain uncredited despite Aldrich's bitter fight with the Writers Guild on Butler's behalf. Aldrich claims he was just "too dumb or too young to be a communist," that when he worked with these men "the heat was already on and they weren't looking for recruits."[2] However, the blacklist continued to have an indirect influence and occasionally to impinge on his projects. For example, an original screenplay, "The Gamma People," was written by Aldrich for John Garfield and Irving Allen in 1950, but Garfield was on the "greylist" and ultimately could not make the picture. Allen later sold the property and the picture was produced, several rewrites later, in England in 1956, without Aldrich having an opportunity for further participation.

In the early fifties, television, being filmed or broadcast live in New York, desperately needed directors, particularly since most established film directors refused to go east and work for the minimum salaries offered them. Walter Blake (who has been associate producer on many Aldrich films) stretched the truth and convinced the producers of the Proctor and Gamble shows that Aldrich had codirected Chaplin in *Limelight* (1952) and was a budding genius. Proctor and Gamble offered Aldrich a weekly half-hour series entitled "The Doctor," and he went to New York. Subsequently Aldrich directed Dan Duryea in the "China Smith" series and several programs for

"Four Star Playhouse." In 1953 he began making television pilots ("Adventures in Paradise" and "The Sundance Kid"), not only because they paid more but also because their production schedules were longer and gave him more time for creative work.

Meanwhile, in Hollywood, Herbert Baker (who had written *So This Is New York,* on which Aldrich was assistant director in 1948) was working with MGM producer Matthew Rapf on a screenplay for *The Big Leaguer.* Baker recommended Aldrich as a "very bright guy" directing television in New York who also knew both the Hollywood industry and athletes. Aldrich got the job as director of the film. The picture was shot quickly in Florida, and Aldrich returned to New York television work.

During a four week break in the "China Smith" series, Aldrich and the crew (including cinematographer Joe Biroc) convinced the series' producer, Bernard Tabakin, to make a feature on the same set. They shot the resulting film, *World For Ransom,* in ten and a half days--a day and a half over schedule. To get money for completion of the picture, Aldrich and his crew shot several beer and "Eversharp" razor blade commercials and pooled their salaries. Aldrich's first of many clashes with establishment censors came with *World For Ransom* (1954). The film originally opened with a shot of a couple's embrace that gradually revealed that the female lead (Marian Carr) was kissing another woman. The scene was deleted.

Despite its low budget and short schedule *World For Ransom* convinced Harold Hecht and Burt Lancaster of Aldrich's ability to direct their upcoming project, *Apache,* later that year. Aldrich had worked with Hecht on *Ten Tall Men* in 1951 and had originally wanted to buy the novel by Paul I. Wellman but couldn't afford it. Instead, Aldrich made himself affordable to Hecht and Lancaster. Aldrich feels he didn't do as well as he should have in directing the film because he was compromised. Originally, Aldrich and Lancaster agreed that the Apache, Massai (played by Lancaster) should be shot in the back by Federal troops. United Artists preferred that Massai walk away from the soldiers unharmed and insisted they shoot both endings. Aldrich learned that "If you shoot two they will always use the other one, never yours."[3]

The association with Hecht-Lancaster continued through 1954-55 with *Vera Cruz.* For the first time, Aldrich had two weeks of rehearsals, a method he has used whenever possible since then. While the actors rehearse, Aldrich walks the set and experiments mentally to gather a visual impression of the effectiveness of the scene. Aldrich also draws a modified storyboard he calls a "worksheet," listing his action cuts, which gives him a sense of working continuity to carry him through the necessarily out-of-sequence filming.

Vera Cruz was highly successful commercially and gave Aldrich bargaining power. He could now afford to choose his next project. *Kiss Me Deadly* was offered to Aldrich by Victor Saville, who owned the rights to Mickey Spillane's works and became executive producer of the film. As Aldrich explains it, he kept the title, threw the book away, and had Al Bezzerides write a "sensational" script.[4] *Kiss Me Deadly* (1955) and the plot's "great whatsit" unleashed critical praise for Aldrich, especially in France, which later caused Aldrich to comment that he regretted making the picture because he was apprehensive that it was not as good as some people thought. While the film's references to classical and romantic myths may have rated extensive critical discussion, Aldrich again caught the attention of the censors, and the Legion of Decency demanded the exclusion of a scene in which Madie Comfort sings while caressing a microphone.

Aldrich used the commercial success of *Kiss Me Deadly* to gain another measure of independence. In 1955 the "Associates and Aldrich Company" was formed with Walter Blake and others to produce *The Big Knife*. It remained in existence for twelve subsequent features through 1972. *The Big Knife*, Clifford Odets' play about Hollywood corruption, was reworked by Aldrich and James Poe and led to the Golden Lion Directorial Award at the 1955 Venice Film Festival, a confirmation of growing critical esteem for Aldrich's work in Europe. The following year Aldrich signed a two-year contract with Columbia Pictures, whose President, Harry Cohn, did not realize that it was Aldrich who had directed the caricature of him in *The Big Knife*.

Aldrich's first picture for Columbia was *Autumn Leaves,* which Aldrich considers a "classy soap opera,"[5] made because he wanted to direct something other than cruelty and violence. At first Joan Crawford and Aldrich were at odds over the screenplay. She demanded that Aldrich use her writer or she would not report to the studio. Aldrich refused; and Crawford appeared but would not speak to him for five days. Finally, when she saw that her portrayal of a scene had brought tears to his eyes, she embraced him, and they remained friends until her death.

Cohn and Aldrich could not decide on a subsequent project at Columbia, so Aldrich, a believer in keeping a large stock of projects, independently produced and directed *Attack!* as adapted by James Poe from the play "Fragile Fox" by Norman Brooks. Despite the lack of armed forces assistance--the Army refused to loan tanks to the production because, among other things, it disapproved of a plot involving cowardly officers and "fragging"--*Attack!* was completed on schedule in 1956.

Prior to their release, Aldrich took both *Attack!* and *Autumn Leaves* to the 1956 summer film festivals in Berlin and Venice. *Autumn Leaves* won Aldrich the Silver Bear for Best Direction in Berlin, and *Attack!* won several awards in Venice. François Truffaut had interviewed Aldrich in Venice after the success of *The Big Knife* in 1955, and they met often during the summer of 1956.

When Aldrich returned to the U.S. he began work in New York on *The Garment Jungle* for Columbia. At about the same time Harry Cohn realized Aldrich had mocked him in *The Big Knife* and, not unexpectedly, felt tricked.

Problems began on *The Garment Jungle* when Aldrich learned that the script had not been "cleared" to prevent harassment from the underworld [see Appendix p. 159]. Shaken, Aldrich returned to Hollywood, where Cohn smoothed out the problems temporarily. Then Lee J. Cobb protested the unsympathetic attitude of his character, Walter Mitchell, and Cohn became more apprehensive about Aldrich's tough exposé of the New York garment industry and urged him to "soften" the script. Aldrich refused, and when he fell ill with flu and missed one day of filming, Cohn used it as an excuse to replace him with Vincent Sherman. Aldrich claims he has never seen the finished film.[6]

Columbia was required by contract to continue to pay Aldrich's salary, but he returned home without any projects and constrained by Cohn from finding other work in Hollywood. Finally he was offered *The Phoenix,* an English novel to be produced by Michael Carreras for Hammer-Seven Arts and to be shot in Europe with an American cast.

For the next five years (1957-62) Aldrich became an international director. *The Phoenix*, retitled *Ten Seconds To Hell* in the U.S., was shot in Berlin; *The Angry Hills* in Greece; *The Last Sunset* in Mexico; and *Sodom And Gomorrah* in Morocco and Rome. He considers *Sodom And Gomorrah* a marvelous experience but has labeled the others as "awful, just awful."[7]

While in Berlin, Aldrich met Sibylle Siegfried, a German fashion model, whom he married in 1966. Aldrich's previous marriage, from 1941 to 1965, had been to Harriet Foster, with whom he had four children: Adell, born 1943; William, born 1944; Alida, born 1947; and Kelly, born 1952. Adell has worked as script supervisor on several Aldrich films and is now directing motion pictures; William is a professional motion picture producer; Kelly is a Teamster driver captain for motion pictures; and Alida is also involved with Aldrich Co. productions and assisted her sister on a feature film made for television.

During this European period and for several years following, Aldrich first made public his dissatisfaction with the American motion picture industry through a number of published interviews and articles. One article written by Aldrich candidly explained his problems working in Europe and the financial and critical failure of his four pictures.[8] Still, Aldrich sought a blockbuster. Two projects, "Taras Bulba" and "The Czar's Bride," both about Asia in the sixteenth century, excited him a great deal; but both needed the cooperation of the Soviet Union. *Taras Bulba* was finally planned for production in Yugoslavia and England, to star Anthony Quinn; but United Artists withdrew financing, leaving Aldrich almost bankrupt. To retain his home, Aldrich sold the proposed film property for $75,000. Unwittingly, however, he sold it to United Artists and Burt Lancaster, whom Aldrich had previously approached to play Taras. The film was ultimately made in Argentina, starring Yul Brynner and directed by J. Lee Thompson. This was a particularly disappointing turn of events for Aldrich, who feels akin to the character and has said "I *am* Taras."[9]

Aldrich returned to Hollywood in 1962 to make *What Ever Happened To Baby Jane*. Contrary to industry opinion regarding the incompatibility of long-established female stars, he teamed Bette Davis with Joan Crawford in the film. They were his only choices for the parts, and he succeeded in gaining their enthusiastic participation. It was Davis's idea, for instance, to wear chalky makeup. *Baby Jane* grossed $12,000,000 over its $825,000 negative cost. This gave Associates and Aldrich back the financial independence lost in the Columbia dispute and overseas work.

After *Baby Jane*, Aldrich's Hollywood reputation was reestablished. He had no trouble packaging *Four For Texas* (1963), with Frank Sinatra and Dean Martin, and *Hush...Hush Sweet Charlotte* (1964), a sequel to *Baby Jane* with Bette Davis and Olivia De Havilland in a part Joan Crawford gave up due to illness. *The Flight Of The Phoenix* (1966), however, failed commercially.

His next film, *The Dirty Dozen* (1967), became the success Aldrich had wanted. It has grossed over $30,000,000. The sale of his residual ten percent interest in the picture allowed Associates and Aldrich to make "The Dream Deal."[10] At a cost of more than a million dollars, they purchased and remodeled the educational film studio of John Sutherland in east Hollywood, a studio originally built in 1913 to house Famous Players-Lasky. The Aldrich Studios opened in August 1968; it was planned to produce between eight and sixteen features there over a five year period. In 1970, Aldrich announced further expansion of his studio and business interests. Associates and Aldrich asked the Securities Exchange Commission for permission to offer $63,000,000 of stock after combining with two diversified companies holding tax shelter interests. This combine would have supported production and distribution of the Aldrich Studio pictures, but the plan was abandoned. The initial productions, *The Legend Of Lylah Clare* (1968), *The Killing Of Sister George* (1968) (with additional problems incurred by a lengthy dispute over its "X" rating and the loss of a lawsuit against the media for refusal to run advertising), and the $140,000 experiment on a "mini-picture" to sell the script and test a new actress for *The Greatest Mother Of 'Em All* (1969), proved unprofitable. This forced Aldrich into a four picture coproduction contract with ABC-Palomar *(Too Late The Hero* [1970]; *The Grissom Gang* [1971]; *Whatever Happened To Aunt Alice?* [1969]) which was terminated after the third picture. In 1972, the last Aldrich Studios production, *Ulzana's Raid*, barely broke even and could not save the studio. Aldrich felt he had "devised a better mousetrap but there weren't any more mice."[11] He admitted the studio was a disaster and sold it to Video Cassette Industries for an undisclosed sum in July 1973.

Aldrich had begun production of *Emperor Of The North Pole* for 20th Century-Fox a year prior to the sale of his studios, and it was released over the fourth of July weekend in 1973. Its lack of public response confounded Aldrich, who was willing to take the blame for financial "dogs"[12] such as *The*

Legend Of Lylah Clare, in which instance he believed his work as a producer was poor, but could not understand the box office failures of *Emperor Of The North Pole, The Grissom Gang,* and *The Flight Of The Phoenix*, which he felt were expertly crafted in all aspects.

Aldrich had been announced to direct *The Yakuza* for Warners, but its star, Robert Mitchum, disapproved, and Aldrich was dropped. "If *Emperor Of The North Pole* had taken off in its New York opening, I'd have dropped him, he wouldn't have dropped me."[13] claims Aldrich, who would have preferred Lee Marvin for the lead in *The Yakuza.*

Instead, Aldrich concentrated on *The Longest Yard*, from a story written by Al Ruddy in the early 1970's. Only after Ruddy's success as producer on *The Godfather* was he able to sell the idea of a prisoner-versus-guards football game to Paramount. Aldrich read the script by Tracy Keenan Wynn; a self-avowed "football nut," he believed it took someone who had played football and was "freaked out" about it to direct the picture.[14] Aldrich found the film's star, Burt Reynolds, an ideal choice, because the actor had played college football at Florida State before an injury prevented him from becoming a professional player. The picture was originally planned for production in Florida; but difficulties with penal authorities there made it necessary to move to Georgia, where then-Governor Jimmy Carter smoothed out all problems, ultimately inviting Aldrich to join the state's Film Advisory Committee.

While completing *The Longest Yard*, Reynolds became interested in a script entitled "City of the Angels" by Steve Shagan, author of *Save The Tiger*. Reynolds and Aldrich formed "RoBurt Productions" and collectively bought the script. After several title changes, it became *Hustle*. Because Aldrich believed U.S. audiences would not accept an American actress playing a call-girl heroine, he and Reynolds traveled to Paris and offered the female lead to Catherine Deneuve, who accepted. *Hustle* (1975) became the first picture which Aldrich had shot on location in Los Angeles since *The Big Knife.*

In July 1975, while at work on *Hustle*, Aldrich was elected president of the Directors Guild of America for a two-year term succeeding Robert Wise. His major concerns were the DGA conflict with the Writers Guild over writer's and director's credits and the DGA Trust and Retirement Fund. Aldrich hoped that the Inter-Guild Council, a new federation of the Screen Actors, Writers, Directors and Producers Guilds which he had helped form would provide a forum for airing differences between these organizations.

Both *The Longest Yard* and *Hustle* were commercially successsful pictures, returning Aldrich to a relatively independent financial position. His major project for 1976 was *Twilight's Last Gleaming*, an international picture coproduced by Lorimar Productions and Bavaria-Atelier in Munich. This film created controversy among distributors and critics because of the political intentions of the production; but its mediocre box office returns convinced Aldrich that despite his belief, often stated by General Dell in the film, that "the people should know," the people "just don't want to."[15]

Nonetheless, Lorimar Productions had already engaged Aldrich to direct Joseph Wambaugh's screenplay of his best-selling novel about Los Angeles policemen, *The Choirboys*. Additionally, Aldrich reorganized his "Aldrich Company."

The first well published action of Aldrich's initial two-year term as President of the Directors Guild of America was a dispute between the DGA and the Writers Guild of America over "possessory" screenplay credit. Historically, screenwriters have little control over the final version of a shooting script. The WGA was attempting to change this situation for their membership by negotiating for strict rewrite provisions in renewed contracts with signatory producers of The Alliance[16] and of the Association of Motion Picture and Television Producers. The DGA threatened to strike if certain of these provisions guaranteeing that only the screenwriter could change the screenplay during production were accepted by the producers. The DGA claimed these stipulations would make it impossible for a director to work. Ultimately, the Writers Guild was forced to withdraw their demands.

Shortly after, Joseph Wambaugh discovered that Aldrich was making changes in the screenplay of *The Choirboys* and immediately took action to have his screenwriter credit removed from the film. Wambaugh also has filed suit against Lorimar Productions for $1,000,000, claiming that they had promised to leave his script intact; but Aldrich has never worked that way with a script.

After being elected to a second term as President of the DGA, Aldrich prepared for difficult negotiations with The Alliance and the Association of Motion Picture and Television Producers over the renewal of the Directors Guild contract which expired December 31, 1977. He was quoted as saying that he accepted the new term because he was assured the DGA membership would, if necessary, follow him through to a strike to achieve their goals.[17] Aldrich hired a team of professional bargaining agents to assist the DGA members in negotiations. A strike proved unnecessary when the Producers' Association granted the Directors Guild the most extensive increase in salaries and benefits in industry history. Since then Aldrich has brought plans before the membership for a new headquarters building to include both offices and a massive inter-guild complex of screening and conference rooms.

The Choirboys was released at the end of 1977 and proved both a critical and financial failure. In early 1978, Lorimar concluded the Wambaugh suit with an undisclosed but reputedly substantial out-of-court settlement.[18] Aldrich had anticipated that *The Choirboys* would at least be financially successful. This second box-office failure in a row led Aldrich to a reassessment of his personal projects in the first months of 1978, and in the second half of that year he accepted an offer from Warner Bros. to replace Richard Donner as director of a Gene Wilder comedy-Western entitled *No Knife.*[19] As this book went to press, Aldrich was in the process of editing *No Knife* for release in the summer of 1979 and has tentatively agreed to undertake another project for the producer of *No Knife* in late 1979.[20]

NOTES

1. Pierre Sauvage, entry 178, p. 56.
2. Appendix.
3. Joel Greenburg, entry 107, p. 9.
4. Charles Higham, entry 153, p. 19.
5. Charles Higham, entry 153, p. 19.
6. Joel Greenburg, entry 107, p. 10.
7. Pierre Sauvage, entry 178.
8. Robert Aldrich, entry 859.
9. Harry Ringel, entry 155, p. 12.
10. A.D. Murphy, entry 108.
11. Harry Ringel, entry 155, p. 14.
12. Harry Ringel, entry 154, p. 167.
13. Harry Ringel, entry 155, p. 16.
14. Charles Higham, entry 153, p. 20
15. Bridget Byrne, entry 768.
16. A bargaining unit formed by Paramount Studios and Universal-MCA after their withdrawal from the A.M.P.T.P. in 1975.
17. Army Archerd, entry 186.
18. *Los Angeles Herald Examiner,* entry 787.
19. Army Archerd, *Daily Variety* (5 September 1978), p. 2.
20. *Daily Variety* (16 January 1979), p. 3.

The Director: Critical Survey

Robert Aldrich's films concentrate on the most basic situation: man attempting to survive in a hostile universe. Like most filmmakers, Aldrich uses and reuses such general devices as narrative tension between subjective and objective viewpoints and frustration or fulfillment of the audience's genre expectations. There is nothing unusual or distinctive in this process as such. Generally speaking, all films can be classed by genre and narrative mode. What isolates Aldrich, like any author, is his choice of narrative elements, which might also be called his thematic preoccupations or world view, and the organizing structure (style) which he imposes upon them.

In order to survive, certain Aldrich heroes can be more consistently vicious, self-centered and cynical than any villain. "You're the kind of person that has only one true love: you" (Hammer in *Kiss Me Deadly,* 1955). "I'm not sick, I'm in love...with me" (Zarkan in *The Legend of Lylah Clare,* 1968). Others like Massai in *Apache,* Joe Costa in *Attack!,* and Phil Gaines in *Hustle* are driven by an irreducible and essentially idealistic personal code to behavior that is perhaps even more extreme than either Hammer's or Zarkan's. Characters who are in narrative terms basically antagonists, like Joe Erin in *Vera Cruz* and Wirtz in *Ten Seconds to Hell,* may both reflect on and try to explain their compulsive destructiveness by telling stories that recount the murder of an adolescent father figure who had taught them to look out for number one. In films such as these, the presence of a ruthless pragmatism in one of the two principals would normally promise a clear-cut alignment into hero and villain, into Erin versus Ben Trane, Karl Wirtz versus Eric Koertner, black versus white. The actual result is ambiguous: each film is less than absolute in its definition of a moral man yet is absolute in its definition of morality. In *Vera Cruz* and *Ten Seconds to Hell,* the protagonist does finally defeat the antagonist; but the triumph is more societal than personal. In *Flight of the Phoenix* (1966) and *Too Late the Hero* (1970), the moral distinctions between the members of a group are so finely drawn that the chance or haphazard manner deciding which of them live and which die constitutes the pervasive irony of the films. As Major Reisman counsels the prisoner Wladislaw early in *The Dirty Dozen,* innocence or guilt, reward or condemnation, are purely matters of circumstance. "You only made one mistake," he says, pausing by the cell door and grinning back at the man sentenced to death; "you let somebody see you."

In this sense, Aldrich is a rigorous determinist. His fables about bands of outsiders, including *Attack!, Ten Seconds to Hell, The Flight of the Phoenix, The Dirty Dozen, Too Late the Hero, Ulzana's Raid, The Longest Yard,* and *Twilight's Last Gleaming,* all isolate a group of men in a specific, self-contained and threatening universe: soldiers behind enemy lines; a bomb disposal unit in postwar Berlin; passengers on a plane down in the Sahara; inmates of a prison; ex-convicts in a missile silo. In such situations they undergo an inexorable moral reduction, in which both the idealists and the decadents--the social extremists--perish. Usually, the conflicts are between men and nature and between men and other men. In the few films that do focus on women *(The Killing of Sister George, Whatever Happened To Baby Jane, Hush...Hush, Sweet Charlotte),* the focus is on the deviate and the psychotic.

An interior consistency of theme and style accounts for the fact that Aldrich's films are difficult to classify according to genre. Erin and Wirtz relate their twisted, parallel histories in the context of an adventure Western and a return-from-the-war melodrama respectively. Zarkan is a retired film director, Hammer is a private detective: yet their self-love, their egocentric disdain for the lives and feelings of others, and their inability to rectify this attitude even when presented with second chances are traits which mark them as sibling personalities despite radically different genre backgrounds.

Aldrich's visualization also transcends the stylistic conventions of genre. Strong sidelighting, angles of unusual height or lowness, foreground clutter, and staging in depth appear as frequently in his Westerns as in his war pictures or his neo-Gothic thrillers and are as readily integrated into the stark, action milieu of a fifties *film noir* like *Kiss Me Deadly* as they are into the richly colored frames of a sixties psychological melodrama like *The Legend of Lylah Clare.* Transmuting and expressing in sensory terms the physical and emotional makeup of the situation, of the characters caught in these frames, remains the basic dynamic of an Aldrich picture regardless of genre. More often from a disturbingly high or low angle than from a natural eye level, Aldrich's camera will capture a figure crouching behind a lamp (Charlies Castle's favorite retreat in *The Big Knife)* or lurking at the edge of a pool of light (like Lily Carver in *Kiss Me Deadly).* Grimacing faces or dark objects will suddenly intrude into the foreground of medium long shots, disturbing previously flaccid compositions, possibly in anticipation of a violent turn in plot events. Recurring high angle medium shots peer down from behind ceiling ventilators (in *World for Ransom, The Angry Hills, Hush...Hush, Sweet Charlotte,* and *Too Late The Hero)* so that the dark blades slowly rotating above the characters' heads become an ominous shorthand externalizing the tension whirring incessantly inside them. Conversely, the hissing sound of man's life leaking out *(Kiss Me Deadly)* or a *post mortem* burst of gunfire

(*Attack!*) become objective correlatives to the dissipation of the audience's tension.

In a subjective manner, the characters sometimes "choose" to situate themselves within the frame. For the guilt-ridden Charles Castle, the lamps about the room have a symbolic value which unconsciously draws him back to them again and again. Or characters may be placed objectively: Lily Carver at the edge of the light is simultaneously in a figurative darkness appropriate to her mental state. The overhead ventilators are variable metaphors: in *World for Ransom* the fan in the room where Mike Callahan is interrogated by an underworld figure is not only a distracting influence at the frame's center but casts multiple shadows on the surrounding walls and defocuses the reading of the shot away from the human figures to create a visual confusion appropriate to Callahan's emotions. In *The Angry Hills,* a crane down to eye-level from an opening position behind a similar fan diminishes the object's importance as a distraction and suggests an unwinding, an impending detente rather than a knotting up of plot events. In both these pictures, Aldrich adapts the photographic styles of *film noir* to make specific visual statements about characters and events. In Callahan's initial movements through the somber streets, alleys, and stairwells of Singapore, angle and editing shift the wedges of light and the dim boundaries of narrow passageways as if he were travelling through a dark maze, anticipating for the audience the uncertainty of his actual, emotional condition. In *The Angry Hills,* Aldrich's characteristic low light and sidelight cast long shadows on interior walls and floors and form rectangular blocks to give the frame a severe, constricting geometry which can symbolize the director's moral determinism. For instance, when Gestapo chief Heisler tries to be a nonparticipant in a brutal interrogation, sitting in the foreground with his back to the camera while an underling administers a beating in the rearground, the fixture and geometry of the composition require the participation of Heisler's figure to complete the overall pattern of the shot and will not allow him to be a mere spectator.

While Aldrich's definition of milieu may be superficially realist (and must be so, as the overall context of the films themselves is superficially realist), selection of detail is the most readily applicable method by which figurative meaning may be injected. In *The Legend of Lylah Clare,* the contrast between Barney Sheean's office and Lewis Zarkan's home, between autographed black and white photos of various stars on the walls and lustrous oil paintings of Lylah, between evenly distributed fluorescent light on flat white surfaces and candelabras glistening off the broken texture of wood paneling--all this is not merely a contrast of setting, but of sensibility as well. Both are established within a stylized conception of "producer's office" and "director's home" that is ambivalent, being both serious and satirical, descriptive and analytical. Subject/object versions of reality, genre preconceptions, and sensory input are all in play. Decor and camera angle inform character, character affects angle and decor; and the recognition of type reconciles or estranges the audience to the aptness or inaptness of these interactions. If there is an indisputable cynicism in Aldrich's presentation of figures like Zarkan and Sheean, it is bifocal, acting as both directorial opinion and directorial conjecure of what the world's opinion of such men might be. If there is any vulgarity in the way they are presented, it is less a formal deficiency than an appropriate reflection of the life-style in which they are trapped. Ultimately, characterization and caricature, like all of Aldrich's thematic and stylistic components, refocus on the basic question: survival.

In *Hustle,* Lt. Phil Gaines's partner remarks as the two watch pornographic home movies featuring a suicide victim that her action was rash because "her survival wasn't threatened." Gaines's reply is, "It depends on how you define survival." Because survival is the key definition for Aldrich, there is no overriding morality in his work, no sense of good and evil to which all must conform to be sanctioned. There are, however, personal codes and personal moralities. In many ways, his judgment of Ben Trane or Eric Koertner, of Zarkan or Joe Costa is more severe than the judgment he passes on characters less idealistic or with less sense of honor. The former are foolish enough to place their faith in societal institutions, which collapse around them or betray them. They repress personal values for the vaguely postulated good of society at large; their disillusionment and sometimes fatal alienation is the price that must be paid. Not that the "mealy-mouthed" compromisers such as Charlie Castle or Erskine Cooney fare any better. Aldrich and most of his heroes are caught in that almost Manichaean perception of the world as a dichotomy between natural and artificial, between chaotic and ordered, between instinctual and institutionalized conduct that impels the unaware or unprepared into indecision and can short-circuit a saving or creative act into an impotent and deadly vacillation.

The ending of *Ten Seconds to Hell* is a montage of the introductory close-ups of the members of the bomb-disposal unit and shots of a rebuilt city. A quick reading might be that those who died did so meaningfully, for a purpose; but in the context of what has gone before, the conclusions of *Ten Seconds To Hell* and of *The Dirty Dozen*--which closely resembles the former film, featuring flashbacks of the commando unit at the celebration before the mission that will kill most of them--merely recapitulate the fact that many have miscalculated and perished.

Being wrong is not a moral deficiency in Aldrich's work; it neither mitigates nor insures salvation. What it does is put the "offender" on the outside, because, as Reisman tells Wladislaw, getting caught being wrong *is* a violation of acceptable social conduct. "Pilot error" is what Frank Towns enters into his log as the cause of the crash in *Flight Of The Phoenix;* but that film, and *Too Late the Hero, The Grissom Gang, Ulzana's Raid,* and *The Longest Yard* are, in their own ways, explorations of the infrastructure of error. What they make progressively clearer are the conditional limitations of attributing blame so that the bitter and defensive accusations of Towns ("If you hadn't made a career of being a drunk, if you hadn't stayed in your bunk to have that last bottle, you might have checked that engineer's report and we might not be here") give way gradually to the resignation of Fenner in *The Grissom Gang*, McIntosh in *Ulzana's Raid*, and Crewe in *The Longest Yard*. McIntosh's comment on his adversaries--"Ain't no sense hating the Apaches for killing, Lieutenant. That'd be like hating the desert for being thirsty"--is a realization on a conscious level of the causality at work in most Aldrich films. The reasons for the crash in *The Flight of the Phoenix* are as arbitrary, as free of pure causality, as the dangerous assignments in *Too Late the Hero* and *Ulzana's Raid*, the kidnapping in *The Grissom Gang*, or the football game in *The Longest Yard*.

In these later films particularly, characters begin to regard the organizing structures that compel their actions with a degree of sardonic humor: "I got a story for the *Daily Mirror* when I get back: 'How I Stopped Smoking in Three Days' " *(The Flight of the Phoenix)*; "You put a hell of a lot of trust in a man who can't tell an inside curve from a three-legged horse!" *(Ulzana's Raid)*; or finally, "Don't you know what country you live in? Can't you smell the bananas? You live in Guatemala with color television" *(Hustle)*. As Aldrich's heroes begin explicitly to question the manifestations of inversion which seem to control their destinies, they discover a limited number of alternatives to such situations: escape, death, or perhaps madness (Trucker Cobb in *Flight of the Phoenix*; Mrs. Riordan in *Ulzana's Raid)*. For the escapees like Koertner, Towns, and Hearne *(Too Late The Hero)*, there is, if necessary, expiation and reintegration. For the dead, time and circumstances permitting, there is a burial. Only the dying, such as McIntosh, seem to have any choice. But, when offered the possibility of interment, he disdains both burial in a cemetery ("Being another one of them little markers back at the fort don't appeal to me") and in the open country ("I don't fancy sitting around passing the time of day with no gravediggers"), preferring to wait for the vultures. Presented with a conventional moral value, he makes the only answer that an outsider can.

From Mike Callahan's rejection by the perverse and aptly named Frennessey in *World for Ransom* through the chilling freeze-frames at the end of *The Legend of Lylah Clare* and *The Grissom Gang*, to Gaines's offhanded death in *Hustle*, the one constant in Aldrich's work is that ultimately no one is untouched by the savagery of the surrounding world. For those who expose the more visceral layers of their psyche to it, the risk is always annihilation or, perhaps worse, descent into an unfulfilled, insensate existence. If, in the final analysis, Aldrich's sympathy resides most with individuals who are antiauthoritarian, men like Massai in *Apache* or Reisman in *The Dirty Dozen*, it resides there because these are men who survive by resolving all the conflicting impulses of nature and society, of real and ideal, of right and wrong, in and through action.

The Films: Synopses, Credits and Notes

A. FILMS DIRECTED BY ROBERT ALDRICH

*1 THE BIG LEAGUER   (1953)

Synopsis

"Hans" Lobert (Edward G. Robinson) is the coach of a Spring training camp for major league hopefuls (the camp is that of the New York Giants' in Florida). Among the rookies is Adam Polachuk (Jeff Richards), who has come to the tryouts secretly because his father (Mario Siletti) disapproves of baseball and believes him to be away at college. Despite the encouragement of Lobert and the romantic sympathy of Lobert's niece Christy (Vera Ellen), Polachuk's apprehension and guilt over deceiving his father cause his self-assurance to deteriorate. Just as he is on the verge of abandoning baseball, Lobert arranges for his father to witness a game during which Adam's natural ability convinces Mr. Polachuk that he may have been wrong in opposing his son's interest.

Credits and Notes

Producer:	Matthew Rapf [M.G.M.]
Screenplay:	Herbert Baker, based on a story by John McNulty and Louis Morheim
Photography:	William Mellor
Art Direction:	Cedric Gibbons, Eddie Imazu
Musical Direction:	Alberto Colombo
Sound:	Douglas Shearer
Editor:	Ben Lewis
Assistant Director:	Sid Sidman
Technical Advisor:	John B. (Hans) Lobert
Cast:	Edward G. Robinson (John Lobert), Vera-Ellen (Christy), Jeff Richards (Abraham Polachuk), Richard Jaeckel (Bobby Bronson), William Campbell (Julie Davis), Carl Hubbell (Himself), Paul Langton (Brian McLennan), Lalo Rios (Chuy Aguilar), Bill Crandall (Tippy Mitchell), Frank Ferguson (Wally Mitchell), John McKee (Dale Alexander), Mario Siletti (Mr. Polachuk),

Al Campanis, Bob Trocolor, Tony Ravis (Themselves), Robert Calwell (Pomfret), Donald "Chippie" Hastings (Little Joe)

Filmed on location near Melbourne, Florida and at MGM Studios in Culver City beginning February 16, 1953.

Completed: March 4,1953.
Cost: $800,000
Distribution: Metro-Goldwyn-Mayer
Running time: 71 minutes
Released: August 19, 1953 (Los Angeles)

This film has not been viewed by the authors. Synopsis was written from information contained in entries 191-196.

2 WORLD FOR RANSOM   (1954)

Synopsis

Mike Callahan (Dan Duryea) is an Irish emigre and war veteran working as a private investigator in Singapore. He is summoned by a wartime love named Frennessey (Marian Carr) to the nightclub where she works. There she confides to him that her husband, Julian March (Patric Knowles), may be engaged in some illegal activities and asks Callahan to disentangle him if he can. After questioning March and being forcibly questioned himself by a local gangster, Callahan discovers that a black marketeer named Alexis Pederas (Gene Lockhart) has recruited March for a scheme involving a renowned nuclear physicist, Sean O'Connor (Arthur Shields). While Callahan searches for further information, March, impersonating a major, kidnaps O'Connor at the airport. Pederas then sends a message to the British command that he is offering O'Connor to the highest bidder, whether Russian, Chinese, or Western.

A photographer and informant of Callahan's who had taken a picture of March and O'Connor driving through town comes to Callahan with the snapshot; but March, aware of the incident, alerts Pederas, who has the man killed and the incriminating material planted in Callahan's room. Inspector McCollum (Douglas Dumbrille) comes to question Callahan and discovers the false clue; but Callahan surprises him with a blow and escapes. After spending the night at Frennessey's, Callahan plans to slip out of town and go to a deserted jungle village where O'Connor may be hidden. He is spotted by Major Bone (Reginald Denny) of British Intelligence, who, uncertain of Callahan's role, decides to follow at a distance. In the process Bone loses immediate contact with a support force and finds himself alone with Callahan at the village. They ascertain that March and Pederas's men are indeed there with O'Connor and decide not to wait for help. Bone is wounded in the assault, but Callahan succeeds in slipping into March's bunker and holding the captors at bay with two grenades. Since O'Connor is out of the room,

Callahan reacts to March's threatening gesture by throwing both charges and ducking for cover. All are killed except Callahan and O'Connor.

Callahan returns to Frennessey, having failed to save her husband but hoping to take his place. She rejects him violently, explaining that she never loved Callahan or his physical advances and suggesting that March's platonic affection was what she wanted because men are physically repellent to her. As she loses control, Callahan leaves and returns to the streets of Singapore.

Credits and Notes

Producers:	Robert Aldrich and Bernard Tabakin [Plaza Productions]
Associate Producer:	A. E. Houghton, Jr.
Screenplay:	Lindsay Hardy and [uncredited] Hugo Butler
Photography:	Joseph Biroc
Art Direction:	William Glasgow
Set Direction:	Ted Offenbacher
Music:	Frank DeVol
Song:	"Too Soon" by Walter Samuels
Sound:	Jack Solomon
Editor:	Michael Luciano
Production Manager:	Jake R. Berne
Assistant Director:	Nate Slott
Cast:	Dan Duryea (Mike Callahan), Gene Lockhart (Alexis Pederas), Patric Knowles (Julian March), Reginald Denny (Major Bone), Nigel Bruce (Governor Coutts), Marian Carr (Frennessey), Doublas Dumbrille (Inspector McCollum), Keye Luke (Wing), Clarence Lung (Chan), Lou Nova (Guzik)

Filmed at the Motion Picture Center Studios in Hollywood in eleven days beginning April 13, 1953

Completed:	September 1, 1953
Cost:	$100,000
Distribution:	Allied Artists
Running time:	82 minutes
Released:	January 27, 1954 (Los Angeles)

3 APACHE (1954)

Synopsis

At the final surrender of Geronimo and his band, one Apache warrior, Massai (Burt Lancaster), tries to disrupt the proceedings and die gloriously in a solitary assault on the entrenched U.S. Cavalrymen. Despite the assistance of Nalinle (Jean Peters), who slips through the surrounding troops, Massai is frustrated in his attempt, captured alive, and taken off in chains. An escape also fails when Chief Scout Al Sieber (John McIntire) intercepts Nalinle's attempt to pass Massai a weapon at the railroad station where several Apaches are gathered en route to relocation in Florida under the guardianship of a corrupt Indian agent, Weddle (John Denner). During a stopover in St. Louis, Weddle is persuaded by a newspaper man to pose with his notorious prisoners for a photograph. The confusion created by the powder flash enables Massai to escape unnoticed.

After severing his handcuff chains under the train wheels, Massai wanders through metropolitan St. Louis confused and frightened by the modern sights and sounds. Stowing away on various vehicles, he reaches Oklahoma, where he unknowingly breaks into the barn of a reservation Cherokee named Dawson (Morris Ankrum). When Dawson discovers Massai, he gives him food and points out to him the merits of survival as a farmer rather than death as a warrior. Massai leaves Dawson's farm unconvinced but with a token bag of Cherokee seed corn.

On Massai's return to New Mexico, he seeks rest in the tent of Nalinle and her father Santos (Paul Guilfoyle), who is Chief in Geronimo's absence. Santos sells Massai to Hondo (Charles Buchinsky [Bronson]), an Indian cavalryman who is courting Nalinle, for liquor. Weddle and an aide reassume the duty of transporting the newly captured Massai with two renegades, but Weddle plans to fake an escape attempt by the Indians and kill them. Massai surprises Weddle first, killing the aide but sparing Weddle to deliver his "declaration of war" to the cavalry fort. After kidnapping Nalinle, Massai circles back to the fort, cutting telegraph wires and blowing up a wagon. He arrives in time to send an arrow into Weddle's back as he stands in the commandant's office delivering Massai's message. Massai also sets fire to the stables.

Nalinle and he flee from the fort, and she eventually convinces him that she was not party to her father's treachery. They perform their own marriage ceremony and continue their flight. They are followed by Sieber and Hondo, but at the snowline the cavalrymen are forced to abandon their pursuit for the winter.

The next spring Nalinle, bearing Massai's child, is inspired by the growth of a stalk from the Cherokee corn which Massai had flung away the previous winter. She goes down to a mountain trading post for more seed. Several weeks later, Sieber visits the post while trying to pick up Massai's trail and recognizes Nalinle from the trader's description. Massai sees Sieber and his men coming up the mountain and readies himself for a last battle; Nalinle is in labor as he goes out to meet them. After storming through the soldiers' position, Massai is wounded and retreats into the tall stalks of corn he has grown from Nalinle's seed. Sieber follows him in, but as they fight hand to hand, Massai hears a baby's cry. He stands and starts back to their cabin. Sieber surmises that Massai "just called off the war" and leaves the mountain with his men.

Credits and Notes

Producer:	Harold Hecht [Hecht-Lancaster Productions]
Screenplay:	James R. Webb, based on the novel *Bronco Apache* by Paul I. Wellman
Photography:	Ernest Laszlo (*Technicolor*, 1.85:1)
Art Direction:	Nicolai Remisoff
Music:	David Raksin
Sound:	Jack Solomon

Editorial Supervision: Alan Crosland, Jr.
Technical Consultant: Leonard Doss
Assistant Director: Sid Sidman
Cast: Burt Lancaster (Massai), Jean Peters (Nalinle), John McIntire (Al Sieber), Charles Buchinsky [Bronson] (Hondo), John Denner (Weddle), Paul Guilfoyle (Santos), Ian MacDonald (Clagg), Walter Sande (Lt. Col. Beck), Morris Ankrum (Dawson), Monte Blue (Geronimo)

Filmed on location in New Mexico and at Keywest Studios, Hollywood, in thirty-four days beginning October 19, 1953.

Completed: January 15, 1954
Cost: $1,240,000
Distribution: United Artists
Running time: 89 minutes
Released: June 28, 1954 (Chicago); July 21, 1954 (Los Angeles)
Original Title: *Bronco Apache*

4 VERA CRUZ (1954)

Synopsis

Joe Erin (Burt Lancaster) and Ben Trane (Gary Cooper) have both come to Mexico as hired guns. Erin, a professional killer with a band of outlaws as his associates, meets Trane, an expatriate Confederate veteran, while fleeing from local thieves. After trying and failing to take Trane's horse, Erin proposes an alliance for their mutual benefit and increased chance of survival. When they are captured by troopers, they sell their services to Maximilian (George Macready) and, after putting on a sharpshooting display during an imperial party, are assigned as bodyguards to a favorite of the court, Countess Marie Davarre (Denise Darcel). As they escort her carriage to the coast, Trane notices from the wheel ruts that it is very heavily laden, although it has little visible cargo. Investigation discloses that the coach is filled with gold, with which the Countess has been charged to purchase more men for Maximilian's shrinking army. While Erin makes one bargain with Trane, he strikes another with the countess. His plans backfire when Nina (Sarita Montiel), a young mestizo woman who has been travelling with the column, alerts the Juaristas and enlists Trane in their cause. After Trane and Erin betray the Federal troops, they have a showdown over the gold. Trane outdraws Erin and delivers the gold to Nina and her compatriots.

Credits and Notes

Producer: James Hill [Hecht-Lancaster Productions]
Executive Producer: Harold Hecht
Screenplay: Roland Kibbee and James R. Webb, based on an original story by Borden Chase
Photography: Ernest Laszlo (*Technicolor; SuperScope*, 2:1)
Music: Hugo Friedhofer

Orchestrations:	Raul Lavista
Song:	"Vera Cruz," music by Hugo Friedhofer, lyrics by Sammy Cahn
Sound:	Manuel Topeta, Galdeno Samperio
Editor:	Alan Crosland, Jr.
Assistant Director:	Jack R. Berne
Cast:	Gary Cooper (Ben Trane), Burt Lancaster (Joe Erin), Denise Darcel (the Countess), Cesar Romero (the Marquis), Sarita Montiel (Nina), George Macready (Maximilian), Ernest Borgnine (Donnegan), Morris Ankrum (Ramirez), Henry Brandon (Danette), Charles Buchinsky [Bronson] (Pittsburgh), Jack Lambert (Charlie), Jack Elam (Tex), James McCallion (Little-Bit), James Seay (Abilene), Archie Savage (Ballard), Charles Horvath (Reno), Juan Garcia (Pedro)

Filmed on location in Cuernavaca, Mexico, and in Los Angeles beginning March 3, 1954.

Completed:	May 12, 1954
Cost:	$3,000,000
Distribution:	United Artists
Running time:	94 minutes
Released:	January 12, 1955 (Los Angeles)

5 KISS ME DEADLY (1955)

Synopsis

While returning to Los Angeles at night, private investigator Mike Hammer's (Ralph Meeker) car is flagged down by a woman named Christina (Cloris Leachman). She tries to evade Hammer's questions about where she is escaping from--barefoot and wearing only a trenchcoat--but he learns that she is from a nearby asylum. Nonetheless, he takes her through a roadblock. A few miles beyond, after a stop for gas at which she tells him that, should anything happen, he is to "remember me," Hammer's car is run off the road. Hammer is semiconscious while Christina is tortured and killed, and he is thrown clear when his car is pushed off a cliff.

Hammer returns to consciousness in a hospital, where his secretary Velda (Maxine Cooper) and a detective of his acquaintance (Wesley Addy) inform him that a Federal investigators' board wants to question him. Their interest and Christina's cryptic message prompt him to ignore all warnings and begin his own investigation. He follows up a number of disconnected leads, all of which point to a conspiracy against a murdered scientist named Raymondo, organized by a local gangster, Carl Evello (Paul Stewart). The conspirators attempt to buy Hammer off with a conciliatory phone call and a new sports car, from which he has his mechanic (Nick Dennis) remove two bombs. When he visits Evello's house, Evello's sister Friday (Marian Carr) tries to seduce Hammer, and after subduing Evello's thugs, he is offered money by Evello. Hammer refuses; he traces Christina's roommate, Lily Carver (Gaby

Rogers), and hides her in his apartment. Before he can go further, Nick the mechanic is killed and Hammer is abducted by Evello's men. At the gangster's beach house he encounters Dr. Soberin (Albert Dekker), whose voice Hammer recognizes as that of Christina's killer. Overcoming the influence of pentathol administered by Soberin, Hammer overpowers Evello and kills one of his men then returns home to find Velda missing; but with Lily Carver he decodes Christina's message through a poem by Rossetti. From a morgue attendant, Hammer obtains a key which leads to a locker containing what Velda had dubbed "the great whatsit." He leaves it in the locker but goes out to find Carver gone. At his apartment, the police are waiting; he is told that the box contains radioactive material being sought by foreign agents. When the locker is found empty, Hammer again follows his own lead to a patient of Soberin and gets Soberin's address from a prescription bottle. Arriving at Soberin's beach house, Hammer discovers that Lily Carver has killed him to gain sole possession of the box. Carver shoots Hammer and opens the container. The radioactive material sets her on fire and begins a chain reaction. Hammer struggles through the house, finds Velda, and frees her. Together they stumble into the surf as the house explodes.

Credits and Notes

Producer:	Robert Aldrich [Parklane Productions]
Executive Producer:	Victor Saville
Screenplay:	A. I. Bezzerides, based on the novel *Kiss Me Deadly* by Mickey Spillane
Photography:	Ernest Laszlo (1.85:1)
Art Direction:	William Glasgow
Music:	Frank DeVol
Song:	"Rather Have the Blues," lyrics and music by Frank DeVol; sung by Nat "King" Cole
Editor:	Michael Luciano
Assistant Director:	Robert Justman
Cast:	Ralph Meeker (Mike Hammer), Albert Dekker (Dr. Soberin), Paul Stewart (Carl Evello), Maxine Cooper (Velda), Gaby Rodgers (Gabrielle/Lily Carver), Wesley Addy (Pat), Juano Hernandez (Eddie Yeager), Nick Dennis (Nick), Cloris Leachman (Christina), Marian Carr (Friday), Jack Lambert (Sugar), Jack Elam (Charlie Max), Jerry Zinneman (Sammy), Percy Helton (Morgue Doctor), Fortunio Bonanova (Carmen Trivago), Silvio Minciotti (mover), Leigh Snowden (girl at pool), Madi Comfort (singer), James Seay (FBI man), Mara McAfee (nurse), Robert Cornthwaite (FBI man), James McCallian ("Super"), Jesslyn Fax (Mrs. "Super"), Mort Marshall (Piker), Strother Martin (truck driver), Marjorie Bennett (manager), Art Loggins (bartender), Bob Sherman (gas station man), Keith McConnell (Athletic Club clerk), Paul Richards (attacker), Eddie Real (side man)

Filmed on location in Los Angeles and at the Sutherland Studios in twenty-one days beginning November 27, 1954.

Completed:	December 23, 1954
Distribution:	United Artists
Running time:	105 minutes
Released:	May 18, 1955 (Los Angeles)

6 THE BIG KNIFE (1955)

Synopsis

Charlie Castle (Jack Palance), a former Broadway actor and current star of Hoff International Pictures, does not want to renew his contract. Dissatisifed with the type of parts he has been given, he has told his agent Nat Danziger (Everett Sloane) to inform producer Stanley Hoff (Rod Steiger) of his decision. Additionally, Charlie's insecurity and alcoholism have estranged him from his wife Marion (Ida Lupino), to whom he hopes to be reconciled after breaking with Hoff.

Through his aide Smiley Coy (Wendell Corey), Hoff sends Charlie word of his displeasure and offers him more money if he reconsiders. Charlie refuses but lapses into depression, seeking solace in drink and dalliance with Connie Bliss (Jean Hagen), the wife of an associate. Not understanding Charlie's behavior, Marion makes plans to leave him. Hoff appears in person and, after histrionic appeals have failed, resorts to blackmail. He threatens to expose Charlie as the drunk driver of a car which killed a pedestrian in an accident for which Buddy Bliss (Paul Langton) had taken the blame. Faced with this threat, Charlie agrees to sign. In the aftermath of the confrontation, Charlie confides to Smiley Coy that he is concerned about Dixie Evans (Shelley Winters), a bit player who had been with him at the time of the accident. Smiley promises to take care of this problem.

Smiley's method is to get Dixie drunk and then push her in front of a car. Her violent death and his wife's departure throw Charlie into an even blacker depression. Charlie is visited on the set by Hank Teagle (Wesley Addy), who confesses that he hopes to marry Marion after her divorce. Charlie returns home and makes one last appeal to Marion to stay with him. Just after she decides she will stay, Marion discovers that Charlie has slit his wrists in the bath and died.

Credits and Notes

Producer:	Robert Aldrich [Associates and Aldrich]
Screenplay:	James Poe, based on the play *The Big Knife* by Clifford Odets
Photography:	Ernest Laszlo (1.85:1)
Art Direction:	William Glasgow
Music:	Frank DeVol
Sound:	Jack Solomon
Editor:	Michael Luciano
Production Supervisor:	Jack R. Berne
Assistant Directors:	Nate Slott, Bob Justman

Cast: Jack Palance (Charlie Castle), Ida Lupino (Marion Castle), Wendell Corey (Smiley Coy), Jean Hagen (Connie Bliss), Rod Steiger (Stanley Hoff), Shelley Winters (Dixie Evans), Ilka Chase (Patty Benedict), Everett Sloane (Nat Danziger), Wesley Addy (Hank Teagle), Paul Langton (Buddy Bliss), Nick Dennis (Mickey Feeney), Bill Walker (Russell), Mike Winkelman (Billy Castle), Mel Welles (bearded man), Robert Sherman (bongo player), Strother Martin (stillman), Ralph Volke (referee), Michael Fox (announcer), Richard Boone (narrator)

Filmed at the Sutherland Studios, Los Angeles, in fifteen days beginning April 25, 1955.

Completed: May 14, 1955
Cost: $425,000
Distribution: United Artists
Running time: 111 minutes
Released: November 25, 1955 (Los Angeles)

7 AUTUMN LEAVES (1956)

Synopsis

Millicent Wetherby (Joan Crawford) is an attractive "forty-ish" woman unable to have a fulfilling relationship with a man. She is self-employed as a manuscript typist and her only visible acquaintance is Liz (Ruth Donnelly), the manager of the court apartments where she resides. With Liz, Milly self-deprecatingly analyzes her solitary life and unescorted "dates," her name for personal excursions to concerts and movies.

Following a concert, she encounters a young veteran, Burt Hanson (Cliff Robertson), in a local coffee shop. His enthusiasm allows him to succeed in picking her up. He courts her vigorously and proposes marriage. Milly rejects him, ostensibly because he is too young but equally because of a sense of her own emotional vulnerability. He drops out of her life for several weeks; when he returns, her renewed loneliness during his absence has convinced Milly to risk marriage.

While living with Burt is physically and emotionally satisfying, Milly begins to notice inconsistencies both in what he tells her of his past and what he relates of his day to day activities. Additionally, he continues to bring her gifts which he cannot afford on his salary as a store clerk. Milly's suspicions are abruptly confirmed by a visit from Virginia Hanson (Vera Miles), who claims to be a former wife whom Burt has never mentioned to Milly. She also reveals that Burt's father, whom he has told Milly is dead, is still alive. When questioned by Milly, Burt admits that he has stolen gifts for her and lied about his past but says that he cannot remember all the circumstances which caused him to break with Virginia and his father; he only recalls returning home one day, going upstairs and inexplicably suffering a blackout. Under Milly's urging, Burt agrees to meet with his former wife and father at a local hotel, to which Milly precedes him and discovers the sexual relationship between Virginia and Burt's father (Lorne Greene). Burt arrives to find the three exchanging angry words and collapses into manic depression. Milly attempts to care for him herself, but he becomes more and more uncommunicative while gradually transferring his anger to her and menacing her physically. Milly consults a psychiatrist and agrees to commit Burt, despite apprehension that a complete cure would dissipate his emotional attachment to her. She works long hours for the next several months to pay the bills for his care and finally goes to visit him prior to his release, resigned to losing him. Burt rejects her offer of freedom and convinces Milly that he wants to stay with her, not out of gratitude but genuine love.

Credits and Notes

Producer:	William Goetz [Wm. Goetz Productions]
Screenplay:	Jack Jevne, Lewis Meltzer, and Robert Blees
Photography:	Charles Lang, Jr. (1:85:1)
Art Direction:	William Glasgow
Set Decoration:	Eli Benneche
Music:	Hans Salter
Conductor:	Morris Stoloff
Song:	"Autumn Leaves," music by Joseph Kosma, original French lyrics by Jacques Prevert, English lyrics by Johnny Mercer; sung by Nat "King" Cole
Sound:	Ferol Redd, John Livadary
Costumes:	Jean Louis
Editor:	Michael Luciano
Assistant Director:	Jack R. Berne
Cast:	Joan Crawford (Millicent Wetherby), Cliff Robertson (Burt Hanson), Vera Miles (Virginia), Lorne Greene (Hanson), Ruth Donnelly (Liz), Shepperd Strudwick (Dr. Couzzens), Selmer Jackson (Mr. Wetherby), Maxine Cooper (Nurse Evans), Majorie Bennett (waitress), Frank Gerstle (Mr. Ramsey), Leonard Mudie (Col. Hillyer), Maurice Manson (Dr. Masteson), Bob Hopkins (clerk)

Filmed at Columbia Studios, Los Angeles, beginning August 31, 1955.

Completed:	November 21, 1955
Running time:	107 minutes
Distribution:	Columbia
Released:	September 11, 1956 (Los Angeles)
Original title:	*The Way We Are*

8 ATTACK! (1956)

Synopsis

During an assault of a German bunker during World War II, nineteen men from the platoon of Lt. Joe Costa (Jack Palance) are lost. Costa holds the commander of his company, Captain Erskine Cooney (Eddie Albert), responsible for failing to respond to his calls for assistance. After this skirmish, while the men discuss Cooney's cowardice and Costa takes out his anger at a blacksmith forge, Lt. Woodruff (William Smithers) arranges a meeting with the battalion chief, Colonel Bartlett (Lee Marvin). Woodruff convinces Costa to join Bartlett, Cooney and himself in a card game. Costa cannot resist taunting Cooney during the game, and they exchange angry words. While Cooney is sulking, Bartlett asks Costa and Woodruff not to issue a formal complaint, confessing that he must cover up for Cooney because of his father's political connections but advising them that the company will sit out the rest of the war in the rear. Costa is unconvinced but agrees not to file charges.

Bartlett fails to reckon on the Germans, who begin a counterattack that becomes the Battle of the Bulge. Cooney's company is told to hold where they are, and he sends Costa's platoon to a forward point as spotters. Before he leaves, Costa promises Cooney that if he fails to get needed support he will return to kill him, and Woodruff promises Costa that he personally will go in if needed.

Costa's men advance down a hill towards the outskirts of a town. When they are met by machine gun and mortar fire, most fall back. Costa and a handful reach an outlying house. While they are watching the town, they discover two Germans, a captain (Peter Van Eyck) and a sergeant (Steven Geray), from whom they learn that heavy armor is approaching. By the time Costa's men have eliminated a sniper in a bell tower who had them pinned down, the German tanks have arrived. Costa radios for support so that they may fall back. Claiming that he cannot commit any more men, Cooney refuses. Woodruff prepares to take his own platoon out, but Cooney orders him to remain. Infuriated by Cooney's silence and the German captain's deception, Costa pushes the enemy officer out the door to be cut down by his own forces. He and his men scramble out the back under heavy fire from the tanks. Costa is hit in the leg but stops to pick up a wounded man. By the time he has limped back up the hill carrying him on his shoulders, the man is dead.

Meanwhile, other armored units are assaulting the rest of the company in town. Cooney has lost all semblance of command and retreated to his room, where he cries hysterically. Believing Costa is dead, Woodruff goes out to organize resistance; when he returns to inform Bartlett of the situation, Cooney, fortified by alcohol, has disappeared. As Woodruff learns that three survivors from Costa's platoon are pinned in a cellar, Costa himself appears in the doorway looking for Cooney. When Costa hears that his men are trapped, he goes back to find them.

Costa encounters a tank in the street but, taking a bazooka from a fallen man, succeeds in killing its crew. However, the machine's momentum carries it forward towards Costa, pinning him in a doorway and running over his arm. Having lost contact with Costa, Woodruff reaches the cellar where Tolliver (Buddy Ebsen), Bernstein (Robert Strauss), and Snowden (Richard Jaeckel) have taken cover. As they discuss how to get out with Bernstein, who has broken his leg, Cooney appears. Brandishing a gun, he orders the men out into the street. While they hesitate, Costa arrives, his arm a bloody mass but his rifle leveled at Cooney. Unable to pull the trigger, he collapses and dies from loss of blood. When Cooney turns to gloat, Woodruff shoots him in the back. As relief appears, the three other men fire a round into Cooney's body and tell Woodruff to say he died from enemy fire. Woodruff is tempted by this suggestion, but when Colonel Bartlett arrives and assumes Costa killed Cooney, Woodruff tells him the truth. Bartlett offers to cover it up if Woodruff will recommend Cooney for a citation. Woodruff refuses. He stands for a moment by Costa's agonized death mask and goes in to call the divisional commander.

Credits and Notes

Producer:	Robert Aldrich [Associates and Aldrich]
Screenplay:	James Poe, based on the play *Fragile Fox* by Norman Brooks
Photography:	Joseph Biroc (1.85:1)
Art Direction:	William Glasgow
Set Decoration:	Glen Daniels
Music:	Frank DeVol
Sound:	Jack Solomon
Editor:	Michael Luciano
Associate Producer:	Walter Blake
Production Supervisor:	Jack R. Berne
Assistant Director:	Robert Justman
Technical Supervisor:	Bud Cokes
Special Effects:	David Koehler
Sound Effects:	Robert A. Reich
Makeup:	Robert J. Schiffer
Casting Supervisor:	Jack Murton
Dialogue Director:	Robert Sherman
Production Assistant:	Adele Strassfield
Cast:	Jack Palance (Lt. Costa), Eddie Albert (Capt. Cooney), Lee Marvin (Col. Bartlett), William Smithers (Lt. Woodruff), Robert Strauss (Pfc. Bernstein), Richard Jaeckel (Pfc. Snowden), Buddy Ebsen (Sgt. Tolliver), Jon Shepodd (Cpl. Jackson), Jimmy Goodwin (Pfc. Ricks), Strother Martin (Sgt. Ingersol), Peter Van Eyck (German officer), Steven Geray (German non-Com), Louis Mercier (Frenchman), Judson Taylor (Pvt. Abramowitz), Ron McNeil (Pfc. Jones)

Filmed on location at the Albertson Ranch, Triunfo, California, and at RKO-Pathe and Universal Studios beginning January 16, 1956.

Completed:	February 14, 1956
Distribution:	United Artists
Running time:	107 minutes
Released:	October 17, 1956 (Los Angeles)
Original title:	*The Fragile Fox*

9 THE GARMENT JUNGLE (1957)

Synopsis

Korean war veteran Alan Mitchell (Kerwin Matthews) returns to New York to join his widowed father Walter Mitchell's (Lee J. Cobb) dress manufacturing business. The garment industry itself is under pressure from local unions to sign shop contracts; and Alan is suspicious that this turmoil may be connected with the death of his father's partner from a fall down an elevator shaft.

Alan is somewhat alienated by his father's insistence on keeping out the union and his long-term liaison with a young buyer, Lee Hackett (Valerie French). Eventually Alan learns that Walter has been paying protection money to a small union-busting syndicate run by Artie Ravidge (Richard Boone). Alan decides to go to the union to learn their side of the issue and, if possible, get more information about Artie Ravidge's mob. There he meets Tulio Renata (Robert Loggia) and his wife, Theresa (Gia Scala). Tulio's arguments for unionization are fully as emotional as Walter Mitchell's against it; Tulio appeals to Alan's liberalism, urging him to break with his father and help them organize the Mitchell employees. Alan decides to try to convince his father to unionize or, at least, break with Ravidge. Walter, believing he can control his hired thugs, still refuses and passes on what he learns from Alan to Ravidge. The result is Tulio's brutal murder in a dark alley near his home. This radicalizes Alan, and he promises to get evidence to connect Ravidge (and possibly his father) with the crime. Walter himself is shocked by Ravidge's violence and implicit admission that he killed Mitchell's partner because he was pro-union. He admits his error to his son and Lee Hackett, to whom he proposed marriage, and begins an attempt to disconnect himself from Ravidge. This leads only to his own murder at the hands of Ravidge's men. Alan, who has already assumed some responsibility for Theresa and her child, now finds himself head of the Mitchell firm but still unable to implicate Ravidge. Freed from a promise of secrecy by Walter's death, Lee admits to Alan that she has his father's record of payoffs to Ravidge. While that material is taken to the district attorney, Alan goes to vent his anger and frustration in a physical confrontation with Ravidge. His fight is broken up by the arrival of Theresa with the police, who arrest the beaten Ravidge.

Credits and Notes

Producer:	Harry Kleiner [Columbia]
Directors:	Vincent Sherman and [uncredited] Robert Aldrich
Screenplay:	Harry Kleiner, based on a series of articles, "Gangsters in the Dress Business," by Lester Velie
Photography:	Joseph Biroc (1.85:1)
Art Direction:	Robert A. Peterson
Set Decoration:	William Kiernan, Frank A. Tuttle
Music:	Leith Stevens
Orchestrations:	Arthur Morton

Sound:	John Livadary
Costumes:	Jean Louis
Editor:	William Lyon
Assistant Director:	Irving Moore
Makeup:	Clay Campbell
Hairdressing:	Helen Hunt
Cast:	Lee J. Cobb (Walter Mitchell), Kerwin Matthews (Alan Mitchell), Gia Scala (Theresa Renata), Richard Boone (Artie Ravidge), Valerie French (Lee Hackett), Robert Loggia (Tulio Renata), Joseph Wiseman (Tony), Adam Williams ("Ox"), Wesley Addy (Mr. Paul), Willis Bouchey (Dave Bronson), Robert Ellenstein (Fred Kenner), Celia Lousky (Tulio's mother)

Filmed on location in New York and at Columbia Studios beginning October 13, 1956.

Completed:	December 20, 1956
Distribution:	Columbia
Running time:	88 minutes
Released:	May 22, 1957 (Los Angeles)
Original title:	*The Garment Center*

Note: Vincent Sherman replaced Aldrich as director on December 4, 1956, five days before the scheduled completion of shooting and sixteen days before the actual completion. Aldrich has never seen the finished picture and is uncertain of how much of his footage was reshot.

10   THE ANGRY HILLS   (1959)

Synopsis

Mike Morrison (Robert Mitchum) is an American war correspondent trapped in Athens by a sudden German advance. Morrison's agreement with the British to acquire a list of contacts in the Greek underground and deliver it to British Intelligence puts him in jeopardy of being captured and executed as a spy. Konrad Heisler (Stanley Baker), the Gestapo chief, is under intense pressure from his superiors to obtain a copy of this list, and he commissions the quisling Tassos (Theodore Bikel) to discover its whereabouts. Tassos tracks down Morrison but only succeeds in wounding him.

Morrison escapes from Athens and reaches a village of partisans, where he is cared for by Eleftheria (Gia Scala). After his recovery he joins her brother, Leonides (Peter Illing), in an abortive raid which is betrayed by a German spy posing as an escaped British soldier (Patrick Jordan). Leonides is killed and Eleftheria leads Morrison to a convent where he must hide until arrangements can be made to get him out of the country. From the convent he is taken to Lisa Kryiakides (Elisabeth Mueller), a widow and a double agent who was also Heisler's mistress. Fearing that Tassos, who has had Eleftheria tortured and killed, will soon follow the trail to her, Lisa makes hurried arrangements. A miscalculation causes Heisler to learn of her participation, and he takes her children to compel her to betray Morrison. Instead she exchanges herself for them. While she distracts Heisler, an agent named Chesney (Sebastian Cabot) kills Tassos and puts Morrison with Lisa's children on a boat leaving the country.

Credits and Notes

Producer:	Raymond Stross [Raymond Stross Productions]
Screenplay:	A. I. Bezzerides, based on the novel *The Angry Hills* by Leon Uris
Photography:	Stephen Dade *(CinemaScope)*
Art Direction:	Ken Adam
Music:	Richard Bennett
Conductor:	Dock Mathieson
Sound:	A. W. Watkins, Stanley Smith
Editor:	Peter Tanner
Associate Producer:	Victor Lyndon
Production Manager:	Clifton Brandon
Assistant Director:	Buddy Booth
Cast:	Robert Mitchum (Mike Morrison), Elisabeth Mueller (Lisa Kyriakides), Stanley Baker (Conrad Heisler), Gia Scala (Eleftheria), Theodore Bikel (Tassos), Sebastian Cabot (Chesney), Peter Illing (Leonides), Leslie Phillips (Ray Taylor), Donald Wolfit (Dr. Stergion), Marius Goring (Commander Oberg), Jackie Lane (Maria), Kieron Moore (Andreas), George Pastell (Papa Panos), Patrick Jordan (Bluey), Marita Constantiou (Cleopatra), Alec Mango (Phillibos)

Filmed on location in Greece beginning June 14, 1958.

Completed:	December 10, 1958
Distribution:	Metro-Goldwyn-Mayer
Running time:	105 minutes
Released:	July 29, 1959

11 TEN SECONDS TO HELL (1959)

Synopsis

Six German demolition experts, recently released from prisoner of war camps, are recruited by the Allies to form a bomb squad. The risks are high but the pay good, and the six men decide they will work at it for three months. To insure that those who survive will be solvent, they attach a grisly rider to their pact. Each man will contribute half his wages to a joint fund. At the end of the agreed period, the survivors will quit and divide the accumulated money. The unofficial leader of the squad is Eric Koertner (Jack Palance), a former architect who has trouble retaining his idealism as he defuses bombs amidst the rubble of buildings he helped to build. His rival for command of the group, as well as his philosophical antagonist, is Karl Wirtz (Jeff Chandler). Wirtz formulated the idea of a survivor's bonus and won a moral victory over Koertner when the group adopted it. But the focus of their unstated antipathy soon shifts to Margot Hofer (Martine Carol), a widowed resident of the group's boarding house to whom both men are sexually attracted. Although Koertner's advances towards the woman succeed, Wirtz takes solace in the fact that the men of the squad are rapidly being killed off and his belief that Koertner's idealistic despair is likely to lead to a fatal error. Ultimately, only Wirtz and Koertner remain alive. Koertner suggests that they quit now and divide the money. Wirtz refuses and uses the fact that Koertner gave his word to compel him to stay. As the men alternate calls, luck determines who will get the dangerous bombs. Wirtz is the less fortunate, but Koertner concedes that Wirtz has been assigned a two-man bomb and, despite the fact that the agreement absolves him from responsibility, offers to help. Wirtz, however, panics. Fearing that they will both be killed, he tries to blow up Koertner with a trip wire. He fails but allows an enraged Koertner to beat him. Totally disillusioned, Koertner walks away from Wirtz. As he reaches the edge of the site, Wirtz makes a mistake and the bomb explodes.

Credits and Notes

Producer:	Michael Carreras [Seven Arts--Hammer]
Screenplay:	Robert Aldrich and Teddi Sherman, based on the novel *The Phoenix* by Laurence Bachmann
Photography:	Ernest Laszlo (1.85:1)
Art Direction:	Ken Adam
Music:	Kenneth V. Jones
Sound:	Henry Garlowski
Editor:	Henry Richardson
Assistant Director:	Frank Winterstein
Cast:	Jack Palance (Koertner), Jeff Chandler (Wirtz), Martine Carol (Margot), Robert Cornthwaite (Loeffler), Dave Willock (Tillig), Wesley Addy (Sulke), Jimmy Goodwin (Globke), Virginia Baker (Frau Bauer), Nancy Lee (Ruth Sulke), Richard Wattis (Major Haven), Charles Nolte (Doctor)

Filmed on location in Berlin and at UFA Studios beginning February 17, 1958.

Completed:	May 10, 1958
Distribution:	United Artists
Running time:	93 minutes
Released:	September 16, 1959
Title in Great Britain:	*The Phoenix*

12   THE LAST SUNSET   (1961)

Synopsis

Brendon O'Malley (Kirk Douglas), a black-suited gambler whose only sidearm is a derringer, crosses the border into Mexico to avoid arrest. He is pursued by Dana Stribling (Rock Hudson), a Texas sheriff, who holds O'Malley responsible for his sister's suicide. Stribling catches up with O'Malley at the ranch of John Breckenridge (Joseph Cotten), a cattleman planning to drive his herd north to Crazy Horse in Texas for a quick sale.

Since Breckenridge is an ineffectual chief and his ranch hands inexperienced as drovers, he has hired O'Malley as informal trail boss. Breckenridge's wife, Belle (Dorothy Malone), who as a teenager had been seduced by O'Malley, favors replacing him with the newly arrived Stribling. Breckenridge agrees to hire them both, and the drive begins with Belle and her daughter, Missy (Carol Lynley), accompanying them on the chuckwagon.

On the first stopover, Breckenridge is bullied into a barroom brawl and, despite the efforts of O'Malley and Stribling to extricate him, is shot in the back. His death leaves the two men in contention for leadership of the drive and the affections of Belle. Although they establish an informal truce and work together to overcome the hazards of bad weather and raiding Indians, Stribling makes it clear that he will try to arrest O'Malley as soon as the drive is over. Further, Belle's bitterness over her earlier abandonment by O'Malley and physical attraction to Stribling causes more friction between the two men. Missy, however, is greatly attracted to O'Malley and flirts with him constantly. After three down-and-out drovers try to kidnap the two women, O'Malley rescues Stribling from quicksand. This action momentarily eases the tension between them, until, on the eve of crossing the river into Texas, Stribling questions O'Malley about his sister. The latter's reply, that she had been a common bar girl, leads to a fistfight which is broken up by Belle with a rifle. Her clear indication that she prefers Stribling to O'Malley, causes O'Malley to succumb to the inexperienced Missy's advances.

No longer bearing rancor towards Belle, O'Malley tells her that he plans to avoid a showdown with Stribling and leave with Missy, whom he genuinely loves. Belle's revelation that he loves Missy because she is his daughter stuns him. Rather than avoid Stribling, whose plan to marry Belle has caused him to consider allowing O'Malley to escape, O'Malley challenges Stribling to meet him behind the stockyards. After saying farewell to Missy, O'Malley goes with an empty weapon to a gunfight which he could easily win and he is killed.

Credits and Notes

Producer:	Eugene Frenke and Edward Lewis [Brynaprod S.A.]
Screenplay:	Dalton Trumbo, based on the novel *Sundown at Crazy Horse* by Howard Rigsby
Photography:	Ernest Laszlo (*Eastman* Color)
Art Direction:	Alexander Golitzen, Alfred Sweeney
Set Decoration:	Oliver Emert
Music:	Ernest Gold
Conductor:	Joseph Gershenson
Sound:	Waldon O. Watson, Don Cunliffe
Song:	"Pretty Little Girl in the Yellow Dress," music by Dmitri Tiomkin, lyrics by Ned Washington
Costumes:	Norma Koch
Edited:	Edward Mann (supervisor), Michael Luciano
Production Manager:	Joe Behm
Assistant Directors:	Thomas J. Connors, Nate Slott
Cast:	Kirk Douglas (Brendon O'Malley), Rock Hudson (Dana Stribling), Dorothy Malone (Belle Breckenridge), Carol

Lynley (Missy Breckenridge), Neville Brand (Frank Hobbs), Regis Toomey (Milton Wing), Adam Williams (Calverton), Jack Elam (Ed Hobbs), John Shay (Bowman), Rad Fulton (Julesberg Kid), George Trevino (Manuel), Peter Virgo (third man), Jose Torvay (Jose), Margarito de Luna (Rosario), Chihuahua, Jose Frowe, Manuel Vergara.

Filmed on location near Mexico City and Caliente, Mexico, and at Universal Studios beginning May 11, 1960

Completed:	July 29, 1960
Distribution:	Universal-International
Running time:	112 minutes
Released:	June 8, 1961 (Grauman's Chinese Theater, Hollywood)
Original titles:	*The Day of the Gun; The Hot Eye of Heaven*

13 WHATEVER HAPPENED TO BABY JANE (1962)

Synopsis

In the 1920's, Baby Jane Hudson was the idol of millions, a vaudeville superstar whose childish laments and waifish dance routines supported her father, mother, and sister, Blanche, in luxurious style. Fully aware of this, she compelled her father to spoil her shamelessly and neglect Blanche.

But Blanche (Joan Crawford) succeeds in making a name for herself as an actress in the 1930's and insists that the major stuido holding her contract also find vehicles for Jane (Bette Davis). After a director (Wesley Addy) and producer (Bert Freed) review scenes from both sisters' latest films, they agree that Jane has retained none of the appeal or acting ability which once sold Baby Jane dolls by the thousands and that it would be much to the studio's advantage to pursuade Blanche to pursue a career unencumbered by her sister. Their plan is soon dropped, however, when Blanche is permanently paralyzed in an automobile accident and must abandon acting.

Thirty years later, Jane and Blanche are subsisting on insurance and meager residuals from Blanche's days of stardom. Jane, a frustrated and garish spinster, bitterly resents having to care for her invalid sister and depending on her money for support. Those few people who know the two women suspect that the vituperative Jane was somehow responsible for the kindly and uncomplaining Blanche's injury. Since Jane takes Blanche's endorsed checks to the bank and buys the household food, Blanche's only contact with the outside world is the weekly visit of a cleaning woman, Elvira Stitt (Maidie Norman), and an occasional glance of a neighbor, Mrs. Bates (Anna Lee), from her second floor window. Blanche seldom, if ever, visits the ground floor of her house.

For years, despondency and alcoholism have caused Jane to lapse into vivid fantasies of the past. Elvira, alarmed by suspicious actions on Jane's part, feels compelled to warn Blanche that Jane may want to sell the house and place Blanche in a nursing home. The fact that the house is in Blanche's name prompts her to question Jane. To her horror, Blanche learns that Jane does have such notions, but she receives only taunts and vague threats. To further unbalance Blanche, Jane brings up serving trays containing the bodies of a pet bird and a rat. At the same time, she puts in effect her plans for a comeback. She orders full size versions of her Baby Jane dresses and poses with white makeup and rouged cheeks before a full-length mirror. She also places an ad for an accompanist which is answered by Edwin Flagg (Victor Buono), a ne'er-do-well supported by his mother. Flagg is amazed at the spectacle of the "new" Baby Jane but goes along with her in hopes of getting a large enough advance to abandon his mother.

Listening at her door, the terrorized Blanche realizes that Jane has gained control of all Blanche's assets by expertly imitating her voice on the phone and forging her signature. When Jane goes out, Blanche desperately attempts to crawl downstairs and call her doctor. Jane returns, catches her, beats her, and drags her back upstairs, where she locks Blanche in her room. When Elvira comes to clean, Jane fires her and asks for her key. Elvira, pretending to have left the key at home, waits outside until Jane leaves for the bank and enters the house. Finding Blanche's room locked and receiving no answer to her call, Elvira forces the door. Inside, she finds Blanche gagged and tied to the bed. As Elvira struggles with the ropes, Jane returns. While Blanche watches helplessly Jane kills Elvira with a hammer.

After hiding Elvira's body in the trunk of her car, Jane dresses for Edwin Flagg's visit. Following an argument with his mother, Flagg has gotten drunk and is brought to the door by the police, who suspect him of being a prowler. Somewhat unnerved, Jane tells them Flagg has an appointment with her. After they leave, Flagg loudly demands the advance money for his services. Hearing a strange voice, Blanche manages to free an arm and tip over a table. Flagg, insisting on investigating the noise himself, breaks Jane's hold and rushes upstairs. Shocked at seeing the half-starved and beaten Blanche, Flagg runs away.

Fearing discovery, Jane plans to leave the house. By the following morning she has reached the beach, where she has lain Blanche in the sand and excavated a small hole. Blanche pleads for a doctor. When Jane refuses out of fear of being punished, Blanche makes a desperate confession. She admits that she was the cause of her own injury, having been at the wheel of the car attempting to run down Jane. Because of either her drunken state or trauma, Jane had obliterated the memory of this incident. Now, forced to remember, she relapses totally into her childish persona and saunters off to buy the dying Blanche an ice-cream cone. When police, alerted by Flagg, come up to question her, she tells them Blanche is down the beach. Then she notices that a crowd of bathers has gathered and begins to perform her Baby Jane act.

Credits and Notes

Producer:	Robert Aldrich [Associates and Aldrich--Seven Arts]
Executive Producer:	Kenneth Hyman
Screenplay:	Lukas Heller, based on the novel *Whatever Happened to Baby Jane* by Henry Farrell
Photography:	Ernest Haller (1.85:1)
Art Direction:	William Glasgow
Set Decoration:	George Sawley
Music:	Frank DeVol

Song:	"I'm Writing a Letter to Daddy."
Sound:	Jack Solomon
Costumes:	Norma Koch
Choreography:	Alex Romero
Editor:	Michael Luciano
Associate Producer:	Walter Blake
Production Supervisor:	Jack R. Berne
Assistant Director:	Thomas J. Connors
Seven Arts Representatives:	Eliot Hyman, Ray Stark
Script Adaptation:	Harry Essex [uncredited]
Cast:	Bette Davis (Jane Hudson), Joan Crawford (Blanche Hudson), Victor Buono (Edwin Flagg), Marjorie Bennett (Della Flagg), Maidie Norman (Elivra Stitt), Anna Lee (Mrs. Bates), Barbara Merrill (Liza Bates), Julie Aldred (Baby Jane), Gina Gillespie (Blanche as a child) Dave Willock (Ray Hudson), Ann Barton (Cora Hudson), Bert Freed (Producer), Wesley Addy (Director)

Filmed on location in Los Angeles and at Warner Brothers and the Producer's Studios beginning July 9, 1962.

Completed:	September 12, 1962
Cost:	$825,000
Distribution:	Warner Brothers
Running time:	132 minutes
Released:	October 31, 1962 (New York); November 7, 1962 (Los Angeles)

Stock footage from *Parachute Jumper* (Alfred E. Green; Warner Brothers, 1933), *Ex-Lady* (Robert Florey; Warner Brothers, 1933), and *Sadie McKee* (Clarence Brown; M.G.M., 1934)

14   SODOM AND GOMORRAH   (1963)

Synopsis

In their wanderings in search of a permanent home, the Hebrews under Lot (Stewart Granger) pitch temporary camp on a plain outside the cities of Sodom and Gomorrah. The ruler of the cities, Queen Bera (Anouk Aimee), reacts favorably to Lot's personal appeal for permission to remain for at least a full growing season so that the Hebrew's supply of grain may be replenished. Bera's hidden motive is fear of her nomadic neighbors, the Helamites, who are conspiring with her brother, Astaroth (Stanley Baker), to capture her kingdom. With Lot and his people as her *de facto* allies encamped between Sodom and the Helamites' tribal land, she has additional security.

Lot is given Ildith (Pier Angeli), a former slave and personal attendant to Bera, as a concubine. He proposes marriage to Ildith, who accepts because of a genuine attraction to Lot and also because Bera has commissioned her to spy on him. Ildith promises to abandon her old gods in favor of the Hebrew Yahweh. On their wedding day, Astaroth and the Helamites, who have been harassing the Hebrews since their arrival, launch a surprise attack on the Hebrew camp. Although the attackers are repulsed when Lot destroys a dam, flooding the plain and drowning most of the Helamite army, Astaroth kidnaps Sheeah (Rosanna Podesta), one of Lot's daughters, and escapes.

Since the Hebrews have been dispossessed by the floodwaters which destroyed her enemies, Bera allows them to take refuge in her cities. There, under the influence of the luxurious surroundings and sensual pleasure, they fall into the carnal, unproductive mode of life of the Sodomites despite Lot's admonitions. Even Lot himself is tempted until he discovers that Astaroth has reduced his daughter to concubinage and kills him.

Bera must imprison Lot for killing a royal figure, although she is glad to be rid of the threat of Astaroth. Without Lot's leadership, the Hebrews fall further into pagan practice. In Bera's dungeon, two angels appear to Lot and tell him to lead the people out of the city, for God will destroy it that very night. Lot's chains fall to pieces, and he bands together all who will listen to flee with him into the hills. At sunset, an earthquake levels the cities and fire rains from the skies, killing Bera and all her subjects. Ildith, ignoring the warning not to look back, turns around to see and is transformed into a pillar of salt.

Credits and Notes

Producer:	Goffredo Lombardo [A Titanus Production--Embassy, Joseph E. Levine]
Executive Producer:	Maurizio Lodi-Fe
Screenplay:	Hugo Butler and Giorgio Prosperi
Photography:	Silvio Ippoliti, Mario Montuori, Cyril Knowles (*Eastman Color* processed by *De Luxe)*
Art Direction:	Ken Adam, Giovanni D'Andrea
Music:	Miklos Rozsa
Sound:	Kurt Koubrausky
Costumes:	Giancarlo Bartolin Salembeni
Choreography:	Archie Savage
Costumes:	Peter Tanner
Effects Editor:	Leslie Hodgson
Second Unit Direction:	Sergio Leone
Assistant Directors:	Gus Agosti, Franco Gironi
Cast:	Stewart Granger (Lot), Pier Angeli (Ildith), Stanley Baker (Astaroth), Rossana Podesta (Sheeah), Anouk Aimee (Queen Bera), Claude Mori (Maleb), Rik Battaglia (Melchoir), Giacomo Rossi-Stuart (Ishmael), Feodor Chaliapin (Alabias), Aldo Silvani (Nacor), Enzo Fiermonte (Eber), Scilla Gabel (Tamar), Antonio De Teffe (Captain), Gabriele Tinti (Lieutenant),Daniele Vargas (Segur), Massimo Pietroloon (Isaac), Mitsuko Takara (Orpha), Mimma Palmara (Arno), Alice and Ellen Kessler (dancers)

Filmed on location in Morocco and in Rome in 124 days beginning January 23, 1961.

Completed:	June 9, 1961
Cost:	$4,500,000
Distribution:	20th Century-Fox
Running time:	154 minutes
Released:	January 23, 1963 (Los Angeles)

15 FOUR FOR TEXAS (1963)

Synopsis

Zack Thomas (Frank Sinatra) and Joe Jarrett (Dean Martin), passengers on a stagecoach for Galveston, find themselves under attack from a gang of masked riders. After driving off the bandits, Thomas makes the mistake of admitting that they were probably after his carpetbag, which contains $100,000. Jarrett relieves Thomas of the money at gunpoint. Reaching Galveston, Jarrett puts the money in the bank of a local racketeer, Harvey Burden (Victor Buono), who has partially financed Thomas's efforts to control gambling in the area. Meanwhile, Thomas returns to the bordello run by Elya Carlson (Anita Ekberg) and makes plans to steal back his funds. Burden, hoping to eliminate both men and take over the town, sends a gunslinger named Matson (Charles Bronson) to kill Thomas, whose life is saved when Jarrett wounds the assassin.

Refusing Thomas's offer to join forces, Jarrett contacts Maxine Richter (Ursula Andress), owner of a riverboat which might be converted to a gambling ship. Thomas, knowing his money has been used to refurbish the boat, plans to take it over by force. But Maxine and Elya convince the two men to join forces because they suspect Burden may move in to claim the spoils if Thomas and Jarrett fight. The womens' suspicions are confirmed when Matson and his hired guns storm the boat under Burden's orders. But they are defeated, and subsequently Burden is jailed and a double wedding takes place: Jarrett marries Maxine, Thomas weds Elya.

Credits and Notes

Producer:	Robert Aldrich [The S.A.M. Company; for Frank Sinatra, Essex Productions; Dean Martin, Claude Productions; and Associates and Aldrich]
Executive Producer:	Howard W. Koch
Screenplay:	Teddi Sherman and Robert Aldrich, from an original story by Aldrich
Photography:	Ernest Laszlo (*Technicolor*)
Art Direction:	William Glasgow
Set Decoration:	Raphael Bretton
Music:	Nelson Riddle
Orchestrations:	Gil Grau
Sound:	Jack Solomon
Costumes:	Norma Koch
Editor:	Michael Luciano
Associate Producer:	Walter Blake
Makeup:	Robert J. Schiffer
Second Unit Direction:	Oscar Rudolph
Second Unit Photography:	Carl Guthrie, Joseph Biroc, and Burnett Guffey
Script Supervisor:	Robert Gary
Dialogue Supervisor:	Robert Sherman
Property Master:	John Orlando
Stunt Supervisor:	John Indrisano
Assistant Directors:	Thomas J. Connors, Dave Salven

Script Assistant: Adell Aldrich
Cast: Frank Sinatra (Zack Thomas), Dean Martin (Joe Jar-
                      rett), Anita Ekberg (Elya Carlson), Ursula Andress
                      (Maxine Richter), Charles Bronson (Matson), Victor
                      Buono (Harvey Burden), Edric Connor (Prince George),
                      Nick Dennis (Angel), Richard Jaeckel (Mancini), Mike
                      Mazurki (Chad), Wesley Addy (Trowbridge), Jack Elam
                      (Dobie), Marjorie Bennett (Miss Ermaline), Percy
                      Helton (Ansel), Jack Lambert (Monk), Fritz Feld
                      (Maitre D'), Jonathan Hole (Renee), Paul Langon
                      (Beauregard), Jesslyn Fax (the widow), The Three
                      Stooges, Teddy Buckner and his All-Stars

Filmed on location near Mojave, California, and at Warner Brothers Studios, Burbank, beginning April 15, 1963.

Completed: August 1, 1963
Distribution: Warner Brothers
Running time: 124 minutes
Released: December 25, 1963 (Los Angeles)

16   HUSH...HUSH, SWEET CHARLOTTE   (1964)

Synopsis

Charlotte Hollis (Bette Davis) is a recluse living with her housekeeper,
Velma (Agnes Moorehead), in a decaying bayou manor. She has lived alone
since the death of her father under continual taunts from local inhabitants
who believe her guilty of the murder of her married lover, John Mayhew
(Bruce Dern), thirty-five years before. Now Charlotte is under pressure to
leave her home so that a highway can be put through. Taking advantage of
the fact that her mental competence is in question, she manages to keep the
road builders and local authorities at bay with a shotgun. While the sheriff
(Wesley Addy) consults with Dr. Drew Bayliss (Joseph Cotten) regarding
the possibility of having Charlotte committed, her sister, Mirian Deering
(Olivia de Havilland), returns after living for some years abroad. The
impoverished Miriam renews an old affair with Bayliss and, at Charlotte's
invitation, moves into the Hollis house as informal custodian. Charlotte's
mental condition deteriorates as she begins to hear music from the dance at
which Mayhew was killed and see visions of him on the grounds. Velma
suspects that Miriam and Bayliss are responsible for these occurrences and
that they hope to drive Charlotte truly mad and obtain legal control of her
assets. She confides in Harry Wills (Cecil Kellaway), an insurance investigator who has reopened the file of John Mayhew, but before Velma can acquire
any evidence, she falls to her death.

Left under Miriam's influence, Charlotte becomes convinced of Bayliss's
malevolence and shoots him with a gun Miriam has given her. After the two
women have hidden the body in the bayou, Charlotte retreats to her room
and Bayliss reappears, unhurt by the blank load in the gun. As he and Miriam
discuss their plans for Charlotte's money in the garden, Charlotte overhears
them from her balcony. She topples a stone urn over the balcony, crushing

them both. The following day, as Charlotte is removed to an asylum by the sheriff, Willis appears and presents her with Jewel Mayhew's (Mary Astor) confession to her husband's murder.

Credits and Notes

Producer:	Robert Aldrich [Associates and Aldrich]
Screenplay:	Henry Farrell and Lukas Heller, from an original story by Henry Farrell
Photography:	Joseph Biroc (1.85:1)
Art Direction:	William Glasgow
Set Decoration:	Raphael Bretton
Music:	Frank DeVol
Sound:	Herman Lewis, Bernard Fredricks
Editor:	Michael Luciano
Associate Producer:	Walter Blake
Assistant Directors:	William McGarry, Sam Stranglis, William F. Sheehan
Cast:	Bette Davis (Charlotte Hollis), Olivia de Havilland (Miriam Deering), Joseph Cotten (Dr. Drew Bayliss), Agnes Moorehead (Velma Cruther), Cecil Kellaway (Harry Willis), Victor Buono (Big Sam Hollis), Mary Astor (Jewel Mayhew), William Campbell (Paul Marchand), Wesley Addy (Sheriff Luke Standish), Bruce Dern (John Mayhew), Frank Ferguson (Editor), George Kennedy (Crew boss)

Filmed on location near Baton Rouge, Louisiana, and in Los Angeles. Production began June 1, 1964 and was suspended from July 2 to July 21 and from July 29 to September 9 because of a lawsuit and restraining order against Bette Davis and the illness of Joan Crawford, who was originally to portray Miriam Deering.

Completed:	November 22, 1964
Distribution:	20th Century-Fox
Running time:	133 minutes
Released:	December 24, 1964 (Los Angeles)
Original title:	*Whatever Happened to Cousin Charlotte*

17 FLIGHT OF THE PHOENIX (1966)

Synopsis

A twin-engine plane carrying several oilrig workers and British soldiers from a remote desert station for a few weeks' leave is caught in a sandstorm, loses power, and crashes. The survivors find themselves in uncharted desert, without radio contact or any bearing with which rescuers might be guided. After much discussion, the reality of their situation sinks in, and Frank Towns (James Stewart), the pilot, accepts the offer of Captain Harris (Peter Finch) to set off on foot with as many supplies as can be spared in search of an outpost. Harris is to be accompanied by Sgt. Watson (Ronald Fraser), but he feigns a leg injury in order to remain behind, believing the captain is marching to certain death. The captain sets off and is secretly followed that night by one of the oil workers, Trucker Cobb (Ernest Borgnine), who had offered to go along but was ordered to stay behind due to his recent nervous breakdown while working. The next morning, Towns feels compelled to find Cobb and reluctantly leaves the group in charge of his navigator, Lew Moran (Richard Attenborough), whom he suspects caused their plight by being drunk and failing to check a weather report before departure. Towns finds Cobb dead of heat stroke and returns to the plane after a day.

While they are awaiting the results of Harris's trek, Heinrich Dorfmann (Hardy Kruger), a passenger who claims to be an aircraft designer, shows Towns some plans he has drawn up for constructing a single-engine plane from the existing wreckage. Towns dismisses it as impossibly farfetched: but when Harris stumbles back into camp after having marched in a wide circle, Towns is under pressure to come up with a plan.

As supplies run low, the men discover a small group of Bedouins camped beyond a nearby knoll. Fearful that they may be bandits, they are reluctant to approach them *en masse*. Harris volunteers to walk around and approach them from the other side: Watson, no longer able to claim injury, mutinously refuses to go along, so Dr. Renaud (Christian Marquand) replaces him. The following morning, the Bedouins have departed, leaving Harris and the doctor with their throats cut.

Desperately, Towns agrees to Dorfmann's scheme. It is only after many days of exhausting labor, when the "Phoenix" is almost ready, that Towns inadvertently learns that Dorfmann is a designer of model airplanes. Convinced that a plane designed by a "toymaker" will never get off the ground, Towns nevertheless agrees to complete work. The following morning the engine turns over, and with the men clinging to the wings, the "Phoenix" takes off. Circling to the west with limited fuel, Towns spots a pumping station with its own oasis and sets the plane down.

Credits and Notes

Producer:	Robert Aldrich [Associates and Aldrich]
Screenplay:	Lukas Heller, based on the novel *The Flight of the Phoenix* by Elleston Trevor
Photography:	Joseph Biroc (*De Luxe* Color)
Art Direction:	William Glasgow
Set Decoration:	Lucien Hafley
Music:	Frank DeVol
Orchestrations:	Al Woodbury
Song:	"Senza Fine," music and Italian lyrics by Gino Paoli, English lyrics by Alec Wilder; sung by Connie Francis
Costumes:	Norma Koch
Editor:	Michael Luciano
Associate Producer:	Walter Blake
Second Unit Director:	Oscar Rudolph
Aerial Sequences:	Paul Mantz
Special Photography:	L. B. Abbott, Howard Lydecker
Makeup:	Ben Nye (supervisor), Jack Stone, William Turner, Terry Miles, Ed Butterworth, Frank Westmore
Script Supervisor:	Robert Gray
Dialogue Supervisor:	Robert Sherman
Construction Coordinator:	John LaSalandra

Property Master:	John Orlando
Assistant Directors:	William F. Sheehan, Cliff Coleman, Allan Callow
Cast:	James Stewart (Frank Towns), Richard Attenborough (Lew Moran), Peter Finch (Captain Harris), Hardy Kruger (Heinrich Dorfmann), Ernest Borgnine (Trucker Cobb), Ian Bannen (Crow), Ronald Fraser (Sgt. Watson), Christian Marquand (Dr. Renaud), Dan Duryea (Standish), George Kennedy (Bellamy), Gabriele Tinti (Gabriele), Alex Montoya (Carolos), Peter Bravos (Tasso), William Aldrich (Bill), Barrie Chase (Farida)

Filmed on location near Yuma, Arizona, and Pilot Knob, California, and at 20th Century--Fox Studios, Los Angeles, beginning April 26, 1965.

Completed:	August 13, 1965
Cost:	$3,500,000
Distribution:	20th Century--Fox
Running time:	148 minutes
Released:	January 20, 1966 (London) [First shown in Los Angeles for one week only beginning December 15, 1965 to qualify for Academy Award consideration.]

18 THE DIRTY DOZEN (1967)

Synopsis

A few months before the planned invasion of Europe, Major Reisman (Lee Marvin) is summoned before a special board of Army officers. After reprimanding Reisman for his unconventional behavior and repeated violations of accepted army procedures, the board offers him an opportunity to remove the black marks from his service record. He is to lead a commando group in a raid behind enemy lines and, since the odds are against anyone returning, Reisman must use "volunteers" from the prisoners on death row in the Army stockade. But the board makes it clear that this assignment is not optional for Reisman.

Reisman goes to interview his recruits and, after witnessing an execution, moves from cell to cell making the same proposition to each man: hard work preparing for an extremely perilous mission, little chance of returning alive, and no promise of clemency for those who survive. One by one, Franko (John Cassassavetes), the petty gangster; Jefferson (Jim Brown), the angry black man; Posey (Clint Walker), the mentally deficient giant; Maggott (Telly Savalas), the sexual psychopath; Wladislaw (Charles Bronson), the railroaded noncom; and seven others are blackmailed, cajoled, or lured into volunteering.

As their training begins at an isolated camp, guarded by Sgt. Bowren (Richard Jaeckel) and an elite group of M.P.'s, Reisman makes it clear that they will work as a group or not work at all. Although most face the alternative of capital punishment, individuals continue to be unresponsive. Reisman has a particular method to bring each man into line: he humiliates Jiminez (Trini Lopez), beats Posey in hand to hand combat, and threatens to abandon Maggott to a "headshrinker." Captain Stuart Kinder (Ralph Meeker), who gives them all psychological exams, is appalled by the results. He offers to intervene for Reisman and allow him to weed out the worst misfits. Reisman, who by now has accepted the challenge to his own leadership ability, refuses.

As the men begin to break under Reisman's persistent tactics, the Major seeks permission from General Worden (Ernest Borgnine) for his unusual unit to take part in upcoming war games in which Reisman's major antagonist is the pompous Colonel Everett Dasher Breed (Robert Ryan), head of an elite corps of paratroops. Reisman had previously humiliated Breed by taking his unshaven, ragtag squad on a tour of Breed's camp and having one of them, Pinkley (Donald Sutherland), pass as an incognito general and review the men. During the games, Reisman's "Dirty Dozen" (so named because they refused to shave or bathe when Reisman cut their hot water privileges) easily move through "enemy" lines with a variety of illegal ruses and capture Breed's entire command post.

As the group returns triumphantly to their compound for a graduation dinner, Reisman proffers a special reward for their performance: a busload of prostitutes imported from London. In the midst of their entertainment, their camp is raided by Breed and his men. Aided by a maverick M.P. of Bowren's group, Breed disarms the guards and prepares to interrogate the "Dozen" on their mission. Reisman eludes capture, arms himself, and calls Breed's bluff.

The following night the men parachute out over France. Their objective is a heavily guarded chateau maintained by the German high command for the rest and recreation of its officers. Jiminez is lost in the jump, so Maggott must replace him in the strike group. While Reisman and Wladislaw, who speaks German, enter the castle impersonating Wehrmacht officers, Franco and Maggott grapple their way to the second floor. When one of the German women comes up searching for her lover, Maggott's psychotic mysogyny is set off. He loses control and stabs her, which alerts those below, who flee towards a heavily armored bomb shelter. Reisman and Wladislaw manage to disengage themselves at the last minute, but the cellar door is secured against them. Their only possible counter is to barricade the enemy in. Outside, while Posey and Sawyer (Colin Maitland) guard the crossroads, the rest of the unit is under fire from chateau guards. As his men begin to fall, Reisman orders high explosives stuffed down the ventilators of the cellar bunker. The explosives are dowsed with gasoline and followed by grenades, which sends the entire structure up in flames. Reisman and his remaining men escape in a commandeered armored vehicle.

The only visible survivors of the raid are Reisman and Wladislaw. Visiting their hospital room back in England, General Worden reveals that the men have been given posthumous pardons. Reisman is unimpressed--he just goes on squeezing a rubber ball with his injured arm.

Credits and Notes

| Producer: | Kenneth Human [MKH Productions] |
| Screenplay: | Nunnally Johnson and Lukas Heller, based on the novel *The Dirty Dozen* by E. M. Nathanson |

Photography:	Edward Scaife (*Metrocolor*)
Art Direction:	W. E. Hutchinson
Music:	Frank DeVol
Songs:	"The Bramble Bush," music by Frank DeVol, lyrics by Mack David
	"Einsam," music by Frank DeVol, lyrics by Sibylle Siegfried
Sound:	Franklin Milton, Claude Hitchcock
Editor:	Michael Luciano
Sound Editor:	John Poyner
Associate Producer:	Raymond Anzarut
Production Manager:	Julian MacKintosh
Special Effects:	Cliff Richardson
Camera Operation:	Alan McCabe, Tony Spratling
Makeup:	Ernest Gasser, Walter Schneiderman
Script Supervision:	Angela Allen
Assistant Director:	Bert Batt
Main title design:	Walter Blake
Cast:	Lee Marvin (Major Reisman), Ernest Borgnine (General Worden), Charles Bronson (Joseph Wladislaw), Richard Jaeckel (Sgt. Bowren), John Cassavettes (Victor Franko), Jim Brown (Robert Jefferson), George Kennedy (Mjr. Max Ambruster), Trini Lopez (Pedro Jiminez), Ralph Meeker (Capt. Stuart Kinder), Robert Ryan (Col. Everett Dasher Breed), Telly Savalas (Archer Maggott), Donald Sutherland (Vernon Pickey), Clint Walker (Samson Posey), Robert Webber (Gen. Denton), Tom Busby (Vladek), Ben Carruthers (Gilpin), Stuart Cooper (Lever), Robert Phillips (Morgan), Colin Maitland (Sawyer), Al Mancini (Bravos), George Roubicek (Gardner), Thick Wilson (Worden's aide), Dora Reisser (German girl)

Filmed on location near Chenies, England, and at M.G.M. Studios, London, in sixteen weeks beginning April 25, 1966.

Completed:	October 13, 1966
Cost:	$5,400,000
Distribution:	Metro-Goldwyn-Mayer
Running time:	149 minutes
Released:	June 28, 1967 (Paramount Theater, Hollywood)

Note: Roadshow engagement was in 70mm with six-track Stereophonic sound.

19 THE LEGEND OF LYLAH CLARE (1968)

Synopsis

Bart Langner (Milton Selzer) has discovered a young woman named Elsa Brinkmann (Kim Novak) who bears a striking resemblance to the former Hollywood star Lylah Clare. Langner and his sister, Becky (Jean Carroll), show Elsa a slide collection of Lylah and her director-husband, Lewis Zarkan

(Peter Finch), in an effort to convince her that she would be ideal for a filmed biography of the late star. Unknown to either of them, Elsa is already obsessed with Lylah and stardom; her hotel room is filled with cheap picture books and fan magazines concerning Lylah. Nonetheless, something about the prospect frightens her.

The following morning Langner visits Zarkan to coax him out of retirement and into joining him on the project. Zarkan is skeptical--why should Langner, a "cheap ten percenter," be so anxious to produce a motion picture. Langner confesses that he is dying of cancer and wants to accomplish something significant before the end. He hopes to persuade Zarkan's former producer, Barney Sheean (Ernest Borgnine), to finance the picture. Zarkan is unmoved but, partially because of the goading of his housekeeper, Rosella (Rosella Falk), agrees to meet Elsa. When Elsa is late for the important dinner, Zarkan's impatience turns to savage sarcasm over dessert and coffee. Finally, when Elsa does arrive, Zarkan wants to keep *her* waiting, but Langner rushes out and Rosella follows. Both former intimates of Lylah Clare are struck by Elsa's physical resemblance to the dead actress.

Under Zarkan's insistence, Rosella relates the first flashback version of Lylah's death for Elsa's benefit: pursued home by a young man, shortly after her marriage to Zarkan, Lylah succeeded in killing her attacker but fell to her death, a victim of acrophobia. When Zarkan begins to insult Elsa, she snaps back at him a perfect imitation of Lylah's German-accented voice.

The following day, Langner goes to Sheean with his proposition. When Sheean is dubious, Langner points out that the television value of all of Lylah's old pictures would be greatly enhanced by a successful biography. Sheean agrees to let his designer, Bozo Bedoni (Valentina Cortese), produce some copies of Lylah's old gowns for a press conference but makes no other commitments. He does send his son, Peter (Michael Murphy), to observe the conference.

After days of arduous rehearsal of possible questions, various cosmetic preparations, and a change of name, Zarkan invites the press to his home for an unveiling of Elsa Campbell. Among those in attendance is the crippled gossip columnist, Molly Luther (Coral Browne). The conference goes well until Molly begins her questions, ruthless probes of Elsa's personal life. Assuming the Lylah persona, Elsa launches a verbal attack of her own, until Molly leaves in a huff, pausing only to cast a menacing glance at Barney Sheean, who has arrived late.

Ignoring the fact that his bargaining position may be compromised, Zarkan takes Lylah to dinner at the Brown Derby, where Sheean also happens to be dining. Struck by the first sight of Elsa, Sheean's interest is rekindled; but he uses Luther's antagonism to try to get a better deal. Only Langner's arrival with a preview copy of a *Life* magazine that features Elsa's photo on the cover prevents Zarkan from compromising. The deal is made, but Elsa, who has been ignored all evening, is angered when Zarkan toasts Lylah and not her. She storms off with Sheean's son.

When Elsa returns to Zarkan's house for her things, he confronts her. Attempting to hurt him, she breaks into Lylah's former room which he keeps locked. There she discovers torn bedclothes and slashed furniture, just as Lylah left them. Moved by this evidence of Zarkan's devotion, she allows him to seduce her. Zarkan relates a second version of Lylah's death: she had brought the young man with her to irritate him. After the man fell, Zarkan could not grab Lylah in time to save her from falling also.

As production on the film begins, a weary Elsa comes more under Rosella's influence. A drug addict and former lover of Lylah, Rosella makes Elsa dependent on various pills. As the shooting progresses, the Lylah persona seldom manifests itself; but when it comes to the final sequence, the stabbing of Lylah's assailant, Elsa cannot bring herself to play the scene. Zarkan feigns satisfaction with what he has and ends principal photography. Only after viewing a rough cut does Zarkan reveal his plan for a new ending: Lylah will die in a fall rehearsing for a trapeze film. When Langner protests that this is false and tries to assert himself as producer, Zarkan tells him that the negative of the first ending has mysteriously burned. Elsa, however, sits silently through this discussion and leaves without committing herself.

When Zarkan has reassembled his crew to shoot the added scenes, Elsa is entertaining Zarkan's gardener in her dressing room. Sheean visits the set to remind Zarkan of his promise to finish in six months or forfeit his editing rights. Zarkan goes into Elsa's dressing room to insist that the day's shooting begin immediately and finds that Elsa has lapsed totally into the Lylah persona and knows things about his relationship to Lylah which had never been revealed. Overhearing these revelations, Rosella is somewhat unnerved. Knowing that Zarkan is unpredictable, she threatens to "punish" him if harm comes to Elsa. Meanwhile, Elsa, a former circus performer, has decided to do the trapeze work herself. Over protests from some of the crew, Zarkan and Sheean agree to let her. She performs two jumps, but when Zarkan directs her to look down at the camera, a third flashback passes through her mind. In it, Lylah's assailant is revealed to be a woman and Zarkan forces Lylah to look down, causing her to fall from the stairs. Then, from the trapeze, Elsa/Lylah looks down at Zarkan; she becomes dizzy and falls. She is catapulted off the edge of the net and breaks her neck. Zarkan orders the others to play out the scene as Lylah dies.

At the premiere of Zarkan's film, various industry people are interviewed concerning Elsa's death. Zarkan, realizing his error, is barely coherent. Rosella, watching on television in Zarkan's home, has loaded one of his guns. As she waits for Zarkan, a dog food commercial is run: a housewife sets out a dish so tempting it brings a horde of terrorizing mongrels through the doggie-door, forcing her to flee.

Credits and Notes

Producer:	Robert Aldrich [Associates and Aldrich]
Screenplay:	Hugo Butler and Jean Rouverol, based on a teleplay by Robert Thom and Edward de Blasio [The Du Pont Show of the Month, May 19, 1963, on NBC]
Photography:	Joseph Biroc (*Metrocolor*)

Art Direction:	George W. Davis, William Glasgow
Set Decoration:	Henry Grace, Keogh Gleason
Music:	Frank DeVol
Song:	"Lylah," music by Frank DeVol, lyrics by Sibylle Siegfried
Sound:	Franklin Milton
Costumes:	Renie
Editor:	Michael Luciano
Associate Producer:	Walter Blake
Makeup:	William Tuttle, Robert J. Schiffer
Hairdressing:	Sydney Guilaroff
Dialogue Supervision:	Robert Sherman, Michael Audley
Assistant Director:	Cliff Coleman
Commercial:	Norman Tobak (The Petersen Company)
Cast:	Kim Novak (Lylah Clare/Elsa Brinkmann/Elsa Campbell), Peter Finch (Louie Flack/Lewis Zarkan), Ernest Borgnine (Barney Sheean), Milton Selzer (Bart Langner), Rosella Falk (Rosella), Gabriele Tinti (Paolo), Coral Browne (Molly Luther), Valentina Cortese (Countess Bozo Bedoni), Jean Carroll (Becky Langner), Michael Murphy (Mark Peter Sheean), Lee Meriwether (girl), James Lanphier (legman), Robert Ellenstein (Mike), Nick Dennis (Nick), Dave Willock (D.P.), Peter Bravos (butler), Ellen Corby (script girl), Michael Fox (Premiere M.C.), Hal Maguire (second legman), Queenie Smith (hairdresser), Sidney Skolsky (columnist), Mel and Barbara Ann Markweister (aerialists), Dan Borzage (clown), William Aldrich (assistant M.C.)

Filmed on location in Los Angeles and at M.G.M. Studios in Culver City beginning July 12, 1967.

Completed:	November 20, 1967
Distribution:	Metro-Goldwyn-Mayer
Running time:	130 minutes
Released:	August 21, 1968 (Grauman's Chinese Theater, Hollywood)

20 THE KILLING OF SISTER GEORGE (1968)

Synopsis

June Buckridge (Beryl Reid) is a middle-aged actress who portrays a nurse named "Sister George" in a very successful English television soap opera. June is an alcoholic and insecure about her part, and repeated brushes with fellow cast members and BBC management lead her to suspect that they may plan to write her out of the show. Following a particularly argumentative rehearsal, June stops at a local bar and then attempts to take over a cab carrying two nuns. The nuns, horrified at June's behavior and recognizing her as "Sister George," complain to their superiors.

While June is wallowing in self-pity and abusing her dependent "roommate" and lover, Alice "Childie" McNaught (Susannah York), the Church authorities complain to the network about June's vulgar attack on the nuns. Mrs. Mercy Croft (Coral Browne), a BBC executive, is sent to extract an apology from June. After witnessing June's life-style, Mrs. Croft informs June that "Sister George's" audience appeal is shrinking and that cast changes may be required to bolster the show. Despondently, June drinks more heavily than ever and seeks commiseration from Betty Thaxter (Patricia Medina), a prostitute living next door.

Ultimately, June receives a script in which "Sister George" suffers only a mild illness and quickly recovers. Dressed as Laurel and Hardy, she and Childie celebrate at a local gay bar and even ask Mrs. Croft to join them. Surprisingly, Mrs. Croft accepts. Undismayed by the exclusively lesbian clientele of the bar, Mrs. Croft completely deflates June's exuberance by revealing a new script decision: "Sister George" is to be struck by a car and killed in the next episode. June staggers away and out of the bar, leaving Childie with Mrs. Croft.

After the filming of "Sister George's death," June is given a farewell party and offered a job on a new animated production as the voice of "Clarabelle Cow." Insulted by the proposition, June vehemently refuses. Arriving home to seek solace, June discovers that Mrs. Croft has seduced Childie. After a final argument with June, Childie decides to pack up and move in with the attentive Mrs. Croft. Abandoned by all, June goes back to the sound stage searching for traces of her former success. Enraged at having everything taken from her, she slashes the studio sets, wrecking as much as she can before becoming exhausted. Sitting on a bench in the darkened stage, she realizes what she must do and begins to practice "Clarabelle Cow's" somber "moos."

Credits and Notes

Producer:	Robert Aldrich [Associates and Aldrich]
Screenplay:	Lukas Heller, based on the play *The Killing of Sister George* by Frank Marcus
Photography:	Joseph Biroc *(Metrocolor)*
Location Cameraman:	Brian West [London]
Art Direction:	William Glasgow; Jack Holden [assistant, London]
Set Decoration:	John Brown
Music:	Gerald Fried
Sound:	Dick Church, George Maly, Dean Hodges; Robin Gregory [London]
Costumes:	Renie
Editor:	Michael Luciano
Associate Producer:	Walter Blake
Unit Manager:	Eddie Saeta; David Bennett [London]
Makeup:	Bill Turner
Hairdressing:	Jean Austin
Production Supervisor:	George Tobin
Script Supervisor:	Adell Bravos
Dialogue Supervisor:	Robert Sherman

Property Master: Ignazio Sepulveda
Electricians: Lee Electric Ltd.
Assistant Director: Daisy Gerber; Dennis Robertson [London]
Cast: Beryl Reid (June Buckridge/"Sister George"), Susannah York (Alice "Childie" McNaught), Coral Browne (Mercy Croft), Ronald Fraser (Leo Lockhart), Patricia Medina (Betty Thaxter), Hugh Paddick (Freddie), Cyril Delevanti (Ted Baker), Sivi Aberg (Diana), William Beckley (Floor Manager), Elaine Church (Marlene), Brendan Dillon (Bert Turner), Mike Freeman (Noel), Maggie Paige (Maid), Jack Raine (Deputy Commissioner), Dolly Taylor (tea lady), Meier Tzelniker (Mr. Katz), Cicely Walper (Mrs. Coote), Jack Adams (Byron Webster), Rosalie Williams (Mildred)

Filmed on location in London and at the Aldrich Studios, Los Angeles, beginning June 10, 1968.

Completed: October 10, 1968
Cost: $2,555,000
Distribution: ABC Palomar International
Running time: 138 minutes
Released: December 12, 1968 (Fox Theater, Hollywood)
MPAA Rating: X

21 THE GREATEST MOTHER OF 'EM ALL (1969)

NOTE: In 1969 Aldrich produced a twenty-minute promotional reel in an attempt to raise money from independent backers for a full-length film. The original script by A. I. Bezzerides is dated February 3, 1965. The revised version, which is summarized below, is credited to Bezzerides and Leon Griffiths and dated May 19, 1969.

Synopsis

Dolly Murdock, a middle-aged, grass widow and frustrated actress, is married to a travelling toy salesman, Harv, who is seldom home. Dolly is struggling to keep up payments for her mother's care in a rest home and, at the same time, promote her own daughter's show business career. Although Tricia Murdock is only fifteen, Dolly has her working as an exotic dancer at a local nightclub, hoping that she will be discovered. One night, Gene Frazer, a television producer, visits the club and invites Tricia to his home for a nightcap. His seduction of Tricia is interrupted by the arrival of his wife, Eva, whose bisexuality leads her to join them in bed. Tricia, somewhat dazed by this encounter, is deposited at her doorstep and given five hundred dollars by Frazer's chauffeur. Dolly, after a display of indignation, goes to Frazer's ofices and threatens to charge him with statutory rape. Frazer agrees to "do something" for Tricia's career, beginning with an invitation to a party. That afternoon, while Tricia has gone to the beach to meet with a boyfriend named Jack, Harv Murdock returns after a six-month absence. Inadvertently, he takes some prospective clients to a nightclub and is outraged to discover that his daughter is one of the performers. While Harv goes backstage to create a commotion, Dolly whisks Tricia out and takes her to Frazer's party. On arrival, they encounter Sean Howard, a washed-up feature director reduced to doing hack work for Frazer. After overwhelming Howard with compliments, Dolly systematically touts Tricia's ability to all the guests, much to the dismay of the Frazers. Howard takes Tricia in tow and, when Frazer draws him away, mocks the producer's proposed series in front of her. Infuriated, Frazer tells him he has just lost the job. Howard leaves with Tricia, and a vituperative Frazer tells a gossip columnist that Tricia is underage.

Dolly returns home to find Harv waiting, and a heated argument ensues. Tricia returns home in the middle of it and runs to her room followed by Harv, who locks Dolly out. While they talk, Tricia asks Harv why she shouldn't be beautiful and triggers a brief sexual response from her father. Shocked by the incident, Harv abandons Tricia to Dolly and leaves the next morning. As Dolly drives Tricia to Howard's home in the afternoon, she encourages her to solidify her relationship with him. Tricia willingly complies; but after Howard completes what he believes is his seduction of her, his press agent arrives to show him an item in a trade paper linking him to a juvenile. Howard tells him it is too late for denials; he goes up to find Tricia watching a cartoon show and is overcome by her guilelessness.

Soon the tryst betweeen Howard and Tricia is an item in the scandal magazines, and while Dolly plots to reap financial benefit through blackmail, Howard has other ideas and "abducts" Tricia. Dolly chases his sports car in her own battered vehicle, which ends up out of commission on a canyon road. She goes to the police, but they do not take her seriously.

At Howard's mountain chalet, Tricia has accepted his proposal of marriage but, as he opens a bottle of champagne, Howard collapses and dies from a heart attack. At the funeral, Dolly tries to focus media attention on Tricia's plight and talent, much to the exasperation of the mourners. When Tricia goes to the beach with Jack to try to clear her head of recent events, Dolly tries to sell her diary, detailing her liaison with Howard. That fails, but Tricia arrives home to find a nightclub owner who wants her to dance at a club in the valley. Tricia screams at him to get out and then finds her diary on a table. Realizing her mother's latest scheme, Tricia slaps Dolly and initiates a vicious fight, which ends when Tricia secures the diary and leaves the unconscious Dolly on the floor. Dolly is roused by a visit from Eva Frazer, inviting Tricia to come over to their house again, alone. Dolly takes this news up to Tricia with hopes that Frazer may still put her in a television show.

The following morning Dolly finds Tricia dead of an overdose of sleeping pills. After the funeral, and accompanied by Jack, Dolly visits her mother at the rest home and finds her almost catatonic.

*   *   *

The promotional film includes several scenes shot from the Bezzerides and Griffiths revised script but edited in different sequence, as follows:

1. Tricia's (Alexandra Hay) striptease, coached by Dolly (Ann Southern) and observed by both Frazer (Barry Ruso) and Sean Howard (Peter Finch).
2. A scene [shot by second unit] of Tricia in a park with Jack (Peter Hooten).
3. Tricia's visit to Frazer's home.
4. Tricia meeting again with Jack.
5. Tricia watching cartoons in Howard's bed.
6. The confrontation between Dolly and Howard.
7. Howard's proposal of marriage and subsequent death while at the mountain chalet.
8. Dolly and Collinson (Clark Gordon), owner of the valley nightclub, meeting Tricia.
9. Frazer's seduction of Tricia and the intrusion and participation of Eva (Kate Woodville), ending with a freeze-frame of an anguished Tricia.

Credits and Notes

Producer:	Robert Aldrich [Associates and Aldrich]
Screenplay:	A. I. Bezzerides and Leon Griffiths
Photography:	Joseph Biroc
Art Direction:	James Powell Vance
Song:	"Good Morning, Starshine," music by Galt MacDermot, lyrics by James Rado
Sound:	Dick Church
Choreography:	Alex Romero
Editor:	Frank Urioste
Montage Editor:	Albert Nalpas
Production Supervisor:	George Tobin
Makeup:	Bill Turner
Hairdressing:	Jean Austin
Script Supervisor:	Adell Aldrich Bravos
Dialogue Supervisor:	Robert Sherman
Property Master:	Irving Sandler
Wardrobe:	Charles James
Executive Coordinator:	Johnny LaSalandra
Exterior Director:	Tom Buchanan
Exterior Photography:	Verne Carlson
Cast:	Peter Finch (Sean Howard), Ann Sothern (Dolly Murdock), Alexandra Hay (Tricia Murdock), Kate Woodville (Eva Frazer), Barry Russo (Gene Frazer), Peter Hooten (Jack), Michael Fox (night club comic), Clark Gordon (Collinson), Angel Carter (night club waitress)

Filmed at the Aldrich Studios, Los Angeles, beginning July 28, 1969.

Completed:	August 8, 1969
Cost:	$140,000
Running time:	20 minutes

22   TOO LATE THE HERO   (1970)

Synopsis

Lt. Lawson (Cliff Robertson), a code expert with the American forces in the Pacific, is summoned by his commander, Capt. Nolan (Henry Fonda). Although Lawson is scheduled for stateside leave, Nolan has an assignment for him: liaison officer with a British unit about to raid a Japanese outpost. Lawson attempts to refuse the mission, but Nolan makes it clear that he has no options.

Lawson arrives at the British-held southern tip of a remote island and discovers a small, irregular unit under the command of Col. Thompson (Harry Andrews). Thompson confirms the details given him by Nolan: Lawson will accompany a patrol in to the Japanese-held, northern portion of the island to knock out their ship-watch outpost. Lawson will use his knowledge of Japanese codes to send fake messages and misdirect the enemy fleet.

The fifteen-man detachment is led by Capt. Hornsby (Denholm Elliott). Lawson soon learns that the British soldiers' lack of respect for their field commander stems from their early knowledge of his inability to lead. Yet despite the fact that Hornsby lets them fall into an ambush in which several men are killed, the raiders manage to reach the Japanese radio transmitter. Lawson and Pvt. Hearne (Michael Caine) expect that the guards have been alerted to their presence in the area. Nonetheless, when infiltration at night fails, Hornsby storms the radio shack. Hearne and Lawson hang back, refusing to expose themselves unnecessarily. Hornsby, without Lawson to send messages, elects to destroy the radio but is killed by Japanese troops.

The remnants of the patrol fall back, trailed by the Japanese and their portable loudspeaker system, over which Major Yamaguchi (Ken Takakura) exhorts them to surrender. Finally, three of the weary and hungry Britishers decide to surrender, despite Hearne's and Lawson's warnings that they will be executed. As the messages from the loudspeaker continue, Hearne and Lawson trace the wires back to the microphone. Not realizing that Yamaguchi has kept his promise to spare the other men, they kill him and resume their flight. Finally, they reach a no-man's-land between the Japanese and British perimeters. Encouraged by the onlooking British, they take off across the open stretch but come under machine-gun and rifle fire. A few yards short of the objective, one man is hit and falls. Only when he reaches the British camp does Hearne look back and realize Lawson has been killed.

Credits and Notes

Producer:	Robert Aldrich [Associates and Aldrich--ABC Palomar]
Screenplay:	Robert Aldrich and Lukas Heller, from an original story by Robert Aldrich and Teddi Sherman
Photography:	Joseph Biroc
Art Direction:	James Vance
Set Decoration:	John Brown
Music:	Gerald Fried
Sound:	Frank Milton (supervisor), Dick Church (engineer)
Editor:	Michael Luciano

Associate Producer:	Walter Blake
Production Supervisor:	Fred Ahern; Vicente Nayve
Second Unit Director:	Oscar Rudolph
Makeup:	William Turner, Jack Stone
Special Effects:	Henry Millar, Jr.
Sound Effects:	Milo Lory
Script Supervisor:	Ken Gilbert
Dialogue Supervisor:	Robert Sherman
Property Master:	Ignazio Sepulveda
Wardrobe:	Charles James
Music Editor:	William Saracino
Montage Editor:	Albert Nalpas
Casting:	Lynn Stalmaster
Lighting:	Bill Hannah
Construction Coordinator:	Johnny LaSalandra
Head Grip:	Paul S. Schwake, Jr.
Assistant Directors:	Grayson Rogers, Malcolm Harding
Assistant to the Producer:	William Aldrich
Cast:	Michael Caine (Pvt. Tosh Hearne), Cliff Robertson (Lt. jg. Sam Lawson), Henry Fonda (Capt. John G. Nolan), Ian Bannen (Pvt. Thornton), Harry Andrews (Lt. Col. Thompson), Denholm Elliott (Capt. Hornsby), Ronald Fraser (Pvt. Campbell), Lance Percival (Cpl. McLean), Percy Herbert (Sgt. Johnstone), Michael J. Parsons (Pvt. Rafferty), Harvey Jason (Signalman Scott), William Beckley (Pvt. Currie), Don Knight (Pvt. Connolly), Sean MacDuff (Pvt. Rogers), Martin Dorsey (Pvt. Griffiths), Roger Newman (Pvt. Riddle), Ken Takakura (Major Yamaguchi), Sam Kydd (Sergeant-Major), Patrick Jordon (soldier)

Filmed on location near Subic Bay in the Philippines and at the Aldrich Studios, Los Angeles, beginning January 15, 1969.

Completed:	June 27, 1969
Cost:	$6,250,000
Distribution:	Cinerama Releasing Corporation
Running time:	133 minutes
Released:	May 20, 1970 (Egyptian Theater, Hollywood)
MPAA rating:	GP
Television Title:	*Suicide Run*

Note: Roadshow engagement was in 70mm with six-track Stereophonic sound.

23 THE GRISSOM GANG (1971)

Synopsis

Three petty Kansas City gangsters, Joe Bailey (Matt Clark), Frank Connor (Michael Baselon), and Sam (Alvin Hammer), plan the kidnap of a local heiress, Barbara Blandish (Kim Darby). After she and her boyfriend, Jerry (Alex Wilson), a football player, have an argument and start home from a roadhouse, their car is run off the road. Jerry tries to resist the three assailants and is killed. Barbara is then taken to a run-down farmhouse owned by an ex-fighter named Johnny Hutchins (Dotts Johnson). Acting on a tip, the farmhouse is visited the next day by members of the Grissom Gang, led by Slim Grissom (Scott Wilson). They confront Bailey, a former associate, with their knowledge. In a brief but violent skirmish, the three original kidnappers are killed. Hutchins is spared, and Blandish is taken to the Grissom farmhouse. She remains there while the gang, run by "Ma" (Irene Dailey), waits for a response to its ransom demand.

Barbara's father, John P. Blandish (Wesley Addy), raises and pays one million dollars to recover his daughter. The gang members cover their traces; they murder a street photographer who knew of the original abduction, and Eddie Hagen (Tony Musante) seduces Connor's former girlfriend, Anna Borg (Connie Stevens). Slim, who is inexperienced with women, translates his sexual attraction to Barbara into what he believes is love. "Ma" Grissom had planned to kill Barbara after receiving the ransom money; but Slim will not hear of it. Trying to make the most of a bad situation, "Ma" beats Barbara and tells her that she will be spared if she initiates Slim sexually. Barbara is repulsed by Slim's childish infatuation; but when Slim realizes that he is in control of the situation, he forces her to submit to him.

With the ransom money the gang purchases a nightclub. In an ornately furnished room in the back, Slim installs himself with Barbara. Thinking Slim will eventually tire of her, "Ma" permits this. After several months have passed without the police finding a trace of his daughter or his money, Blandish hires Dave Fenner (Robert Lansing), a private investigator. Following a hunch that the three missing gangsters may have been involved, Fenner seeks interviews with their contacts. Posing as a talent agent, Fenner tricks Anna Borg into revealing what she knew of Connor's participation. This leads him to Johnny Hutchins. While Fenner is on his way to Hutchin's farm, Hagen visits Anna and learns of Fenner's visit. When Anna euddenly realizes Hagen's involvement in the kidnapping, he shoots her. As Fenner is receiving information about Hutchins, Slim and Woppy (Joey Faye) are alerted by Hagen and surround the house. In a shootout, Hutchins and Woppy are killed, but Fenner escapes.

Hagen, realizing that he will be blamed for not eliminating Anna sooner, takes Barbara and returns to the abandoned Grissom farm, hoping to use her to bargain with the police. Slim pursues them there and just as Eddie is about to rape Barbara, Slim stabs him. Returning to the club with Barbara, Slim finds it under siege and flees. The police kill "Ma" and the other gang members inside. In the aftermath they discover Slim and Barbara's room. Disgusted by this evidence of his daughter's liaison with a criminal, Blandish loses interest in her return.

The following morning Slim and Barbara are tracked down to a barn in a nearby farm. As the police surround them, Slim confesses his love for Barbara, which she reciprocates. Taking his gun, Slim goes out to be shot down. As Barbara is taken away by Fenner, reporters crowd around, asking about her relationship to the dead gangster. Her father shuns her, and she rides off silently in Fenner's car.

Producer:	Robert Aldrich [Associates and Aldrich--ABC Pictures]
Associate Producer:	Walter Blake
Screenplay:	Leon Griffiths, based on the novel *No Orchids for Miss Blandish* by James Hadley Chase
Photography:	Joseph Biroc (*Metrocolor*)
Art Direction:	James Vance
Set Decoration:	John Brown
Music:	Gerald Fried
Songs:	"I Can't Give You Anything but Love, Baby," lyrics by Dorothy Fields, music by Jimmy McHugh; sung by Rudy Vallee. "I Surrender, Dear," music by Harry Harris, lyrics by Gordon Clifford
Sound:	Dick Church; Harry W. Tetrick (recording supervisor)
Costumes:	Norma Koch
Choreography:	Alex Romero
Film Editors:	Michael Luciano: Frank Urioste (associate)
Production Supervisor:	Fred Ahern
Makeup:	William Turner
Hairdressing:	Jean Austin
Special Effects:	Henry Millar
Sound Effects:	Milo Lory
Script Supervisor	Robert Gray
Dialogue Supervisor:	Robert Sherman
Property Master:	Ignazio Sepulveda
Wardrobe:	Charles James (men); Lucia de Martino (women)
Music Editor:	Scott Perry
Casting:	Lynn Stalmaster
Construction Coordinator:	Johnny LaSalandra
Production crew:	William Hannah (Gaffer); Paul Schwake (head grip); Robert Merry (best boy); Paul Gilbert (electrician); Maurice Larson (painter); Don Pringle (greensman); Joe Jackson, Orville Hallberg (camera operation)
Assistant Directors:	Malcolm Harding, William Morrison
Production Assistant:	Patricia Heade
Unit Publicist:	Dave Davies
Assistant to the Producer:	William Aldrich
Titles:	Don Record
Jewels:	Laykin et Cie (I. Magnin and Company)
Cast:	Kim Darby (Barbara Blandish), Scott Wilson (Slim Grissom), Tony Musante (Eddie Hagen), Robert Lansing (Dave Fenner), Irene Dailey (Ma Grissom), Connie Stevens (Anna Borg), Wesley Addy (John P. Blandish), Joey Faye (Woppy), Don Keefer (Doc), Dotts Johnson (Johnny Hutchins), Mort Marshall (Heinie), Michael Baselon (Connor), Ralph Waite (Mace), Hal Baylor (Chief McLaine), Matt Clark (Bailey), Alvin Hammer (Sam), Dave Willock (Rocky), Alex Wilson (Jerry McGowen), Elliott Street (gas station boy), John Steadman (old man), Raymond Guth (farmer)

Filmed on location near Sutter Creek and Modesto, California, and at the Aldrich Studios, Los Angeles, beginning July 6, 1970.

Completed:	November 13, 1970
Cost:	$3,000,000
Distribution:	Cinerama Releasing Corporation
Running time:	128 minutes
Released:	May 28, 1971 (Pix Theater, Hollywood)
MPAA Rating:	R

24 ULZANA'S RAID (1972)

Synopsis

As the troopers at a cavalry fort in Arizona play a Sunday game of baseball, an outrider brings word that a party of ten Indians has left the nearby reservation of Chirachua Apache. When a group dispatched to question the reservation dwellers brings back word that the war party is led by Ulzana (Joaquim Martinez), a charismatic leader whose avowed mission is to terrorize all white settlers in his homeland, the commandant assembles a troop to pursue them. Over the objections of his chief scout, McIntosh (Burt Lancaster), the troop is placed under the command of a newly-commissioned and totally inexperienced officer, Lt. Garnett DeBuin (Bruce Davidson). DeBuin, who is still under the moral influence of his father, a fundamentalist minister, disapproves of his scouts, both the rough talking McIntosh, who "lives in sin" with an Indian woman, and the "savage" Ke-ni-tay (Jorge Luke). Despite their warnings, his avowed purpose is to deal with Ulzana in a civilized manner.

Various riders have been sent out to warn the local farmers of the threat from Ulzana and to escort those who wish to come back to the safety of the fort. The detachment of searchers comes across a family on their first day of tracking; a husband and wife murdered, a trooper mutilated after he had taken his own life, but the son spared to live with the trauma of witnessing the massacre. Another settler is found buried up to his neck in front of his smouldering home. Unable to understand the motivation for such atrocities, DeBuin questions Ke-ni-tay on the Apache mentality. The only explanation the scout offers is that Ulzana seeks psychic power and hopes to acquire it from the souls of his victims.

As the pursuit continues, Ke-ni-tay recognizes a ruse of the renegades. Most have abandoned their horses, leaving one or two riders changing mounts every few hours to exhaust the cavalry's horses in following a false trail. McIntosh and Ke-ni-tay ride off in opposite directions at right angles to the cavalry column, planning to intercept the riders as they double back. At dawn, McIntosh spots the Indians; he gives chase and, although his own horse is shot, kills one of the riders and wounds the other. When the troopers arrive, McIntosh informs them that he has killed Ulzana's son. After dark, the soldiers mutilate the body in retaliation for their comrade, which greatly disturbs DeBuin, who orders it to be burned. He also orders a reluctant Sergeant (Richard Jaeckel) to pursue the wounded Apache.

The following day, the pursuers reach another gutted ranch; but here the Indians have left alive the rancher's wife, raped and scarred. The sergeant returns, having lost another man in killing the wounded Indian. McIntosh surmises that Ulzana's tactic is to force them to divide and send an escort back to the fort with the crazed woman which he can attack to replace his lost horses. At McIntosh's suggestion they do divide--McIntosh, the sergeant and five others start back, hoping to lure Ulzana out and hold him until DeBuin can arrive. Ke-ni-tay remains with DeBuin and quickly realizes that Ulzana has posted a lookout to make sure the main force does not double back. While he goes up into the foothills to kill him, DeBuin waits. Meanwhile, McIntosh reaches a narrow pass. Although he knows the Apache are probably above, the group rides on. As they come under fire, a flash from the fieldglasses of Ulzana's lookout confuses DeBuin. Thinking it a signal from Ke-ni-tay, he starts back. The ferocity of Ulzana's attack is too much for McIntosh. The troopers try to hide behind their horses but they bolt away. Ulzana's lookout, who is racing to warn his leader, is caught and killed by Ke-ni-tay; but DeBuin still arrives too late. He finds McIntosh, mortally wounded, protecting the woman, and all the others dead. Ke-ni-tay, coming down from the mountain, never pauses but continues after Ulzana. While the soldiers account for the rest of the Apache, Ke-ni-tay runs down the renegade leader and brings the body back to DeBuin, who orders it burned over protests that the head should be taken back to verify his death. At McIntosh's insistence, DeBuin and his remaining men ride off, leaving him behind to die alone.

Credits and Notes

Producer:	Carter de Haven [De Haven--Associates and Aldrich]
Screenplay:	Alan Sharp
Photography:	Joseph Biroc (*Technicolor*)
Music:	Frank DeVol
Art Direction:	James Vance
Set Decoration:	John McCarthy
Sound:	James Alexander, George Maley
Editor:	Michael Luciano
Production Manager:	Ernie Wehmeyer
Makeup:	Mike Moschella, Tony Lloyd
Hairdressing:	Lorraine Robertson
Special Effects:	Sass Bedig, Jack Fagard
Script Supervisor:	Robert Gary
Property Master:	Ignazio Sepulveda
Wardrobe:	Glenn Wright
Production Crew:	William Hannah (gaffer); Robert Aldridge (key grip); John Flannagan (best boy); Gary Moreno (leadman); Ward Wolton (painter); Paul Schwake; Ken Peach, Gil Hamison (camera operation); Lee Brendle, John Black (dolly grips)
Assistant Director:	Malcolm R. Harding
Cast:	Burt Lancaster (McIntosh), Bruce Davidson (Lt. Garnett DeBuin), Richard Jaeckel (the Sergeant), Jorge Luke

(Ke-ni-tay), Joaquim Martinez (Ulzana), Lloyd Bochner (Captain Gates), Douglass Watson (Major Wainwright), Karl Svenson (Rukeyser), Dran Hamilton (Mrs. Riordan), John Pearce (Corporal), Amy Eccles (McIntosh's squaw), Gladys Holland (Mrs. Rukeyser), Richard Bull (Ginsford), Margaret Fairchild (Mrs. Ginsford), Otto Reichow (Steegmeyer), John McKee (company clerk), Nick Cravat, Ted Markland, R.L. Armstrong, Hal Maguire, Richard Farnsworth (troopers), Hal Baylor (Curtis), Dean Smith (Trooper Horowitz), Chuck Courtney (Trooper Mulhearn), Ross Loney (rider), Walter Scott, Jerry Gatlin, Fred Brookfield, Bill Burton, Tony Epper, Larry Randles (stunt troopers), Steve Leonard, Leslie Ann and Mary Carla Flanagan (Ginsford children), Patty Elder, Alan Gibbs (stunt riders)

Filmed on location near Nogales, Arizona, and Las Vegas, Nevada, beginning January 18, 1972.

Completed: March 14, 1972
Distribution: Universal Pictures
Released: October 18, 1972 (Chicago); November 22, 1972 (Los Angeles)
MPAA Rating: R

25 EMPEROR OF THE NORTH POLE (1973)

Synopsis

In the early years of the depression, Freight Number 19 runs through the Northwest and acquires a reputation among hoboes as an unrideable train. Its brutal guard, "Shack" (Ernest Borgnine), carries a small hammer clipped to his belt and has killed several hoboes without compunction. On this particular day a solitary "bo" named "A No. 1" (Lee Marvin) has hopped No. 19 from a trestle overpass. As he settles in, unaware that Shack has already hurled one hobo from the train and is stalking others, another man runs up alongside and jumps into A No. 1's car. "Cigaret" (Keith Carradine) quickly establishes himself as a boaster; his lack of skill in boarding has caused him to be spotted by Shack, who stands above them, amused by their discussion. Unimpressed by Cigaret, A No. 1 returns to his own thoughts. Shack slams and locks the freight car door, planning to deal with them both in the Willamette yard. Unable to force the door open, Cigaret's bravado evaporates, and he begins to panic. A No. 1 admits that their position looks bad but saves his energy. As they approach the yard, he piles up some straw by the wall of the car and sets it afire. Above them, Shack realizes what is happening and instructs the engineer to hurry into the yard. As soon as the flames have charred and weakened the wall, A No. 1 kicks out a portion and jumps through, tumbling out of the train at the edge of the yard. Cigaret hesitates too long; by the time he jumps, the train has entered the yard, and he is captured.

The yard crew realize that a brash greenhorn like Cigaret could not have engineered the fiery escape from Shack's clutches, and they question him regarding A No. 1. Since most of the yard men have had run-ins with Shack, they wonder if a "bo" has finally materialized who could tarnish Shack's reputation for perfect runs. The yard men establish a betting pool and send one of their number to the hobo jungle to challenge A No. 1. While they continue to discuss the possibilities of A No. 1's attempt, Cigaret takes advantage of their inattention to escape. Arriving at the hobo jungle, Cigaret discovers that A No. 1 has been awarded a hero's welcome by the assembly of bums, who have voted him "Emperor of the North Pole." Cigaret wastes no time in claiming half of A No. 1's empire; but the bums are as capable as the yard men of recognizing a greenhorn and ignore his protests.

After an indecisive morning in which he wanders around dodging police and even getting baptized, A No. 1 decides to accept the yard men's challenge. Shack, aware of the contest, decides to take the No. 19 out of the yard at high speed, but the hoboes break open a switch, sending the freight train into a siding and allowing A No. 1 to clamber aboard. As he prepares his tactics for survival, A No. 1 discovers that Cigaret has also jumped the train. Meanwhile, Shack, infuriated at having his train sidetracked, wastes no time in stopping it to search, forcing the bums to take cover in the surrounding brush. When the No. 19 starts up again, Shack spots them and prevents them from climbing on.

As Cigaret mocks him, A No. 1 demonstrates that he is not yet ready to quit. He greases the track to slow down an oncoming express and rides it right back to where the No. 19 has pulled into a siding to allow it to pass. Shack realizes that is not dealing with any ordinary roadbum, when he again spots A No. 1 aboard his train. He threatens to corner the unarmed hoboes with his deadly hammer, but A No. 1 slams on the emergency brake, enabling both men to leap off. Shack watches from above a boxcar while a defeated A No. 1 catches his breath on the side of the hill and tells Cigaret he has had enough. Sensing a chance to seize A No. 1's meaningless empire, Cigaret scrambles up the hill and gets back on the No. 19. After a moment's pause, in which Shack's attention is diverted to Cigaret, A No. 1 wearily follows. It takes Shack little time to corner the inexperienced Cigaret on a flatcar at the rear of the train and begin to beat him savagely. Reluctantly, A No. 1 interrupts and, after a desperate struggle, wrenches away Shack's weapon and pommels him, finally throwing the semiconscious guard off the flatcar. As Cigaret starts to bluster about "their" victory, A No. 1 pushes him off the train also, yelling back that he doesn't have the right attitude to call himself a hobo.

Credits and Notes

Producer:	Stanley Hough [Inter-Hemisphere Productions]
Executive Producer:	Kenneth Hyman
Screenplay:	Christopher Knopf
Photography:	Joseph Biroc (*DeLuxe* Color; *Panavision*)
Camera Operators:	Joe Jackson; Ken Peach
Art Direction:	Jack Martin Smith
Set Decoration:	Raphael Bretton

Music:	Frank DeVol
Song:	"A Man and A Train," lyrics by Hal David, music by Frank DeVol; sung by Marty Robbins
Sound:	Dick Overton
Film Editors:	Michael Luciano; William Navarro (assistant)
Unit Production Manager:	Saul Wurtzel
Makeup:	William Turner
Special Effects:	Henry Millar, Tom Fisher, Jack Monroe
Script Supervisor:	Howard Hohler
Dialogue Supervisor:	Robert Sherman
Property Master:	Ignazio Sepulveda
Wardrobe:	Ed Wynigear
Construction:	Johnny LaSalandra
Production Crew:	William Hannah (gaffer); Jack Richter (head grip); Phil Sarabia, Paul Schwake, Robert Duncan, O. T. Henderson (grips); Paul Gilbert (electrician); Robert Bells, Robert Woodside, Don Gerrard (lighting); John Flanagan (best boy); Maurice Larson (painter); Stuart MacKenzie (greensman); Tom Pedigo (Leadman); Ray de la Motte, Ed Morey, Joe Thibo (camera assistants); Howard Wilmarth (boom); Don Parker (recorder)
Assistant Director:	Malcolm Harding
Production Assistant:	Betty Berry
Unit Publicist:	Dave Davies
Stills:	Orlando Suero
Associate Editors:	Roland Gross, Frank Capacchione
Dubbing Editor:	Godfrey Marks
Visual Effects:	L. B. Abbott
Sound Effects:	Edward Rossi, William Hartman, Don Isaacs, Don Walden
Second Unit Director:	Michael D. Moore
Second Assistants:	Barry Steinberg, Larry Powell
Sound Rerecording:	Theodore Soderberg
Casting:	Jack Baur
Titles:	Walter Blake (design); Pacific Title
Cast:	Lee Marvin (A No. 1), Ernest Borgnine (Shack), Keith Carradine (Cigaret), Charles Tyner (Cracker), Malcolm Atterbury (Hogger), Simon Oakland (policeman), Harry Caesar (Coaly), Hal Baylor (yardman), Matt Clark (yardlet), Elisha Cook (Gray Cat), Joe di Reda (Dinger), Liam Dunn (Smile), Diana Dye (Prudence), Robert Foulk (conductor), James Goodwin (Fakir), Ray Guth (Preacher), Sid Haig (Grease Tail), Karl Lucas (Pokey Stiff), Edward McNally (yard clerk), John Steadman (Stew Bum), Vic Tayback (yardman), Dave Willock (Groundhog), Ralph Montgomery (Alkee Stiff), Don Blackman (Old Shine), Hal Jon Norman (Pegleg), Harry Hickox (Elder), Danny Big Black (Hobo), Wayne Sutherlin (Gink), Bern Holfman (Halfy), Forrest Wood (station agent), Joe Hayworth (Ash Eater), Jack Collins (dispatcher), Richard Doughty (the Cub), James

Kingsley (machinist), George McFadden (Prairie Special engineer), Ben Dobbins (mechanic)

Filmed on location near Cottage Grove, Oregon, and at 20th Century--Fox Studios beginning July 11, 1972.

Completed:	October 1, 1972
Cost:	$3,800,000
Distribution:	20th Century-Fox
Running time:	118 minutes [126 minutes before general release]
Released:	May 23, 1973 (New York); June 29, 1973 (Los Angeles)
MPAA Rating:	PG

Note: This film was originally released in New York under the title *The Emperor of the North Pole*, but was changed to *Emperor of the North* for the Los Angeles and subsequent runs. [See Bibliography]

26 THE LONGEST YARD (1974)

Synopsis

Former professional football star Paul Crewe (Burt Reynolds) severs his relationship with a Palm Beach heiress (Anitra Ford) in a violent manner. He slaps her around then steals her car and eludes the police, whom she summons to arrest him. After a high speed chase through the central city, Crewe finally pushes the battered vehicle into the river. When two policemen come to question him in a nearby bar, he provokes them into a fight. For auto theft and resisting arrest, Crewe is sentenced to a year at hard labor in Citrus State Prison.

Arriving at the prison, Crewe finds that his reputation has preceded him. Many inmates are openly contemptuous of an athletic super-star who ruined his career by shaving points. Warden Hazen (Eddie Albert), however, feels no compunction about asking Crewe to help his semiprofessional team of guardsmen win a national championship. Opposed to this idea is Captain Knauer (Ed Lauter), coach and quarterback of the team, who warns Crewe with his fists not to accept Hazen's offer. Crewe's compliance with Knauer's threat angers Hazen, who sends Crewe to work on the swamp reclamation detail shackled to a rebellious black prisoner, Granville (Harry Caesar). Crewe tries to keep a low profile while on the chain gang, but he is taunted constantly by guards and fellow inmates, particularly the trustee, Unger (Charles Tyner), one of Hazen's informants. Only "Caretaker" (Jim Hampton) and "Pop" (John Steadman), a lifer who lost all hope of parole when he struck Hazen, are in any way friendly. When Crewe is finally goaded into a fight, the guards urge the men to hurt each other severely. But Crewe redirects his violence at Knauer and, as a result, is sent to solitary.

In order to escape the "box," Crewe tells Hazen he has reconsidered his offer. After watching the guards in practice, he suggests that what they need is a tune-up game. Hazen likes the idea and orders Crewe to organize a team of prisoners for just such a purpose. Reluctantly, with Caretaker as his assistant, Crewe begins putting a team together. The first volunteer is Nate Scarboro (Michael Conrad), an aging former pro. Caretaker acquires prison records to suggest both the likeliest players and the guards' weaknesses. After convincing the largest and meanest white inmates to participate, Crewe appeals to Granville to help recruit the best black athletes. Under the enticement of being able to hit the guards where it hurts, they ultimately accept assignments. Unger, spying for Hazen, badgers Crewe to become assistant coach without success. Meanwhile, Caretaker arranges a tryst between Crewe and Hazen's secretary (Bernadette Peters) in exchange for a film of the guards in action and plaster casts and drugs from the dispensary. He even plans for new team uniforms. The rejected Unger takes revenge by boobytrapping the light bulb in Crewe's cell; but it is Caretaker, coming to get something for Crewe, who is burned to death when the bulb explodes.

Saddened by Caretaker's death, the prisoners' view of the game as an opportunity to even the score for years of abuse is strengthened. They stun the guards just by taking the field in black uniforms labelled "Mean Machine." In the first two quarters, the "Mean Machine" also surprises the guards by its ability. Although they make mistakes which allow the guards to score, the prisoners make offensive moves which keep the score close at half-time, while defensively injuring several of the guards.

Dismayed by his team's poor showing, Hazen calls Crewe to the shower room between periods. While Capt. Knauer earnestly chews out his men in the next room, Hazen fixes the game by telling Crewe he has a confession from Unger which implicates Crewe in Caretaker's death. Hazen threatens to use this information against him unless Crewe throws the game by twenty-one points. Frightened by the chance of life imprisonment for murder, Crewe's play in the third quarter is a succession of poor passes and fumbles, which allows the guardsmen to get a three-touchdown lead. Unknown to Crewe and contrary to their "deal," Hazen lets Knauer encourage the guards to give the inmates all the physical abuse they can deliver. With Granville hurt and the team aware that he is throwing the game, Crewe takes himself out. While he watches the prisoners being brutalized, Crewe catches Pop's look of disapproval and remembers Pop's avowal that hurting Hazen was worth a life term. Crewe returns to the field and is racked several times when "Mean Machine" blockers abandon him. When he does manage to gain ground, his men are convinced Crewe has decided to play to win. Finally, it is the last play of the game, with the inmates' line of scrimmage on the guards' one-yard line. As Crewe rolls out on an option, he spots a hole and plows his way through, scoring a comeback upset at the gun.

At first Hazen is too stunned to speak; then as Crewe walks back alone towards the end zone, Hazen tells Capt. Knauer that Crewe is trying to escape and must be shot. Knauer grabs a rifle and takes aim but hesitates out of newfound respect for Crewe and ignores Hazen's enraged orders to fire. When Crewe bends down to pick up the game ball and heads back, both men make evident their disgust with Hazen; and Crewe goes into the showers uncertain of his fate.

Credits and Notes

Producer:	Albert S. Ruddy
Associate Producer:	Alan Horowitz
Screenplay:	Tracy Kennan Wynn, from a story by Albert S. Ruddy
Photography:	Joseph Biroc (*Technicolor*)
Camera Operator:	Orville S. Halbert
Production Design:	James S. Vance
Set Decoration:	Rafael Bretton
Music:	Frank DeVol
Sound:	Fred D. Faust ()
Sound Rerecording:	John Wilkinson
Sound Effects:	Gordon Daniel, Jim Fritch, Howard Beals
Songs:	Lynyrd Skynyrd's "Saturday Night Special" written by Ronnie Van Zant and Edward Calhoun King. "Teach Me To Cheat," sung by Judy Kester. "Roadside Roses," sung by Jack Barlow. "Paramount on Parade," by Janis and King. "Born Free," by Barry and Black. "You Got to be a Football Hero," by Sherman, Lewis and Fields; performed by the Soul Touchers Band and Chorus
Film Editors:	Michael Luciano; Roy Peterson and Dennis Wooley (assistants); Frank Capacchione, Allan Jacobs, George Hively (football sequences)
Montage Film Effects:	Steve Orfanos
Unit Production Manager:	Russ Saunders
Makeup:	Tom Ellingwood, Guy Del Russo
Special Effects:	Thol Ogden Simonson
Script Supervisor:	Alvin Greenman
Property Master:	Horst Grandt
Wardrobe:	Charles James; Kenneth Harvey (assistant)
Construction:	Arnold Pine
Production Crew:	William Hannah (gaffer); Paul Schwake (head grip); Joe E. Hicks, Donald G. Cowger (grips); Lon Massey, Jr., John Donnelly (best boys); Michael Scoville (cableman); James Contreras (boomman); Frank Cappiello (landscaper); Ralph A. Nelson (property assistant); Richard E. Enoch (transportation); Frederick J. Smith, Henry Harrison, Julian Wilson (camera assistants); Anna Zappia (production secretary); Joan Bennett (director's secretary)
Second Unit Director (car chase) and Stunt Coordinator:	Hal Needham
Second Assistant Director:	Ron Wright
Production Assistant:	Michael Newman
Unit Publicist:	Dave Davies
Stills:	Steve Wever
Second Unit Photography:	Cliff Poland
Technical Advisor:	Patrick Studstill
Casting:	Joyce Selznick

Titles: Walter Blake (design); Opticals West
Cast: Burt Reynolds (Paul Crewe), Eddie Albert (Warden Hazen), Anitra Ford (Melissa), Ed Lauter (Captain Knauer), Harry Caesar (Granville), Ray Nitschke (Bogdanski), Mike Henry (Rassmeusen), Joe Kapp (Walking Boss), John Steadman (Pop), Bernadette Peters (Warden's secretary), Michael Conrad (Nate Scarboro), James Hampton (Caretaker), Pepper Martin (shop steward), Ernie Wheelwright, Jr. (Spooner), Tony Cacciotti (Rotka), Richard Kiel (Samson), Pervis Atkins (Mawabe), Dino Washington (Mason), Charles Tyner (Unger), Mort Marshall (Assistant Warden), Robert Tessier (Schokner), Michael Fox (announcer), Joe Dorsey (bartender), Chuck Hayward (Trooper I), Alfie Wise (Trooper II), Dr. Gus Carlucci (team doctor), Jack Rockwell (trainer), Sonny Shroyer (Tannen), Ray Ogden (Schmidt), Don Ferguson (referee), Tony Reese (Levitt), Steve Wilder (J.J.), George Jones (Big George), Wilbur Gillan (Big Wilbur), Wilson Warren (Buttercup), Joe Jackson (Little Joe), Donald Hixon (Donny), Jim Nicholson (ice man)

Filmed on location at Georgia State Prison, Reidsville (9/10/73); and in Savannah and Brunswick, Georgia; Hilton Head Island, South Carolina; Beverly Hills, California.

Cost: $2,500,000
Distribution: Paramount (U.S.); CIC-American (Great Britain)
Running time: 121 minutes (U.S.); 122 minutes (Great Britain)
Released: August 21, 1974 (Loews State, Orpheum, New York City)
MPAA Rating: R [Certified X in Great Britain]
Title in Great Britain: *The Mean Machine*

27 HUSTLE (1975)

Synopsis

When a bus full of children on a beach outing discovers the body of a young woman (Sharon Kelly) in the surf, Lt. Phil Gaines's (Burt Reynolds) morning off from the Los Angeles Police Tactical squad is interrupted. He leaves the house he shares with French-born Nicole Britton (Catherine Deneuve) troubled by personal problems. Nicole, who came to the U.S. as a highly paid call girl, continues to practice her profession part-time because Gaines, apprehensive after divorcing an unfaithful wife will not make an unqualified emotional commitment to her. Gaines leaves knowing she resents the occasions when his job spoils their time together and may unconsciously retaliate by "turning a trick."

Gaines and his black partner, Sgt. Louis Belgrave (Paul Winfield), establish that the girl may be Gloria Hollinger, a reported runaway of some years earlier; they summon her parents, Marty and Paula Hollinger (Ben Johnson and Eileen Brennan), to the morgue for identification of the corpse. At the sight of Gloria's unclad body unceremoniously rolled out from a cold drawer, Hollinger attacks Gaines and abuses him verbally for not even covering the body. Gaines acknowledges that it was callous of them but feels compelled to tell Hollinger that Gloria most likely died of a self-induced drug overdose following attendance at a party. The detectives also know she was a frequent performer at sex parties and in stag reels.

As Paula Hollinger tries to console her husband in their daughter's long unused room, Gaines goes home and discovers Nicole in an erotic phone conversation with a client. Gaines disconnects the phone and tries once again to express his feelings to Nicole.

The following morning, Gaines and Belgrave are called before Chief John Santoro (Ernest Borgnine) and questioned about Hollinger's allegation to the district attorney that the police are covering up his daughter's murder. Gaines assures him it was suicide; and Belgrave's desire to keep the case open in thwarted. Outside, Gaines does agree to follow up on a photograph found in the dead girl's possession, but his ambivalence about the case is increased by Hollinger's belligerence at the official disposition of the case, when he accuses Gaines of covering up.

Somewhat mollified by Paula Hollinger's thanks and her admission that her husband has not been the same since his wartime experiences, Gaines decides to follow up on the photograph. But before he can begin, he receives a call that a man whom Gaines had once arrested and had institutionalized has been released, killed two women, and taken another hostage in a garment workshop, where he now is demanding to see Gaines. By the time Gaines and Belgrave reach the scene, Gaines is almost out of control in his indignation over a system of justice which not only brushes aside Marty Hollinger because he is, as Santoro says, "Nobody," but which also lets a psychopath go free. Arriving at the garment workshop, Gaines crosses police barricades to join the psychopath on the top floor. Knowing that Gaines will be killed if he exchanges himself for the hostage, Belgrave jumps through a skylight and shoots the psychopath. Gaines sees the man is not dead and puts a bullet in his head to insure that he will never be let loose again.

The results of enlarging the Hollinger girl's photograph disclose her standing next to her roommate, Peggy Summers (Catherine Bach), and a prominent attorney named Leo Sellers (Eddie Albert). Even as Gaines is pondering whether to harass Sellers, who is not only a powerful figure but is responsible for bringing Nicole to Los Angeles, she is spending the afternoon on Seller's yacht. While there, she watches him make a call from a public telephone, not knowing that the connection is with a city in the Midwest and that he is listening to the sound of an explosion signaling the death of a union leader. After the call, Sellers returns to Nicole, unaware that he has made the call on a phone coincidentally tapped by narcotics officers.

While Hollinger, following up on information given him by Gloria's roommate, goes to a nightclub where his daughter once worked as an exotic dancer, the Tactical Squad is given the tape of Sellers' telephone call and Gaines recognizes the voice. After being confronted with the call, Sellers, although he knows the tapes could not convict him of any crime, admits that the Hollinger girl frequented his parties, including one the night before she died. Gaines accepts Sellers' story, which suggests the motive for her suicide was simply fatigue with her dissolute life-style. Sellers also tells Gaines that Nicole was with him when he made the call. This provokes a violent argument when Gaines returns home, which leads to his striking Nicole, then to a tearful reconciliation.

The following morning Gaines is dismayed to learn from Paula Hollinger that Marty has been beaten up by employees of the nightclub where he went to ask questions. Although he is sufficiently outraged to visit the club himself and physically abuse the M.C. (Jack Carter), Gaines confides to Belgrave that if Hollinger follows the trail to Sellers he may be more seriously hurt. After he learns from Hollinger's wife that her infidelity was one of the causes of Gloria's estrangement and that, ironically, she was not even Marty's child, Gaines begins to see too many depressing parallels with his own past. He convinces Belgrave that they must disillusion Hollinger by showing him a stag reel, acquired from Sellers, featuring his daughter. Yet this makes Hollinger even more determined to find the person responsible for Gloria's death. When Gaines and Belgrave learn from Paula that Hollinger has beaten Peggy Summers to learn Sellers' name, they race to Sellers' home only to discover Hollinger has already murdered him. Even as he lectures Hollinger, Gaines tampers with evidence to make it look as if Hollinger acted in self-defense. Shooting the stupefied Hollinger in the arm perfects the alibi, at which point Belgrave realizes that Gaines may well have engineered the entire thing out of jealousy over Nicole. Still, he goes along with Gaines.

Exorcised of the ghosts of his past, Gaines calls Nicole and proposes that they go to San Francisco and rediscover each other. On his way to the airport, he stops at a liquor store, stumbles into a robbery, and is killed. Belgrave appears at the airport to break the news to Nicole.

Credits and Notes

Producer:	Robert Aldrich [RoBurt Productions — Paramount in association with Churchill Service Company]
Executive Producer:	Burt Reynolds
Associate Producer:	William Aldrich
Screenplay:	Steve Shagan
Photography:	Joseph Biroc (*Eastmancolor*)
Camera Operators:	Kenneth Peach, Jr.; Roger Sherman, Jr.
Art Direction:	Hilyard Brown
Set Decoration:	Raphael Bretton
Music:	Frank DeVol
Sound:	Jack Solomom
Songs:	"Yesterday When I Was Young," by Charles Aznavour, English lyrics by Herbert Kretzmer; sung by Charles Aznavour. "So Rare," lyrics by Jack Sharpe, music by Jerry Herst. "A Man and a Woman," by Francis Lai. "Mission Impossible," music by Lalo Schifrin. "Begin the Beguine," by Cole Porter
Film Editor:	Michael Luciano; Dennis Wooley (assistant)
Production Supervisor:	Eddie Saeta

Special Effects: Henry Millar
Script Supervisor: Adell Aldrich
Dialogue Supervisor: Alvin Greenman
Property Master: Horst Grandt
Wardrobe: Oscar Rodriquez (men); Betsy Cox (women)
Makeup: Tom Ellingwood
Hair Stylist: Marlene Williams
Production Crew: William Hannah (gaffer); Paul Schwake (head grip); Don Farnsworth (grip); Ed Reilly (best boy); Paul Wolfe (cableman); Joe Kenworthy (boomman); Patrick Moudakis (leadman); Michael Dunn (property assistant); Fred Smith, Roy Hogstedt, Steve Shank (camera assistants); Anna Zappia (production secretary); Nancy Streebeck (executive producer's secretary); Joan Bennett (associate producer's secretary); Terry Flanagan (director's secretary); Harvey Dorn (transportation); Jack Sanders (D.G.A. trainee); Maurice Larson (painter)

First Assistant
Director: Malcom Harding
Second Assistant
Director: Phil E. Ball
Production Assistant: Walter Blake
Stills: Jack Gereghty
Casting: Jack Baur
Cast: Burt Reynolds (Lt. Phil Gaines), Catherine Deneuve (Nicole Britton), Ben Johnson (Marty Hollinger), Paul Winfield (Sgt. Louis Belgrave), Eileen Brennan (Paula Hollinger), Eddie Albert (Leo Sellers), Ernest Borgnine (Santoro), Jack Carter (Herbie Dalitz), Sharon Kelly (Gloria Hollinger), James Hampton (bus driver), David Spielberg (Bellamy), Catherine Bach (Peggy Summers), Chuck Hayward (morgue attendant), David Estridge (albino), Peter Brandon (minister), Naomi Stevens (woman hostage), Med Flory (albino-beating cop), Steve Shaw (cop in elevator), Dino Washington (cop in elevator), Anthony Eldridge (laugher), John Duke Russo (man in phone booth), Don Billett (cop in tee shirt), Hal Baylor (Police Captain), Nancy Bonniwell (girl in airport bar), Don "Red" Barry (airport bartender), Karl Lukas (Charley), Gene Chronopoulos (bartender), Patrice Rohmer (Linda, a dancer), Alvin Hammer (liquor store clerk), Dave Willock (liquor store clerk), Queenie Smith, Marilyn Moe (customers), Robert Englund (holdup man), George Memoli (foot fetish man), Fred Willard (interrogator), Thad Geer (second holdup man), Kelly Wilder (Nancy Gaines), Ben Young (first detective), Tasso Bravos, Jimmy R. Hampton, Nathan Harding (boys on beach), John Furlong (Waiter), Jason Wingreen (Jim Lang), Ron Nyman (Pan Am clerk), Victoria Carroll (guest)

Filmed on location in Los Angeles, Pasadena and Marina del Rey, California, beginning November 20, 1974.

Completed:	February 11, 1975
Distribution:	Paramount (U.S.); CIC-American (Great Britain)
Running time:	120 minutes (U.S.); 118 minutes (Great Britain)
Released:	December 25, 1975 (multiple run, Los Angeles)
MPAA Rating:	R [Certified X in Great Britain]
Original titles:	*Home Free; City Of The Angels*

28 TWILIGHT'S LAST GLEAMING (1977)

Synopsis

It is Sunday, November 16, 1981. While President David Stevens (Charles Durning) shaves and prepares to receive a former teacher, four men--Dell (Burt Lancaster), Powell (Paul Winfield), Garvas (Burt Young), and Hoxie (William Smithers)--ambush an Air Force truck on a country road. They dispatch the occupants, take their uniforms, and drive towards a nearby Titan missile installation. On a road in Colorado, SAC General MacKenzie (Richard Widmark) is driven to work and pays no attention to the radio news broadcast about four escaped convicts. At the White House, James Forrest (Roscoe Lee Browne) asks the President not to extradite a political assassin. Stevens refuses; his military aide General O'Rourke (Gerald O'Loughlin) arrives as Forrest leaves and tries to change Stevens' mood with light banter. At the missile base, the convicts pass the questioning of the security guards. Mindful of the television monitors mounted on a central bunker, they stall their truck between two gates and overpower the guards as they try to push it clear. Dell enters the bunker to cover the remaining guard. When Hoxie enters and shoots him, Dell turns and kills Hoxie. Using Dell's unexplained knowledge of the installation, the three remaining convicts complete their descent to the missile control center located 400 feet underground. Posing as the relief team which they have ambushed, Dell and Garvas trick the two launch technicians into opening the massive steel door to the control center. As the convicts burst in, one of the technicians, Captain Towne (Richard Jaeckel), recognizes Dell as a fellow Vietnamese War prisoner; but it is too late to sound an alarm, and he is overpowered. Towne also knows that Dell is a former Air Force general and codesigner of the missile installation, a man convicted on dubious murder charges after threatening to reveal secrets about U.S. military operations in Vietnam. With his technical knowledge, Dell activates the supposedly fail-safe, impeding features in the launch console. He finishes just before a security call from Stratgegic Air Command central control and announces that he has taken control of the site. While General MacKenzie's "beeper" summons him from a church service, Dell pleads for Towne's assistance. Because Hoxie, who had the knowledge to open a wall safe in the control center, has been killed, Dell must have the combination to obtain the keys inside it; and only those keys turned simultaneously can begin the actual launch of the missiles. Towne tells Dell that he is deceiving himself if he thinks that he can beat the system, and he refuses to help. Garvas then tortures the other technician and gets the combination. When MacKenzie reaches the SAC command center and telephones Dell, the former general delivers his ultimatum: a personal line to the President or the missiles will be fired.

MacKenzie, one of the men responsible for Dell's disgrace, verifies through an electronic check that Dell has fully activated the console. Although he still doubts that Dell has the keys, MacKenzie reluctantly picks up his direct line to the White House. Stevens receives the call in the company of O'Rourke and Defense Secretary Guthrie (Melvyn Douglas); then O'Rourke quickly summons other key cabinet members and joint chiefs. In the presence of these advisers, a somewhat incredulous Stevens contacts Dell and hears his demands: ten million dollars, a plane to a neutral country, Presidential publication of National Security Council document 9759, and Stevens himself as hostage.

After Stevens has stalled for time to read the document, which the majority of his advisers believe should not be published, and found Dell adamant on that point despite a counter offer of twenty million dollars, the joint decision is to permit MacKenzie to attack the installation. A number of armored personnel carriers deploy in plain view of the television scanners as a diversionary tactic, so that a helicopter may lower a four-man squad onto the one blind spot directly over the bunker. While Dell opens the silo doors and demands the APC's stop where they are, two men carrying a tactical nuclear weapon climb down the cables in the elevator shaft. As they prepare to arm the bomb just outside the control room door, one of them slips and falls against it, triggering an alarm. Before the convicts can react, the technicians burst through the locked door of their quarters. They are subdued, but Garvas is killed. Enraged at MacKenzie's attempt, Dell and Powell turn the keys, and three missiles rise up out of their silos. MacKenzie asks for permission to detonate the bomb; but Stevens refuses, and the men are withdrawn.

O'Rourke convinces Stevens that only by agreeing to the terms and becoming a hostage can he lure Dell out of the control center, where is is now virtually invulnerable and obviously capable of launching the missiles. Despite his misgivings, Stevens leaves for the installation; but first he secures the promise of Secretary Guthrie that, should Stevens be killed, Guthrie will make public document 9759.

MacKenzie deploys snipers in the abandoned APC's, as Stevens goes down alone to meet Dell. Powell has convinced Dell that even the President's life will be sacrificed before the document is published and that there is little chance of success. But when Dell decides to launch the missiles, Powell refuses to turn the other key; he prefers that small chance to none. Stevens tries to reassure the two convicts that there is no trap awaiting them. Nonetheless they make their way cautiously up to the bunker, and once outside they stand on either side of Stevens and spin around to avoid presenting themselves as clear targets. When the three men are halfway to the Presidential plane, the snipers open fire, killing Dell and Powell but also fatally wounding Stevens. O'Rourke reaches him first, and Stevens has him call Guthrie over. Before he dies, Stevens reminds Guthrie of his promise; and, with O'Rourke cradling the President's body before him, the Defense Secretary is left to ponder whether he will fulfill his promise to the dead man.

Credits and Notes

Producer:	Merv Adelson [Lorimar Productions in association Bavaria Atelier presenting a Geria GmbH Production]
Executive Producer:	Helmut Jedele
Production Executive for Lorimar:	Harry Sherman
Production Executive for Geria:	Lutz Hengst
Production Associate for Aldrich:	Walter Blake
Screenplay:	Ronald M. Cohen and Edward Huebsch, based on the novel *Viper Three* by Walter Wager
Photography:	Robert Hauser (*Technicolor*)
Camera Operators:	Gerhard Fromm, Dieter Matzka
Production Designer:	Rolf Zehetbauer
Art Direction:	Werner Achmann
Music:	Jerry Goldsmith, "My Country 'Tis of Thee," sung by Billy Preston
Sound:	James Willis
Film Editor:	Michael Luciano
Production Supervisor:	Henry Sokal
Special Effects:	Henry Millar
Script Supervisor/ Dialogue Director:	Alvin Greenman
Property Master:	Harry Freude
Wardrobe:	Tom Dawson
Gaffer:	Jack Wilson
First Assistant Director:	Wolfgang Glattes
Second Assistant Director:	Peter Eitzert
Technical Advisor:	H. Andrew Erwin
Cast:	Burt Lancaster (Lawrence Dell), Richard Widmark (General Martin MacKenzie), Charles Durning (President David T. Stevens), Melvyn Douglas (Zachariah Guthrie), Paul Winfield (Powell), Burt Young (Garvas), Joseph Cotten (Arthur Renfrew), Roscoe Lee Browne (James Forrest), Gerald S. O'Loughlin (General Micahel O'Rourke), Richard Jaeckel (Captain Towne), Vera Miles (Victoria Stevens), William Marshall (William Klinger), Charles Aidman (Colonel Bernstein), Leif Erickson (Ralph Whittaker), Charles McGraw (General Crane), Morgan Paull (Lieutenant Cannellis), Simon Scott (Phil Spencer), William Smith (Hoxey), Bill Walker (Willard)

Filmed on location near Munich, West Germany, beginning February 16, 1976.

Completed:	May, 1976
Cost:	$6,500,000
Distribution:	Allied Artists
Running time:	143 minutes

Released: February 9, 1977 (multiple run, Los Angeles)
MPAA rating: R
Original titles: *Viper Three; Silo III*

29   THE CHOIRBOYS   (1977)

Synopsis

In Vietnam in 1969, two American soldiers stumble into a cave in search of concealment from pursuing guerillas. As the enemy throws flames into the cave, one of the Americans, Sam Lyles (Don Stroud), experiences a psychotic episode in which he imagines that he cannot breathe.

In 1975 the nightwatch reports for roll call at a police precinct house. Sgt. Yanov (Charles Haid) checks off various patrol teams: the oldest man, Whalen (Charles Durning), and his partner, Slate (Perry King); Van Moot (Stephen Macht) and Sartino (Chuck Sacci); Lyles and Bloomguard (James Woods); Motts (Lou Gosset) and Tanaguchi (Clyde Kusatsu); Rules (Tim McIntire) and Proust (Randy Quaid). When the watch commander, Lt. Grimsley (George DiCenzo), appears, Whalen takes the opportunity to air several gripes. Grimsley replies with a threat to bust Whalen before his upcoming completion of twenty years' service and retirement eligibility. Yanov concludes by inviting the men to "choir practice" at his home that evening. In the narrow parking lot, the men back out a dozen patrol cars simultaneously, which infuriates the ineffectual Grimsley.

At "choir practice," a noisy post-watch party at which the men concentrate on drinking and playing cards, Whalen gropes at a policewoman in the pool, and she storms away to dress and leave. While she is sitting on a glass-top table combing her hair, a drunken Sartino crawls in and begins to kiss the glass beneath her, until she discovers him and becomes hysterical.

The following night, Rules and Proust receive a call concerning a woman perched on a roof ledge. When the reach the scene, Proust recommends waiting for the sergeant, but Rules insists on talking to the woman, first seductively then abusively. When Rules tells her to go ahead and jump, she does. When the sergeant does arrive, Rules claims that they were unable to reach the roof in time to speak with her.

While Grimsley is eating at a coffee shop, a woman enters and engages him in small talk. Then she leads him back to a motel where Whalen and Slate are staked out. They burst in on Grimsley's "on duty" interlude. Grimsley realizes that he has been set up but tacitly agrees to stop riding Whalen.

The following afternoon when the alternate watch commander, Lt. Finque (David Spielberg), opens his locker, he is attacked by a duck that has been placed inside. He is forced to appear at roll call with his face bruised and bandaged.

As patrol begins, Slate and Whalen stop at a local striptease club, where Slate introduces Whalen to Foxy (Phyllis Davis), one of the performers. Afterwards Whalen advises Slate not to get involved with that sort of woman; but Slate confesses a compulsion to do just that. The next "choir practice" is at MacArthur Park. Rules has fallen into a drunken sleep, and Tanaguchi shows the others how he has lured a duck out of the lake and up to Rules' body with breadcrumbs. He has also opened Rules' fly and closed it again on the duck's head. The animal's thrashing finally rouses Rules, who jumps up screaming and falls into the lake. The others then take his pants and leave him handcuffed to a tree. A homosexual who is walking his poodle finds Rules but is scared off by his shouting. When the others return to release him, Rules pulls out a gun and begins shooting, until Whalen knocks him down.

At the following watch, Bloomguard, Lyles, and Slate report to Vice Sgt. Scuzzi (Burt Young) for temporary assignment. While Bloomguard picks up two prostitutes, one of whom is pregnant, Lyles and Slate stake out a department store men's room, where they wait for vice officer Zoony (Vic Tayback). Rules, who has been summoned to arrest a shoplifter, comes in unknowingly to use the restroom. When Zoony comes in shortly afterwards, he initiates an impromtu prank, making sexual advances towards Rules. This ends in a brawl. While Lyles and Slate are separating Zoony and Rules, Bloomguard is chasing the two women down a residential street, as they shout "Rape!" Scuzzi is somewhat disenchanted wih his new charges, so the next day he sends all three to stake out an apartment believed to be used by a highly-paid prostitute specializing in "bondage." Slate thinks that the form of the woman in the window is familiar but does not discuss it further with his companions. Meanwhile, Zoony brings in a young man who has solicited him in the park. After encouraging him to get counseling, Scuzzi lets him go.

Later that evening, Rules and Proust answer a call in a low-rent building where black and Chicano laborers are fighting. Rules antagonizes each man in turn with racial slurs, until both turn on the policemen and beat them. The following afternoon, roll call is held outside so that the precinct Captain and a Deputy Chief can issue the monthly citation for outstanding service--to Rules. Despite the catcalls which accompany Rules' acceptance, Deputy Chief Riggs praises his aggressiveness and encourages the other men to do likewise.

Lyles and Bloomguard return to regular patrol, and Lyles drives by the apartment which they had previously staked out. When they see signs of activity, they decide to stage their own raid. The woman turns out to be Foxy; and while Bloomguard holds her in the outer room, Lyles discovers that the customer tied up in her "torture chamber" is Slate. Lyles frees Slate but is too disturbed to agree to meet him later and discuss his behavior. The next day's roll call begins with Yanov's announcement that Slate has been found dead by his own hand. Lyles gets up and leaves the room.

That evening's "choir practice" has become a wake by the time Rules arrives in the precinct's paddy wagon. He tells the others that he has learned that Slate's body was covered with whip marks but is prevented from elaborating when Lyles lunges at him. Bloomguard deduces what happened the previous night but is unable to persuade Lyles to stop consuming alcohol and pills. Eventually Lyles staggers semi-consciously into the back of the paddy wagon, where the others have already deposited a drowsy Van Moot. Rules finds them there and latches the door. When he is unable to get out,

Lyles fantasizes that he is back in the Vietnamese cave. The young man whom Scuzzi had freed and who has returned to the park, hears Lyles' shouts and goes to open the door. As Van Moot ducks for cover, the frenzied Lyles draws his gun and shoots the young man. When the others arrive and are unable to resuscitate him, they decide to concoct a story to cover up the killing.

Riggs (Robert Webber) suspects that Bloomguard story is a fabrication, but he is unable to get anything from Lyles, who has been committed. Grimsley, who now works for Riggs, suggests that he bring in Whalen alone and interrogate him personally. When Riggs gives Whalen the alternatives of immunity or dismissal from the force without his pension, Whalen agrees to name everyone involved. After he has taken his retirement and gone north to operate a fishing boat, Whalen receives a letter from Motts containing a newspaper clipping which reveals that Riggs has merely perpetuated the coverup and given all the men six-month suspensions. Whalen returns and threatens to go to the press with the real story. Riggs relents, and all the "choirboys" are reinstated.

Credits and Notes

Producer:	Merv Adelson, Lee Rich [Lorimar--P.A.C. Cinematografica]
Executive Producers:	Pietro Bregni, Mario Bregni, Mark Damon
Associate Producer:	William Aldrich
Screenplay:	Christopher Knopf and Joseph Wambaugh [uncredited], based on the novel by Wambaugh
Photography:	Joseph Biroc (*Technicolor*)
Camera Operator:	Kenneth Peach, Jr.
Art Direction:	Bill Kenney; Sig Tinglof (designer)
Set Decoration:	Raphael Bretton
Music:	Frank DeVol
Sound:	James Contreras
Film Editor:	Maury Weintrobe; Joe Guresky (assistant)
Production Supervisor:	Eddie Saeta
Special Effects:	Henry Millar
Script Supervisor:	Adell Aldrich
Dialogue Supervisor:	Alvin Greenman
Property Master:	Horst Grandt
Wardrobe:	Tom Dawson (men); Yvonne Kubis (women)
Makeup:	Tom Ellingwood
Production Crew:	Bill Shaw (gaffer); Lee Krosskove (head grip); Robert Shaw (best boy, electric); Elisha Harris, Edward Nedin, John Wilson, Richard McConihay (electricians); William Gillespie (second grip); Howard Hagedorn, Kris Krosskove (dolly grips); Robert Kyte, Lowell Brown (boommen); Tom Tomlinson (property assistant); Tim Wade, Charles Minsky, Steve Smith (camera assistants); Robert Krume (construction coordinator); Wayne Fisher (lead man); Ward Welton (painter); Ken Hardie (craft service); Charles Randazzo (driver captain); Lynn Guthrie (Lorimar representative); Vivian Cooper, Joan

Bennett (secretaries); Jonathan Zimmerman (D.G.A. trainee); Arthur L. Wilde (unit publicist)

First Assistant Director:	Malcolm Harding
Second Assistant Director:	Cheryl Downey
Production Coordinator:	Teresa Stokovic
Location Manager:	Lynn Kuwahara
Production Assistant:	Walter Blake
Transportation Coordinator:	Kelly Aldrich
Stills:	Orlando Suero
Casting:	Jack Baur; Barbara Miller (consultant)
Cast:	Charles Durning (Spermwhale Whalen), Lou Gosset (Calvin motts), Perry King (Baxter Slate), Burt Young (Scuzzi), Randy Quaid ("Whaddayamean" Dean Proust), Clyde Kusatsu (Francis Tanaguchi), Stephen Macht (Spencer Van Moot), Tim McIntire (Roscoe Rules), Chuck Sacci ("Father" Sartino), Don Stroud (Sam Lyles), James Woods (Harold Bloomguard), Charles Haid (Nick Yanov), Barbara Rhoades ("No Balls" Hadley), Robert Webber (Deputy Chief Riggs), Jeanie Bell (Fanny Forbes), Blair Brown (Kimberly Lyles), Michele Carey (Ora Lee Tingle), Joe Capp (hod carrier), Jim Davis (Drobeck), Phyllis Davis (Foxy), Jack DeLeon (Quigley), George De Cenzo (Grimsley), David Spielberg (Finque), Vic Tayback (Zoony), Michael Wills (Blaney), Susan Batson (Sabrina), Claire Brennen (Carolina Moon), Gene Chronopoulos (card player), Dianne Dixon (carrier's wife), Lani Kaye Harkless (secretary), Louise Lorimer (Fox), Dimitri Logothetis (card player), Bob Minor (hod carrier No. 2), Maria O'Brien (carrier No. 2's wife), John Steadman (Odello). Cheryl Smith (Tammy), Maile Souza (Sheila), Lomax Study (businessman), Ta-Tanisha (Melissa), Hatsuo Uda (soldier), Bill Walker (Tilden), Ben Young (vice officer), Suzanne Zenor (blonde), Alex Brown, Howard Curtis, Gary Davis, Jon K. Greene, James Halty, Jim Kingsley, John R. McKee, Jim Winburn, Dick Ziker (policemen)

Filmed on location in Los Angeles and at M.G.M. Studios, Culver City, beginning March 28, 1977.

Completed:	June 20, 1977
Cost:	$6,500,000
Distribution:	Universal--M.C.A.
Running time:	119 Minutes
Released:	December 23, 1977 (Los Angeles)
MPAA Rating:	R

29A NO KNIFE (1979)

Synopsis

In 1850 the head of a Polish rabbinical school selects one of his poorest pupils, Avram Mutz (Gene Wilder), to emigrate to San Francisco and establish a congregation among Jewish "forty-niners." At a farewell gathering, Mutz is entrusted with an antique Torah for the new temple.

Mutz lands in Philadelphia and learns that the ship he was to take around the Horn has already sailed. Having been told by the head rabbi that San Francisco was situated close to New York, Avram hires a wagon to take him north. The owners of the wagon, Darryl and Matt Diggs (George Di Cenzo and William Smith) and their fellow traveler Jones (Raymond Bieri) transport Avram just outside Philadelphia where they rob and beat him. Shaken by the loss of his funds and a silver plate that had been attached to the Torah, Avram wanders over the unfamiliar countryside and stumbles onto an Amish settlement. The Amish dress is so similar to his own that Mutz assumes he has somehow found an immigrant Jewish enclave. He faints when he discovers that they wear crosses.

The Amish give Avram train fare to Akron, Ohio. In a pullman men's room, Avram first crosses the path of Tommy Lillard (Harrison Ford), a thief. While Avram uses the toilet, Lillard robs the other passengers. When Mutz emerges, he suddenly realizes that it is the Sabbath eve and that he is forbidden to ride by Jewish law, so he gets off the train. To acquire money to complete his journey, the rabbi takes a job working on the railroad. He proves so inept at hammering ties that he is demoted before he can earn enough to purchase his own covered wagon. He buys a horse instead and decides to follow a wagon train westward; but after the first night's encampment, he awakens to find that the train has gone off without him.

As he rides around aimlessly, Avram reencounters Tommy Lillard. The outlaw is amused by the spectacle of Avram alone on the prairie and cursing in Yiddish. On a whim, he agrees to put the rabbi back on the proper trail. After traversing the plains, Lillard recommends that they hole up for the winter. Mutz refuses to delay his trip any longer, and Lillard reluctantly helps him cross the snow-bound Rocky Mountains. When they finally reach a town, Lillard decides to replenish his funds. He asks Avram to hold the horses while he goes into a bank. He returns with a bundle of stolen money, and before Avram can protest they are galloping out of town. The next day, the rabbi is also forced to compromise his scruples about riding on the Sabbath in order to elude a posse.

The two men evade the posse but a fall into the hands of hostile Indians. They are about to be tortured, when Avram's chanted Hebrew prayer catches the attention of the Chief (Val Bisoglio). He is so intrigued by Avram that he initiates him into one of the tribe's hallucinogenic rituals. After an evening of dancing and singing, Avram faints again. He awakens in a monastic retreat, where Lillard has taken him to recuperate.

The two men ultimately arrive in San Jose. While Lillard goes in search of a brothel, Mutz wanders into the local saloon and spots his assailants from

Pennsylvania at the roulette table. Outraged, Avram tears the silver Torah plate from around the neck of Matt Diggs. Before anyone can react, Lillard arrives and, under the threat of his gun, Avram's money is returned. The following morning, Mutz and Lillard reach the Pacific Ocean. As they celebrate the completion of their trek by plunging in, the Diggs brothers and Jones surprise them. When Matt Diggs contemptuously kicks the Torah into a campfire, Avram dives frenziedly to save it. This distraction allows Lillard to grab his gun. He kills Jones and wounds Matt but is shot himself by Darryl Diggs. Avram is too preoccupied with his book to hear Lillard's pleas for help until Darryl levels his shotgun at him. Finally Avram picks up a revolver but panics. Diggs' derisive laughter brings the rabbi to his senses, and Avram kills him.

The next day, Avram attempts to deposit the Torah inconspicuously at the home of Samuel Bender (Jack Somack), the leader of San Francisco's Jewish community. When he is surprised by Bender's daughter, Rosalie (Penny Peyser), Avram claims to be Tom Lillard delivering the book for someone else and hurries off. When he rejoins Lillard at a saloon, Mutz confesses to having lost his faith and apologizes for momentarily placing the Torah above Lillard's life in importance. While Lillard argues with him, Bender and part of his congregation arrive and convince Avram to assume his post.

The Jewish community's celebration is interrupted by Matt Diggs' reappearance; but he is overcome by Avram's nonviolent resistance. Bender decides to cement Avram's ties to his new congregation by offering him Rosalie's hand in marriage. Avram accepts and is suddenly struck by the magnitude of all that has happened to him in America, now culminating in his unexpected wedding with a bank robber serving as his best man.

Note: *No Knife* was not completed as this study went to press. This synopsis is based on a revised draft of the shooting script.

Credits and Notes

Producer:	Mace Neufeld
Executive Producer:	Howard Koch, Jr.
Associate Producer/ Assistant Director:	Mel Dellar
Screenplay:	Michael Elias, Frank Shaw
Photography:	Robert B. Hauser
Camera Operators:	Mike St. Hilaire, John F. Kiser
Production Design:	Terence Marsh
Set Decoration:	Marvin March
Music:	Frank DeVol
Sound:	Jack Solomon
Film Editors:	Maury Weintrobe; Dennis Lew (assistant)
Production Manager:	Edward Teets
Special Effects:	Henry Millar, Jack Monroe
Script Supervisor:	Doris Grau
Property Master:	Victor Petrotta
Wardrobe:	Dennis Fill, Michael Harte, Edward Marks, George Little, Violet Cane
Make-up:	Leo Lotito, Giannia Bush

Production Crew:	Victor Nikaido, Lynn Tomes, Douglas Olivares (camera assistants); Jack Wilson (gaffer); Duane Smith (best boy, electric); Dan Cady (TBS electric); Bill Beaird (key grip); Eugene Mendez (second grip); Joe Kenworthy (boom-man); John Ramos, Michael Casey (property assistants); Hank Wynands (construction coordinator); Nick Caparelli (leadman); Gavin Cowie (painter); Dale Covey (greens); Glenn Dunn (craft service); Jim Thornsberry, Dean Quisenberry (driver captains); Richard Liebegott (secretary); Herb Adelman (D.G.A. trainee); Rudy Ugland (ramrod); Jerry Young, Kim Burhe, Fred Davidson (wranglers); Susan Pile (unit publicist); Leland Crawford (hairstylist)
Stunt Coordinators:	Chuck Hayward, Mickey Gilbert
Second Assistant Director:	Peter Bergquist
Location manager:	Joe O'Har
Dialogue Director:	Alvin Greenman
Choreographer:	Alex Romero
Technical Advisors:	George American Horse; Rabbi Steven Robbins
Stills:	Jack Shannon
Cast:	Gene Wilder (Rabbi Avram Mutz), Harrison Ford (Tommy Lillard), George Di Cenzo (Darryl Diggs), William Smith (Matt Diggs), Ramon Bieri (Jones), Jack Somack (Bender), Eda Merin (Mrs. Bender), Beege Barkett (Sarah), Penny Peyser (Rosalie), Kenny and Warren Selko (the boy), Leo Fuchs (head Rabbi), Ben Kahlon, Michael Elias, Rolfe Sedan, Rusty Blitz, Sam Nudell, Gabriel Curtis, Larry Gelman, Zachary Berger, Martin Garner (Rabbis), Paul Smith (Mishkin), Carol Helvey (young woman), John Steadman (booking agent), Allen Rich (Bialik), Steffen Zacharias (Rosensheine), Brad Neufeld (Julius), Henry Rowland, Richard Dunham, Walter Janowitz (Amish men), Bret Briggs, Brad Briggs, Chip Frye (Amish boys), Linda Stearns (mother), Heidi Stearns (Jane), Steve Levine (conductor), Jacques Hampton, Roy Kaye (fishermen), Catherine Chase (woman on train), June Constable (Amish woman), Tom Peru, Lou Bell, Howard Gudmundson, Marty White, Dwaine Thompson, James Boswell, T.W. Spear, John Ware (railroad job applicants), Chuck Hayward (wagonmaster), George Barrows (ticket-seller), Gloria Hayes (Indian woman), Alex Romero (old man), Clyde Kusatsu (Ping), Shay Duffin (O'Leary), Joe Kapp (Monterano), Robert Padilla (medicine man), Cliff Pellow (Daniels), Hal Baylor (proprietor), Frank DeVol (piano player), Henry Olek (immigrant), Joe Massengale, Richard Kennedy, Dick Dickinson, Allan Keller (cowboys), Val Bisoglio (Chief Gray Cloud), Ian Wolfe (Father Joseph), Vincent Schiavelli (Brother Bruno), Tom Lillard (Sheriff), Karl Lucas (bartender), Young Jue (waiter), Christine Glazer (dance hall girl), Tina Menard (Avram's mother), Alvin Greenman (wed-

ding guest), Henry Robinson (croupier), Mickey Gilbert, Kim Burke, Bob Herron, Bill Hart, Bob Terhune (stunt doubles), Nick Dimitri, John Hudkins, Fred Carson, Tom Huff, Ken Endoso, George Wilbur, R.L. Tolbert, Walter Scott (stuntmen)

Filmed on location in Rio Rico, Arizona; Greeley, Colorado; and Jenner, California beginning November 2, 1978.

Completed:	January 25, 1979
Cost:	$10,000,000
Distribution:	Warner Brothers
Release date:	July 13, 1979

B. FILMS PRODUCED BY ROBERT ALDRICH

30 THE RIDE BACK   (1957)

Synopsis

A small border town is shaken by the arrival of Hamish (William Conrad), a U.S. marshall, seeking a man. A local priest (Victor Millan) tells Hamish he is concerned about the moral influence of a self-exile named Kallen (Anthony Quinn) on his parishioners, particularly Elena (Lita Milan), who lives with Kallen. Despite his lack of authority, Hamish arrests Kallen and prepares to take him back across the border to Mexico. On the first leg of the journey they are pursued by Elena, who attacks Hamish and tries to free Kallen. When she fails, Kallen tries to appeal to Hamish's sympathy, but the marshall is unrelenting. After they cross the border, Hamish and Kallen discover a farmhouse burned by a raiding party of Indians; the only survivors are two young children. Taking the children with them, the men continue on until attacked by members of the same raiding party. With Kallen's aid, Hamish beats them off, although he is wounded in the process. Kallen takes him to the outskirts of town and is willing to accompany him in; but Hamish, convinced of Kallen's reform, tells him to return to his home.

Credits and Notes

Producer:	William Conrad [Associates and Aldrich]
Executive Producer:	Robert Aldrich
Director:	Allen H. Miner and [uncredited] Oscar Rudolph
Screenplay:	Anthony Ellis
Photography:	Joseph Biroc (1.85:1; printed with a Sepia tint)
Art Direction:	William Glasgow
Set Decoration:	Glen Daniels
Music:	Frank DeVol
Song:	"The Ride Back," by Frank DeVol; sung by Eddie Albert
Sound:	Joseph L. Edmonson
Editor:	Michael Luciano
Associate Producer:	Walter Blake
Assistant Director:	Jack R. Berne

Cast: Anthony Quinn (Kallen), William Conrad (Hamish),
                         George Trevino (border guard), Lita Milan (Elena), Vic-
                         tor Millan (Padre), Ellen Hope Monroe (the girl), Joe
                         Dominguez (Luis), Joe Towers (boy)

Filmed on location in Northern Mexico beginning September 21, 1956.

Completed: October 12, 1956
Distribution: United Artists
Running time: 79 minutes
Released: May 1, 1957

Note: Oscar Rudolph directed ten days of added scenes, retakes, and stunts after
completion of principal photography.

31 WHAT EVER HAPPENED TO AUNT ALICE (1969)

Synopsis

Mrs. Claire Marrable (Geraldine Page) murders her husband for his
money, only to discover that his "estate" consists of a solitary stamp album.
Nevertheless, she is determined to acquire substantial means for her retirement and moves to a small desert community in Arizona where she hires a
succession of rich but lonely women as companion/housekeepers. After she
gains each one's confidence and fortune she murders them, burying them in
her garden. Ultimately she hires Alice Dimmock (Ruth Gordon), who is
investigating the death of Mrs. Marrable's previous victim, Miss Tinsley
(Mildred Dunnock). Alice is assisted by her nephew, Mike Darrah (Robert
Fuller), and Mrs. Marrable's next-door neighbors, the Vaughns (Rosemary
Forsyth and Michael Barbera). Just as they begin to substantiate their suspicions, Mrs. Marrable discovers Alice's ruse and, after beating her
unconscious, places her in a car and pushes it into a lake. Then, Mrs. Marrable attempts to silence the Vaughns by setting their home on fire. But the
Vaughns are rescued, and Mrs. Marrable awakens the next morning to discover that her victims have been exhumed and that her husband's stamp
album was worth $100,000.

Credits and Notes

Producer: Robert Aldrich [Associates and Aldrich--ABC
                         PALOMAR]
Director: Lee H. Katzin and [uncredited] Bernard Girard
Screenplay: Theodore Apstein, based on the novel *The Forbidden
                         Garden* by Ursula Curtiss
Executive Producer: Peter Nelson
Photography: Joseph Biroc (*Metrocolor*)
Art Direction: William Glasgow
Set Decoration: John Brown
Music: Gerald Fried
Sound: Dick Church
Costumes: Renie

Editor:	Michael Luciano (supervising); Frank Urioste
Production Supervisor:	Fred Ahearn
Casting:	Lynn Stalmaster
Unit Manager:	Eddie Saeta
Assistant Director:	Daisy Gerber
Titles:	Don Record and Associates
Cast:	Geraldine Page (Mrs. Marrable), Ruth Gordon (Mrs. Dimmock), Rosemary Forsyth (Harriet Vaughn), Robert Fuller (Mike Darrah), Mildred Dunnock (Miss Tinsley), Joan Harrington (Julia Lawson), Peter Brandon (George Lawson), Michael Barbara (Jim Vaughn), Peter Bonerz (Mr. Bentley), Richard Angarola (Sheriff Armijo), Claire Kelly (Elva), Valerie Allen (Dotty), Martin Garralaga (Juan), Jack Bannon (Olin), Seth Riggs (Warren), Lou Kane (telephone man)

Filmed on location near Tuscon, Arizona, and at the Aldrich Studios, Los Angeles, beginning October 23, 1968.

Completed:	January 5, 1969
Cost:	$1,650,000
Distribution:	Cinerama Releasing Corporation
Running time:	101 minutes
Released:	August 20, 1969
MPAA Rating:	M

Note: Bernard Girard resigned as director after four weeks of filming on November 25, 1968 because of a production dispute. Lee Katzin replaced him on November 27, 1968 and completed the picture.

Writings About Robert Aldrich

A. GENERAL ARTICLES AND BOOKS

1953

32 ANON. "Success Story." *New York Times* (19 April).
[Aldrich to direct *World For Ransom*.]

33 McCLAY, HOWARD. " 'No China Dolls,' Says Director Aldrich..."
Los Angeles Daily News (5 February).
[On "China Smith."]

1954

34 ANON. *"Los Angeles Daily News* (3 September).
[Aldrich is signed by Hecht-Lancaster; Parklane schedules "Kiss Me
Deadly" and "My Gun Is Quick."]

35 ANON. "Independent." *New York Times* (4 November).
[Aldrich announces "The Way We Are," original title of *Autumn
Leaves*.]

36 McCLAY, HOWARD. "Aldrich Will Get Spillane Film." *Los Angeles
Daily News* (3 September).

1955

37 BITSCH, CHARLES et al. "Dictionnaire des Realisateurs Americains
Contemporains." *Cahiers du Cinema,* No. 54 (Noel), p. 47, illus.
[Special Noel issue. Brief biography-filmography-critique on Aldrich.]

38 PRYOR, THOMAS M. "Hollywood Canvas." *New York Times* (7
August), p. X5.
[Aldrich announces "Kinderspiel" and Machine for Chuparosa."]

39 RIVETTE, JACQUES. "On Revolution." *Cahiers du Cinema* No. 54
(Noel), p. 18, illus.
[Special Noel Issue. Article about young American directors.]

40 TRUFFAUT, FRANÇOIS. "La Photo du Mois." *Cahiers du Cinema,* No. 53 (December), p. 37, illus.
[Photograph and brief career analysis of Aldrich]

41 WEILER, A. H. "By Way of Report--New Films on Aldrich Slate-- Other Items." *New York Times* (13 November).
[Aldrich announces "Potluck for Pomeroy"; "Tyranny"; "Candidate for President"; "Fragile Fox" (working title of *Attack*).]

1956

42 BITSCH, CHARLES. "Bio-Filmography de Robert Aldrich." *Cahiers du Cinema,* No. 64 (November), pp. 59-60.
[Filmography through 1956.]

43 _____. "Addenda." *Cahiers du Cinema,* No. 65 (December), p. 40.
[Biography update through 1956.]

44 FENIN, GEORGE. "An Interview with Robert Aldrich." *Film Culture,* 2, No. 4 [No. 10] (July-August), 8-9.

45 TAILLEUR, ROGER. "Avenement du Cinema *Americain.*" *Positif,* 16 (May), 11-24.
[Career analysis.]

46 TRUFFAUT, FRANÇOIS. "Interview with Robert Aldrich." *Cahiers du Cinema,* No. 64 (November), pp. 2-11.
[Career interview through 1956.]

1957

47 D'AMICO, SILVIO, ed. *Enciclopedia deglo Spettacolo, Supplement.* Rome: Casa Editrice Le Maschere, p. 26.
[Filmography.]

48 MICHA, RENE. *Robert Aldrich.* Brussels: Club du Livre de Cinema.

1958

49 ANON. "Aldrich Script Too 'Anti-Gallic' So Brit Co Buys It." *Daily Variety* (14 May).
[Concerning *The Undefeated* by I.A.R. Wylie.]

50 TRUFFAUT, FRANÇOIS. "Interview with Robert Aldrich." *Cahiers du Cinema,* No. 82 (April), pp. 4-10, illus.
[Career update through 1958.]

1959

51 ANON. *Daily Variety* (9 April).
[Announces Associates and Aldrich production of *The Ride Back.*]

52 ANON. "Quinn as 'Taras Bulba.' " *Hollywood Reporter* (26 January), p. 1.
[Announces Aldrich's production of "Taras Bulba" in association with Avala Films of Yugoslavia with budget of $6,000,000.]

53 ANON. *Hollywood Reporter* (23 June), p. 2.
[Aldrich joins jury of the Berlin Film Festival.]

54 ANON. "Hecht's 'Taras Bulba' Yugo Co-Production." *Variety* (2 December), p. 17.
[Announces Hecht and Avala Films' production of "Taras Bulba" to be shot in Yugoslavia. Robert Aldrich mentioned as a previous owner of project before selling it to Joseph Kaufman.]

55 *Filmlexicon degli Autori e delle Opera.* Volume I. Centro Sperimentale di Cinematographia. Rome: Edizioni di Bianco e Nero, p. 74.
[Filmography.]

1961

56 JARVIE, IAN. "Hysteria and Authoritarianism in the Films of Robert Aldrich." *Film Culture,* 22-23 (Summer), 95-111.

1962

57 *Dictionnaire du Cinema.* Collection Seghers. Paris: Editions Seghers, p. 12.

1963

58 ANON. "Aldrich Planning Distribution." *Hollywood Reporter* (17 December), p. 1.

59 ANON. "Full Slate." *New York Times* (3 November).
[Aldrich announces "Cross of Iron"; "Whatever Happened to Cousin Charlotte" (working title of *Hush...Hush Sweet Charlotte*); "Brouhaha"; "The Tsar's Bride."]

60 ANON. "De-Subsidized Producers Abroad Forced Out of Specialized Film Market; Boon for Yanks--Aldrich." *Variety* (25 December), p. 1.

61 CAMERON, IAN and MARK SHIVAS. "Interview and Filmography." *Movie,* No. 8 (April), pp. 8-11.

62 FLYNN, HAZEL. "Aldrich Wants to Make Dream Film." *Hollywood Citizen News* (31 October).

63 MAYERSBERG, PAUL. "Robert Aldrich." *Movie,* No. 8 (April), pp. 4-5.

64 SARRIS, ANDREW. *Film Culture,* No. 28 (Spring), p. 18.

1964

65 ANON. "Aldrich Plans Eight Films to Cost $14,000,000." *Boxoffice* (4 November).
[Aldrich announces "Paper Eagle," "Genghis Khan's Bicycle," "There Really Was a Gold Mine" (semisequel to Vera Cruz), "Now We Know," "Vengeance is Mine," "The Strong Are Lonely," "Pursuit of Happiness," "Mister Man" (television series).]

66 ANON. "Aldrich Has Over $250,000 Invested in Three Films." *Boxoffice* (14 November).
[$80,000 invested in development of "The Legend of Lylah Clare," $50,000 in "Sheik of Araby" (originally titled "Brouhaha"), $50,000 in "The Greatest Mother of 'Em All."]

67 ANON. *Boxoffice* (16 November).
[$100,000 option on "The Legend of Lylah Clare," "Greatest Mother of 'Em All" scripts completed by Bezzerides.]

68 ANON. "Son Making Debut." *Hollywood Reporter* (21 July), p. 2.
[Twelve-year-old Kelly Aldrich to play in *Hush...Hush Sweet Charlotte.*]

69 ANON. "Ill and Injured." *Hollywood Reporter* (6 December).
[Aldrich hospitalized for exhaustion while completing *Hush...Hush Sweet Charlotte.*]

70 ANON. "Producer Sues for Divorce." *Los Angeles Times* (14 August).

71 ANON. "Robert Aldrich Signs for Two at 20th-Fox." *Los Angeles Times* (10 October).
[Aldrich announces "The Sheltering Sky."]

72 ANON. Los Angeles Times (10 November).
[Aldrich announces "The Sheltering Sky."]

73 ANON. "Keep Spare Plots in Your Cupboard." *Variety* (18 November), p. 18.
[Aldrich's advice.]

74 BITSCH, CHARLES and TAVERNIER, B. "La Fonction de Producer." *Cahiers du Cinema,* Nos. 150-151 (December-January), pp. 78-84, illus.
[Interview with Aldrich discussing the difficulties with his European producers on questions of casting and final cut.]

75 CHABROL, CLAUDE. "Directed By:" *Cahiers du Cinema,* Nos. 150-151 (December-January), pp. 113-114, illus.
[Biography-filmography-critique entry in issue's "Dictionary of American Directors."]

76 CURRIE, GORDON. "Gordon Currie's 'Faces of Fame.' " *Hollywood Reporter* (10 December), p. 4.
[Caricature of Aldrich.]

77 GRAHAM, PETER. *Dictionary of the Cinema.* New York: A. S. Barnes and Company, Inc., p. 7.
[Filmography.]

78 HOUSTON, PENELOPE. *Sight and Sound,* 33, No. 4 (Autumn), 165.

1965

79 ANON. "Film Leader R. B. Aldrich is Divorced." *Hollywood Citizen News* (17 June).

80 ANON. "Aldrich in TV Deal with Larry Cohen." *Hollywood Reporter* (17 June).
[Aldrich plans to produce Cohen's one-hour suspense drama television series "Nightmare."]

81 ANON. "Aldrich Adds Novel to 20th-Fox Slate." *Hollywood Reporter* (11 July).
[*Monte Walsh* by Jack Schaefer.]

82 ANON. "No Middle-Aged Hitchcock." *Variety* (20 January).
[Aldrich refuses to be stereotyped as a "suspense-horror" director.]

83 GILETTE, DON. *Hollywood Reporter* (9 June), p. 1.
[Aldrich makes multi-lingual trailers for *Flight of the Phoenix.*]

84 SADOUL, GEORGES. *Dictionnaire des Cineastes* Paris: Editions de Seuil, pp. 8-9.
[Biography-filmography]

1966

85 ANON. "Hitching Post." *Daily Variety* (17 March), p. 11.
[Robert Aldrich marries Sibylle Siegfried.]

86 ANON. "Wedding Bells." *Hollywood Reporter* (17 March), p. 6.
[Robert Aldrich married Sibylle Siegfried in Rome two weeks ago.]

87 ANON. "Bob Aldrich has 3 Films in European Production." *Hollywood Reporter* (16 May), p. 2.
["The Dirty Dozen," "Sunset Trail," and an untitled historical spectacular.]

88 BESSY, MAURICE and CHARDANS, JEAN-LOUIS. *Dictionnaire du Cinema.* Volume I. Paris: Jean-Jacques Prevert, p. 51.
[Biography-filmography.]

1967

89 ANON. "Aldrich and Jacobs to get NATO Awards." *Boxoffice* (16 October).
[Aldrich receives "Director of Year" award for *Dirty Dozen* from National Association of Theatre Owners.]

90 ANON. "Aldrich to Biopic Mex. Gen. Huerta." *Daily Variety* (25 May), p. 1.
[Announces "Rebellion" on the life of Mexican-Indian General Victoriano Huerta.]

91 ANON. *Daily Variety* (8 September), p. 1.
[Ernest Borgnine and George Kennedy cast in "Rebellion," to be filmed in late 1968.]

92 ANON. "Bob Aldrich to Make 4 Pix for Palomar." *Daily Variety* (3 October), p. 1.

93 ANON. "Aldrich, Aide Buy 21000 MGM Shares." *Hollywood Reporter* (14 April), p. 1.

94 ANON. "S. F. Fest Honors Robert Aldrich on 25th Film Anny." *Hollywood Reporter* (22 September), p. 1.

95 ANON. "Women Easier to Direct." *Los Angeles Herald Examiner* (8 June).
[Aldrich quoted as saying women are easier to direct.]

96 ANON. "Czar Beats a Committee." *Variety* (21 June), p. 7.

97 ANON. "Frisco Fest to Honor Bob Aldrich Oct. 21." *Variety* (21 September).

98 ORNSTEIN, BILL. "Associates and Aldrich Co. Hopes to Make 4-6 Pictures Per Year." *Hollywood Reporter* (24 April), p. 1.

99 WINDELER, ROBERT. "To Shut Up and Take Your Lumps?" *New York Times* (3 September).
[Interview.]

100 _____. "Critics Out of Touch." *Kansas City Star* (17 September).
[Interview.]

1968

101 ANON. "Bob Aldrich Takes Wraps Off Studio." *Daily Variety* (9 August), p. 6.

102 ANON. "Break Ground Today on Aldrich Studio." *Hollywood Reporter* (25 June).
[Screen test for Alexandra Hay.]

103 ANON. "Aldrich Dedicates Studios." *Hollywood Reporter* (7 August), p. 10.

104 ANON. *Hollywood Reporter* (4 December).
["X" rating given to *Killing of Sister George* by the Motion Picture Producers Association.]

105 ANON. "Aldrich Buys Pic Rights to 'Coffee, Tea.' " *Hollywood Reporter* (4 December), p. 3).
[Announces purchase of novel *Coffee, Tea, or Me: The Uninhibited Memoirs of Two Airline Stewardesses.*]

106 BLEVINS, WINFRED. "A Fine New Studio On a Fine Old Site." *Los Angeles Herald Examiner* (14 August).

107 GREENBURG, JOEL. "Interview with Robert Aldrich." *Sight and Sound,* 37, No. 1 (Winter 1968-69), 8-13, illus.

108 MURPHY, A. D. "Bob Aldrich's 'Dream Deal.' " *Daily Variety* (4 January), p. 1.)
[Concerning purchase of studio for Associates and Aldrich.]

109 _____. "Robert Aldrich Bankrolling New $1,000,000 Studio Acquisition with 15% Profit Slice of *Dirty Dozen.*" *Variety* (10 January), p. 7.

110 MUSCO, DON. "Aldrich Dedicates New Lot for His Own, Rental Pictures." *Hollywood Reporter* (12 August), p. 4.

111 ORNSTEIN, BILL. "Aldrich Plans Small Pic Chain." *Hollywood Reporter* (4 January), p. 1.

112 SARRIS, ANDREW. *The American Cinema: Directors and Directions, 1929-1968.* New York: E. P. Dutton and Company, Inc., pp. 84-85.
[Brief critique and filmography.]

113 THOMAS, KEVIN. "Major Independent: Touch of Film Past at Studio Dedication." *Los Angeles Times* (12 August).

114 TUSHER, WILLIAM. "Aldrich Challenges Valenti." *Film and Television Daily* (18 December).
[Concerning the "X" rating of *The Killing of Sister George* by the Motion Picture Producers Association.]

1969

115 ANON. "Aldrich's ABC Slate Doubled to 8 Films." *Daily Variety* (28 January), p. 1.
[Announces "Rebellion," "Angry Odyssey," "Coffee, Tea or Me," "No Orchids for Miss Blandish" (working title of *The Grissom Gang*), "Too Late the Hero," "What Ever Happened to Aunt Alice?," "The Greatest Mother of 'Em All," "The Killing of Sister George."]

116 ANON. "Advertising Refused--Newspaper, TV Face Film Suit." *Hollywood Citizen News* (4 February).

117 ANON. "Aldrich Studio Places Plaques." *Hollywood Citizen News* (11 June).

118 ANON. "Aldrich Studios Formal Dedication Attended by Stars."
     Hollywood Reporter (11 June), p. 4.

119 ANON. "Aldrich Plans Enlarge Studio Just Dedicated." *Hollywood
     Reporter* (12 June), p. 10.

120 ANON. *Hollywood Reporter* (20 June), p.1.
     [Aldrich signs Ben Starr to write screenplay for "Coffee, Tea or
     Me."]

121 ANON. "Film Producer Aldrich Files Censorship Suit." *Los Angeles
     Times* (6 February).

122 ANON. "Curb on Ads for X-Pic Cues '*Sis*' Suit by Aldrich." *Variety*
     (5 February), p. 1.

123 ARCHERD, ARMY. "Just for a Variety." *Daily Variety* (21 May), p.
     2.
     [Cites "Rebellion" as most expensive film ever planned by
     Aldrich, who is quoted as saying "not quite in $20 million class."]

124 CHAMPLIN, CHARLES. "Aldrich Weighs Hollywood's Future."
     Los Angeles Times (24 August).

125 GREENBERG, ABE. "Bob Aldrich's Campaign." *Hollywood Citizen
     News* (9 April).

126 _____. "Bob Aldrich Sets Symbol Film Test for Alexandra
     Hay." *Hollywood Citizen News* (25 July).

127 HIGHAM, CHARLES. *The Celluloid Muse: Hollywood Directors
     Speak*. London: Angus and Robertson Ltd.
     [Interview, pp. 21-40; filmography, p. 255; illus. *See also* entry 153
     for update.]

128 TUSHER, WILLIAM. "Aldrich Versus the System." *Film and
     Television Daily* (4 February).

                            1970

129 ANON. "Robert Aldrich Is Planning New Production Company."
     Boxoffice (20 July).

130 BYRNE, BRIDGET. "I'm A Better Director Than People Think I
     Am." *Los Angeles Herald Examiner* (11 October).

131 KNEBEL, FLETCHER. "Hollywood: Broke--And Getting Rich."
     Look (November), p. 46.
     [Capsule articles about various directors, including Aldrich.]

132 MURPHY, A. D. and SETLOWE, RICK. "Aldrich Plots Film Com-
     bine." *Daily Variety* (10 July), p. 1.

133 VERNON, SCOTT. "Aldrich: Blunt, Successful." *Los Angeles
     Herald Examiner* (12 July).

1971

134 ANON. "The Directors Guild Mission to Moscow, Leningrad, Tashkent." *Action,* 6, no. 4 (July-August), 4-9, illus.
[Robert Wise, Robert Aldrich, and and Ralph Nelson on cultural exchange tour to U.S.S.R. *See also* "Impressions of Russia," p. 11.]

135 ANON. "Wise, Aldrich, Nelson on USSR Exchange Visit." *Hollywood Reporter* (22 April), p. 1.

1972

136 ANON. *Hollywood Reporter* (30 June).
[Aldrich announces planned production of *Kill The Dutchman* in conjunction with Universal.]

137 SILKE, JAMES, ed. "Robert Aldrich." *Dialogue On Film,* 2.
[Bibliography, p. 26; filmography, p. 27. Issue is an abridged transcript of the Robert Aldrich Seminar, November 2, 1971, held at the American Film Institute Center for Advanced Film Studies, Beverly Hills. Complete transcript may be read at the Feldman Library at the Center.]

138 SILVER, ALAIN. "Mr. Film Noir Stays at the Table." *Film Comment,* 8, No. 1 (Spring), 14-12.
[Interview. *See* Appendix.]

1973

139 ANON. "Directors Guild Re-Elects Robert Wise and Others." *Boxoffice* (30 July).
[Aldrich elected Second Vice-President]

140 ANON. "W. B. Aldrich Dicker--Lead Holden, Bronson, Marvin?" *Daily Variety* (17 April), p. 8.
[Claims Aldrich's insistence on participation points (percentage of profits) and Lee Marvin as lead are difficulties in production negotiation of *The Yakuza* at Warner Brothers.]

141 ANON. "Aldrich Studios Sold to Video Cassette." *Daily Vareity* (3 July), p. 4.

142 ANON. "Robert Aldrich Feted by French Film Society." *Los Angeles Times* (18 September).
[Cinematheque Francaise presents Aldrich with its Silver Medal in conjunction with Aldrich retrospective.]

143 ANON. "Checklist No. 100, Robert Aldrich." *Monthly Film Bulletin,* 40, No. 478 (November), 238-239.
[Checklist of career credits.]

144 BEAUPRE, LEE. "ABC Films Results: 30 of 36 in Red: Total Loss $47 Mil." *Daily Variety* (31 May), p. 3.

[Article and statistical graph of status of films produced by ABC-Palomar including Aldrich's *Grissom Gang, Too Late the Hero, Killing of Sister George* and *What Ever Happened to Aunt Alice.*]

145 ⸻ . "Aldrich Philosophizes on Biz Where You're 'Only as Good as Your Last Pic.'" *Daily Variety* (21 June).

146 ⸻ . "Bob Aldrich: Candid Maverick." *Variety* (27 June), p. 24.

147 LOYND, RAY. "Director Robert Aldrich: Emperor of An Empty Studio." *Los Angeles Herald Examiner* (1 July).

1974

148 ANON. "Merv Griffin to Honor Robert Aldrich Oct. 9." *Hollywood Reporter* (2 October), p. 5.
[Aldrich, Burt Reynolds, Connie Stevens, Ernest Borgnine appear on the Merv Griffin television program.]

149 ARCHERD, ARMY. "Just for Variety." *Daily Variety* (17 December), p. 3.
[Jimmy Carter, Governor of Georgia, asks Aldrich to be advisor to Atlanta-Southeast Mobil Film Center; Aldrich Agrees.]

150 CHAMPLIN, CHARLES. "Aldrich's Safari in Mogul Country." *Los Angeles Times Calendar* (25 August), pp. 1, 37-38.
[Interview.]

151 CUSKELLY, RICHARD. "Robert Aldrich's Seven Years of Bad Luck are Over." *Los Angeles Herald Examiner* (22 September).

152 DERRY, C. "Robert Aldrich discusses the Horror of Personality Directors." *Cinefantastique,* 3 (1974), 19.
[Interview.]

153 HIGHAM, CHARLES. "Robert Aldrich." *Action*, 9, No. 6 (November-December), 16-21.
[Interview. *See also* entry 127 for expanded interview.]

154 RINGEL, HARRY. "Up to Date With Robert Aldrich." *Sight and Sound*, 43, No. 3 (Summer), 166-169, illus.
[Interview.]

155 ⸻ . "Robert Aldrich: The Director As Phoenix." *Take One*, 4, No. 5 (September), 8-16, illus.
[Career analysis.]

156 ROBINSON, G. "Three by Aldrich." *The Velvet Light Trap,* No. 11 (Winter), pp. 46-49.
[Analysis and credits on *Attack!, The Big Knife,* and *Kiss Me Deadly.*]

1975

157 ANON. "Officers and Board of Directors 1975-77." *Action,* 10, No. 4 (July-August), 24-27.
[Aldrich elected President, Directors Guild of America.]

158 ANON. *Boxoffice* (14 April).
[Aldrich appointed to Directors Guild's Educational and Benevolent Foundation.]

159 ANON. "Robert Aldrich Signs with First Artists." *Boxoffice* (26 May).
[Announces "Seven Day Soldiers."]

160 ANON. "Robert Aldrich is Elected Directors Guild President." *Boxoffice* (7 July).

161 ANON. "Robert Aldrich Elected Prez of Directors Guild." *Daily Variety* (1 July), p. 1.
[Article states Aldrich was the only nominee for President of Guild and has been active in DGA since 1941.]

162 ANON. "Aldrich Retro at Crist's Tarrytown Pic Festival." *Daily Variety (14 November),* p. 4.
[Judith Crist's Film retrospective series at Tarrytown, Pennsylvania.]

163 ANON. "Aldrich to Produce, Direct 'Soldier.' " *Hollywood Reporter* (12 May), p. 3.
[Announces "Seven Day Soldiers," script by Lukas Heller from Tony Kendrick's novel.]

164 ANON. "Robert Aldrich Elected DGA Prexy." *Hollywood Reporter* (1 July), p. 1.

165 ANON. "Aldrich Succeeds Wise as Directors Guild President." *Los Angeles Times* (3 July).

166 ANON. "Aldrich on 'Soldiers.' " *Variety* (21 May).
[Announces "Seven Day Soldiers," script by Lukas Heller from Tony Kendrick's novel.]

167 ANON. "Robert Aldrich Heads Directors Guild; Recall His Upset of DeMille." *Variety* (2 July), p. 40.
[Article reports that after Aldrich's election, William Wyler reminisced to the DGA membership of Aldrich's opposition to the 1950 candidacy of Cecil B. DeMille as DGA president, which lead to the successful election of Joseph Mankiewicz as president. *Note:* According to *Variety* (10 October 1950) DeMille only led an unsuccessful attempt to recall Mankiewicz during his presidency.]

168 FAGIN, STEVE. "Robert Aldrich." *Film Reader*, 1 (1975), 70-72, 119.
[Brief career analysis and filmography.]

1976

169 ANON. "Aldrich, Lorimar Acquire 'Chefs.' " *Daily Variety* (15 September), p. 1.
[The Aldrich Co. and Lorimar Productions announce acquisition of film rights to *Someone Is Killing the Great Chefs of Europe,* a best-selling comic mystery novel written by Nan and Ivan Lyons.]

170 ANON. *Hollywood Reporter* (15 September).
[The Aldrich Co. and Lorimar Productions acquire film rights to the novel *Someone Is Killing the Great Chefs of Europe* by Nan and Ivan Lyons.]

171 CHISSELL, KID. "Kid Chissell Reports." *Los Feliz Hills News* (8 April).
[Comments on Aldrich's affection for boxing and how he has used many ex-boxers in his films, notably "Young" Freddie Welch, Hal Baylor and Med Florey.]

172 COMBS, RICHARD. "Worlds Apart: Aldrich Since *The Dirty Dozen*," *Sight and Sound,* 45, No. 2 (Spring), 112-115, illus.
[Career analysis.]

173 DUVAL, B. "Aldrich le Rebelle." *Image et Son*, No. 306 (May), pp. 25-44, illus.
[Career analysis.]

174 EYQUEM, OLIVER. "Bio-filmographie de Robert Aldrich." *Positif* No. 182 (June), pp. 18-24, illus.
[Filmography through 1976.]

175 LEGRAND, GERARD. "Robert Aldrich et l'Incompletude du Nihilism." *Positif,* No. 182 (June), pp. 2-5, illus.
[Career analysis through 1976.]

176 MURPHY, MARY. "Call Sheet." *Los Angeles Times,* (10 January).
[Aldrich to produce and direct "Seven Day Soldiers."]

177 SAUVAGE, PIERRE. "Entretien avec Robert Aldrich." *Positif* No. 182 (June), pp. 8-17, illus.
[Career interview through 1976; *see also* English language version, entry 178.]

178 _____. "Aldrich Interview." *Movie,* 23 (Winter 1976-77), 50-64, illus.
[Career interview.]

179 SHERMAN, ERIC. *Directing the Film: Film Directors on Their Art.* Boston: Little, Brown & Co.

[Quotes from Aldrich's November 2, 1971, AFI seminar in several chapters on film directing. *See also* entry 137.]

180 STERRITT, DAVID. "Films." *Los Angeles Herald Examiner California Living* (30 May), pp. 4-5.
[Short interview with Aldrich.]

1977

181 ANON. "Kicking the Habit...DGA's Bob Aldrich Says WGA Unfair; Won't Let Him Resign." *Daily Variety* (24 February), p. 1.
[Aldrich files unfair labor practices suit with the National Labor Relations Board against the Writers Guild of America, who refuse to accept his membership resignation prior to a threatened WGA strike.]

182 ANON. "Directors Guild Re-Elects Aldrich to Prexy Post." *Daily Variety* (14 June), pp. 1, 15.

183 ANON. "Robert Aldrich Reactivating His Production Org." *Daily Variety* (11 July), pp. 1, 7.
[Forthcoming projects announced for re-vitalized "Aldrich Co." include "Memoirs of Hecate County," "The Day That I Die," "Someone is Killing the Great Chefs of Europe," "Bruno Bonelli."]

184 ANON. "Robert Aldrich Re-Elected President of DGA." *Directors Guild of America News*, 1, no. 1 (July), 1, 6.
[Election held at biennial convention of the Directors Guild of America in Kansas City, June 11.]

185 ANON. "Aldrich Co. Now in Development on Four Pictures." *Hollywood Reporter* (11 July), p. 3.
[Memoirs of Hecate County," "The Day That I Die," "Someone is Killing the Great Chefs of Europe," "Bruno Bonelli."]

186 ARCHER, ARMY. "Just for Variety." *Daily Variety* (15 June), p. 3.
[States Aldrich accepted second term as DGA Prexy because "he had assurance that the membership was prepared to strike--for higher wage guarantees 'And particularly for assistant dirctors.' "]

187 BYRON, STUART. " 'I Can't Get Jimmy Carter to See My Movie.' " *Film Comment*, 13, no. 2 (March-April), 46-52, illus.
[Interview.]

188 HARWOOD, JIM. 'WG Demands 'Jurisdictional Piracy,' So Says the Directors Guild, Adding That It Will Strike If Producers Accede to Scribes." *Daily Variety* (20 January), p. 1.
[DGA outlines its dispute with Writers Guild demands.]

189 LEVIN, GERRY. "DGA Comes Out Swinging on New Contract Demands." *Hollywood Reporter* (19 May), p. 1.
[Major points of forthcoming negotiations between the DGA and producers' associations outlined by DGA.]

190 McBRIDE, JOSEPH. "DGA's Threats and Olive Branches--Guild Prez Aldrich Unveils Preliminary Positions for AMPTP, Alliance Pactalks." *Daily Variety* (19 May).
[Major points of forthcoming negotiations for new contract between the DGA and producers' associations outline by DGA.]

B. ARTICLES AND REVIEWS ON INDIVIDUAL FILMS

NOTE: Asterisks [*] indicate entries not examined by authors

THE BIG LEAGUER

191 ANON. *Hollywood Reporter* (14 July 1953), p. 3.
[Review.]

192 ANON. *Los Angeles Times* (20 August 1953).
[Review.]

193 ANON. *Saturday Review* (29 August 1953).
[Review.]

194 ANON. *Time* (28 August 1953).
[Review.]

195 ANON. *Variety* (14 July 1953), p. 3.
[Review.]

196 ANON. *Monthly Film Bulletin,* No. 265 (February 1956), p. 18.
[Review.]

WORLD FOR RANSOM

197 ANON. *Daily Variety* (1 October 1953), p. 5.
[Plaza Productions signs a release agreement with Allied Artists.]

198 ANON. *Hollywood Reporter* (1 October 1953).
[Plaza Productions signs a release agreement with Allied Artists.]

199 McCLAY, HOWARD. *Los Angeles Daily News* (27 May 1953).
[Review.]

200 ANON. *Daily Variety* (27 January 1954), p. 4.
[Review.]

201 ANON. *Hollywood Reporter* (27 January 1954), p. 3.
[Review.]

202 ANON. *Monthly Film Bulletin,* No. 248 (September 1954), p. 137.
[Review.]

203 DEMONSABLON, PHILIPPE. *Cahiers du Cinema,* No. 50 (August-September 1954), pp. 49-50.
[Review.]

APACHE

204 ANON. *Hollywood Reporter* (7 June 1952).
[Purchase of novel rights.]

205 BROWNELL, WILLIAM H. *New York Times* (27 December 1953).
[Report on location shooting.]

206 ANON. *Daily Variety* (30 June 1954), p. 3.
[Review.]

207 ANON. *Monthly Film Bulletin,* No. 248 (September 1954), p. 126.
[Review.]

208 ANON. *Time* (9 August 1954).
[Review.]

209 MAHONEY, JOHN. *Hollywood Reporter* (30 June 1954), p. 3.
[Review.]

210 CHABROL, CLAUDE. *Cahiers du Cinema,* No. 45 (March 1955), pp. 45-46.
[Review.]

211 TAILLEUR, ROGER. *Positif,* Nos. 14/15 (November 1955), p. 11.
[Review.]

212 ANON. *Daily Variety* (8 November 1960).
[Settlement of a lawsuit over the firing of Stanley Cortez as director of photography.]

213 ALLOMBERT, G. "Fureur Apache." *Image et Son,* Nos. 288/289 (October 1974), p. 137.
[Review.]

VERA CRUZ

214 ANON. *Hollywood Reporter* (21 December 1953).
[Aldrich signed by Hecht-Lancaster to direct *Vera Cruz.*]

215 ANON. *Daily Variety* (22 December 1954), p. 3.
[Review.]

216 ANON. *Hollywood Reporter* (26 March 1954), p. 12.
[Location report.]

217 ANON. *Los Angeles Times* (11 April 1954).
[Report on location filming.]

218 MOFFITT, JACK. *Hollywood Reporter* (22 December 1954), p. 3.
[Review.]

219 ANON. *Monthly Film Bulletin,* No. 255 (April 1955), p. 55.
[Review.]

220 ANON. *Pix* (4 May 1955), pp. 13-15.
[Report on stunt work.]

221 ANON. *Saturday Review* (15 January 1955).
[Review.]

222 HILL, DEREK. *Films and Filming,* 1, No. 7 (April 1955), 20.
[Review.]

223 TAILLEUR, ROGER. *Positif,* Nos. 14/15 (November 1955), p. 116.
[Review.]

224 TRUFFAUT, FRANÇOIS. *Cahiers du Cinema,* No. 48 (June 1955), pp. 42-45.
[Review.]

KISS ME DEADLY

225 ANON. *Daily Variety* (20 April 1955), p. 3.
[Review.]

226 ANON. *Monthly Film Bulletin,* No. 259 (August 1955), p. 120.
[Review.]

227 BITSCH, CHARLES. *Cahiers du Cinema,* No. 51 (October 1955), pp. 42-43.
[Review.]

228 CHABROL, CLAUDE. "Evolution du Film Policier." *Cahiers du Cinema,* No. 54 (Noel 1955), pp. 27-33, illus.
[Special Noel issue. Article is analysis of genre including discussion of *Kiss Me Deadly,* p. 32, illus.]

229 MOFFITT, JACK. *Hollywood Reporter* (20 April 1955), p. 3.
[Review.]

230 MYSE, ARTHUR . *Cahiers du Cinema,* No. 53 (December 1955), p. 36.
[Review.]

231 SCHEUER, PHILIP K. *Los Angeles Times* (19 May 1955).
[Review.]

232 DOMARCHI, JEAN. "Le Fer dans la Plaie." *Cahiers du Cinema,* No. 63 (October 1956), pp. 18-28, illus.
[Analysis of recent American films including *Kiss Me Deadly* and *The Big Knife.*]

233 DURGNAT, RAYMOND. "The Apotheosis of Va-va-voom." *Motion,* 1, No. 3 (Spring 1962), pp. 30-34.

234 ANON. *Daily Variety* (9 June 1967), p. 2.
[Article reports that Aldrich disturbed by network cuts made for a telecast of *Kiss Me Deadly.*]

*235 CHEVALIER, J. "En Quatrieme Vitesse." *Image et Son,* No. 299 (October 1975), pp. 118-119.
[Credits.]

*236 LEFEVRE, R. "En Quatrieme Vitesse." *Image et Son*, No. 293 (February 1975), pp. 92-94.
[Notes and credits.]

237 SILVER, ALAIN J. *"Kiss Me Deadly*; Evidence of a Style." *Film Comment*, 10, No. 6 (March-April 1975), 24-30, illus.
[Analysis of film's cinematography.]

See Also: Robinson, George, entry 156.

THE BIG KNIFE

238 ANON. *Daily Variety* (16 September 1955), p. 3.
[Review.]

239 ANON. *Hollywood Reporter* (14 March 1955), p. 2.
[Report on start of production.]

240 ANON. *Hollywood Reporter* (24 October 1955), p. 2.
[Report on reaction of industry to filming.]

241 ANON. *New York Times* (24 April 1955).
[Report on Shooting.]

242 ANON. *The New Yorker* (19 November 1955).
[Review.]

*243 BENAYOUN, ROBERT. "Venise, 1955." *Positif*, No. 16 (December 1955), p. 41.
[Review.]

244 KNIGHT, ARTHUR. *The Saturday Review* (19 November 1955).
[Review.]

245 MOFFITT, JACK. *Hollywood Reporter* (16 September 1955), p. 3.
[Review.]

246 ODETS, CLIFFORD. "In Praise of a Maturing Industry." *New York Times* (6 November 1955).
[Odets commends Aldrich's motion picture production of his play and observes that Hollywood motion pictures, in general, are better than ever.]

247 RAMSAY, HARTLEY. *Films in Review,* 6, No. 9, (November 1955), 466-467.

248 RICHER, JEAN-JOSE. "La Quatrieme Vitesse; *The Big Knife.*" *Cahiers du Cinema*, No. 53 (December 1955), pp. 50-51, illus. cover.
[Credits and review.]

249 SCHEUER, PHILIP K. *Los Angeles Times* (24 April 1955).
[Report on the production.]

250 SCHEUER, PHILIP K. *Los Angeles Times* (18 December 1955).
[Review.]

251 TRUFFAUT, FRANÇOIS. "Venise 1955." *Cahiers du Cinema,* No. 51 (October 1955), p. 20, illus.
[Review.]

252 ANON. *Monthly Film Bulletin,* No. 265 (February 1956), p. 14.
[Review.]

253 AUDIBERTI, JACQUES. "Billet XIV; Coupons en Quatre le Grand Couteau." *Cahiers du Cinema,* No. 55 (January 1956), pp. 20-23, illus.
[Analysis of film.]

254 POE, JAMES. *Cahiers du Cinema,* No. 64 (November 1956), pp. 12-15.
[Screenplay excerpt.]

255 POLLOCK, ROBERT. *Films and Filming,* 1, No. 7 (February 1956), 18-19.
[Review.]

*256 TALLMER, JERRY. *Village Voice,* 1, No. 15 (February 1956), 6.
[Review.]

257 KAEL, PAULINE. *Kiss, Kiss, Bang, Bang.* Boston: Little, Brown and Co., 1968, p. 238.
[Review.]

See also: Domarchi, Jean, entry 232; and Robinson, George, entry 156.

AUTUMN LEAVES

258 ANON. *Daily Variety* (30 July 1954), p. 1.
[Associates and Aldrich buy screen rights to "The Way We Are," original title for *Autumn Leaves.*]

259 ANON. *Daily Variety* (9 September 1954), p. 2.
[Joan Crawford signed.]

260 ANON. *Daily Variety* (13 October 1954).
[Reports deal with Distribution Corporation of America.]

261 ANON. *Daily Variety* (16 March 1955), p. 1.
[Aldrich signs with Columbia.]

262 ANON. *Daily Variety* (6 January 1956).
[Use of French theme song.]

263 ANON. *Daily Variety* (13 April 1956), p. 3.
[Review.]

264 ANON. *Monthly Film Bulletin,* No. 275 (December 1956), p. 152.
[Review.]

265 ANON. *New Yorker* (11 August 1956).
[Review.]

266 ANON. *Saturday Review* (12 May 1956).
[Review.]

267 ANON.   *Time* (20 August 1956).
[Review.]

268 CROWTHER, BOSLEY.   *New York Times* (2 August 1956).
[Review.]

269 GILETTE, DON.   *Hollywood Reporter* (13 April 1956), p. 3.
[Review.]

270 LACHENAY, R.   *Cahiers du Cinema,* No. 61 (July 1956), p. 33.
[Review.]

271 SCHEUER, PHILIP K.   *Los Angeles Times* (17 May 1956).
[Review.]

272 DYER, PETER JOHN.   *Films and Filming,* 3, No. 4, (January 1957),
25.
[Review.]

273 SICLIER, JACQUES.   "Vive le Melodrama." *Cahiers du Cinema,* No.
67 (January 1957), pp. 52-53.
[Credits and Review.]

274 TAILLEUR, ROGER.   *Positif,* 20 (January 1957), 43.
[Review.]

*275 BOURGET, JEAN-LOUP.   "Les Melodrames de Joan Crawford."
Positif, No. 131 (October 1971), p. 34.
[Article.]

ATTACK!

276 ANON.   *Hollywood Reporter* (9 November 1955), p. 6.
[Aldrich purchases rights to "The Fragile Fox," original title of
Attack!]

277 ANON.   *Daily Variety* (3 February 1956).
[Pentagon withdraws script approval.]

278 ANON.   *Daily Variety* (5 September 1956), p. 3.
[Review.]

279 ANON.   *Hollywood Reporter* (31 August 1956), p. 1.
[*Attack!* selected for Venice Film Festival.]

280 ANON.   *Hollywood Reporter* (5 September 1956), p. 3.
[Review.]

281 ANON.   *Los Angeles Times* (31 August 1956).
[Congressman accuses Pentagon of attempting to censor *Attack!*]

282 ANON.   *Monthly Film Bulletin,* No. 274 (November 1956), p. 136.
[Review.]

283 BAKER, PETER.   *Films and Filming,* 3, No. 3, (December 1956),
18-19, 24.
[Review, illustrations.]

284 BITSCH, CHARLES. "Le G.I. Inconnu." *Cahiers du Cinema,* No. 64 (November 1956), pp. 51-52.
[Credits and review.]

285 CROWTHER, BOSLEY. "No Pretty War." *New York Times* (20 September 1956).
[Review.]

286 MOSKOWITZ, GENE. *Cahiers du Cinema,* No. 61 (July 1956), p. 33.
[Review.]

287 TAILLEUR, ROGER. *Positif,* No. 19 (December 1956), p. 29.
[Review.]

See also: Robinson, George, entry 156; and Weiler, A. H., entry 41.

288 KRUEGER, ERIC. "Robert Aldrich's *Attack!*" *Journal of Popular Film,* 2, No. 3, (Spring, 1973), 262-276, illus.
[Critical analysis.]

THE GARMENT JUNGLE

289 ANON. *Daily Variety* (17 November 1955).
[Kleiner set to produce.]

290 ANON. *Daily Variety* (4 December 1956), p. 1.
[Sherman replaces Aldrich as director.]

291 ANON. *New York Times* (21 October 1956).
[Report on location work in New York.]

292 ALPERT, HOLLIS. *Saturday Review* (18 May 1957).
[Review.]

293 ANON. *Daily Variety* (14 April 1957), p. 3.
[Review.]

294 ANON. *Monthly Film Bulletin,* No. 283 (August 1957), p. 102.
[Review.]

295 ANON. *Time* (3 June 1957).
[Review.]

*296 ANON. *Village Voice,* 2, No. 29, (15 May 1957), 6.

297 MOSKOWITZ, GENE. *Positif,* No. 22 (March 1957), p. 29.
[Review.]

298 MOSS, IAN. *Films and Filming,* 5, No. 10, (July 1957), 24.

299 POWERS, JAMES. *Hollywood Reporter* (24 April 1957), p. 3.
[Review.]

*300 SEQUIN, LOUIS. "Racket dans la Couture." *Positif,* No. 29 (July 1957), p. 43.
[Article.]

THE ANGRY HILLS

301 ANON. *Daily Variety* (4 November 1957), p. 14.
[Raymond Stross buys rights.]

302 ANON. *Daily Variety* (1 May 1958), p. 1.
[Elisabeth Mueller signed to costar.]

303 MOSKOWITZ, GENE. *Cahiers du Cinema*, No. 88 (October 1958), p. 47.
[Review.]

304 ANON. *Filmfacts,* 2, No. 27 (5 August 1959), 153-154, illus.
[Review.]

305 ANON. *Monthly Film Bulletin*, No. 302 (March 1959), p. 31.
[Review.]

306 ANON. *Variety* (18 February 1959), p. 6.
[Review.]

307 CANBY, VINCENT. *Motion Picture Herald* (6 June 1959).
[Review.]

308 MOFFITT, JACK. *Hollywood Reporter* (4 June 1959), p. 3.
[Review.]

309 POWERS, JAMES. *Daily Variety* (4 June 1959), p. 3.
[Review.]

310 SCOTT, JOHN L. *Los Angeles Times* (30 June 1959).
[Review.]

311 VAUGHAN, DAI. *Films and Filming,* 5, No. 6 (March 1959), 9, 33.
[Review, illustrations.]

*312 LAUGIER, JEAN LOUIS. "Welles et Rossellini." *Cahiers du Cinema*, No. 105 (March 1960), pp. 56-58, illus.
[Critical analysis and credits.]

See also: Aldrich, Robert, entries 863, 864.

TEN SECONDS TO HELL

313 ANON. *Hollywood Reporter* (29 November 1955), p. 4.
[Bachmann sells novel rights.]

314 ANON. *Sight and Sound,* 27, No. 4 (Spring 1958), 177-178.
[Review.]

315 MOSKOWITZ, GENE. *Cahiers du Cinema*, No. 88 (October 1958), p. 47.
[Review.]

316 ANON. *Daily Variety* (15 July 1959), p. 3.
[Review.]

317 ANON. *Filmfacts,* 2, No. 33 (16 September 1959), 193-194, illus.
[Review.]

318 ANON. *Monthly Film Bulletin,* No. 305 (June 1959), p. 69.
[Review.]

319 ANON. *Motion Picture Herald* (18 July 1959), p. 339.
[Review.]

320 ANON. *Time* (8 August 1959).
[Review.]

321 CONRAD, DEREK. *Films and Filming,* 5, No. 9, (June 1959), 25.
[Review.]

322 MOFFITT, JACK. *Hollywood Reporter* (4 June 1959), p. 3.
[Review.]

323 MOULLET, LUC. "Le Poete et Le Geometre." *Cahiers du Cinema,*
No. 101 (November 1959), pp. 53-54.
[Critical analysis and credits.]

See also: Aldrich, Robert, entries 863, 864.

THE LAST SUNSET

324 ANON. *Daily Variety* (7 July 1960), p. 3.
[Filming in Mexico City.]

325 ANON. *Daily Variety* (20 September 1960), p. 1.
[Dorothy Malone sues for equal billing.]

326 ANON. *Daily Variety* (16 November 1960), p. 2.
[Settlement of Malone suit.]

327 ANON. *Hollywood Reporter* (11 April 1960), p. 4.
[Aldrich returns from scouting locations.]

328 ANON. *Hollywood Reporter* (7 June 1960).
[Location report.]

329 ANON. *Daily Variety* (24 May 1961), p. 3.
[Review.]

330 ANON. *Film Daily* (15 June 1961).
[Review.]

331 ANON. *Filmfacts,* 4, No. 28 (11 August 1961), 167-168, illus.
[Review.]

332 ANON. *Monthly Film Bulletin,* No. 331 (August 1961), pp. 114-115.
[Review.]

333 ANON. *Motion Picture Herald* (27 June 1961).
[Review.]

334 CROWTHER, BOSLEY. *New York Times* (15 June 1961), p. 67.
[Review.]

335 CUTTS, JOHN. *Films and Filming,* 7, No. 11, (August 1961), 27-28.
[Review.]

336 HODGENS, R. M. *Film Quarterly,* 15, No. 1 (Fall 1961), 55.
[Review.]

337 POWERS, JAMES. *Hollywood Reporter* (24 May 1961), p. 3.
[Review.]

*338 OMS, MARCEL. *Positif,* No. 45 (May 1962), p. 52.
[Review.]

339 OPHULS, MARCEL. "De Noir Vetu." *Cahiers du Cinema,* No. 130 (April 1962), pp. 58-60, illus.
[Review.]

WHAT EVER HAPPENED TO BABY JANE

340 ANON. *Daily Variety* (22 August 1961), p. 1.
[Aldrich buys rights to novel.]

341 ANON. *Daily Variety* (3 October 1961), p. 3.
[Joan Crawford signs.]

342 ANON. *Daily Variety* (17 May 1962).
[New agreement with Seven Arts.]

343 ANON. *Daily Variety* (30 August 1962).
[Joseph E. Levine set to produce.]

344 ANON. *Daily Variety* (17 October 1962).
[Start date set for film.]

345 ANON. *Daily Variety* (26 October 1962), p. 3.
[Review.]

346 ANON. *Filmfacts,* 5, No. 41 (9 November 1964), 256-258, illus.
[Review.]

347 ANON. *Saturday Review* (10 November 1962).
[Review.]

348 ANON. *Variety* (7 November 1962).
[Purchase price for novel revealed.]

349 CLARK, ARTHUR. *Films in Review,* 13, No. 10, (December 1962), 622-623, illus.
[Review.]

350 CROWTHER, BOSLEY. *New York Times* (7 November 1962).
[Review.]

351 HOPPER, HEDDA. *Los Angeles Times* (16 September 1962).
[Describes Crawford/Davis rivalry.]

352 MEKAS, JONAS. *Village Voice,* 8, No. 5, (22 November 1962), 13.
[Review.]

353 POWERS, JAMES. *Hollywood Reporter* (26 October 1962), p. 3.
[Review.]

354 ANON. *Cinema*, 1, No. 3 (May-June 1963), 32, illus.
[Review.]

355 ANON. *Hollywood Reporter* 2 (8 January 1963), p. 1.
[Boxoffice record for multiple run.]

356 ANON. *Hollywood Reporter* (11 January 1963), p. 3.
[$12,000,000 predicted gross; $1.500,000 on percentage for Davis and Crawford.]

357 ANON. *Los Angeles Examiner* (12 May 1963).
[Davis at Cannes Festival with *Baby Jane*.]

358 ANON. *Monthly Film Bulletin*, No. 353 (June 1963), pp. 81-82.
[Review.]

359 ANON. *New York Times* (13 May 1963).
[Cannes Festival.]

360 ANON. *Variety* (28 August 1963).
[*Baby Jane* recoups negative cost in eleven days of New York run.]

361 BOREIL, JEAN. *Positif*, No. 56 (November 1963), p. 66.
[Review.]

362 DOUCHET, JEAN. "Cannes 1963." *Cahiers du Cinema*, No. 144 (June 1963), p. 37.
[Brief review.]

363 DYER, PETER. "Meeting Baby Jane." *Sight and Sound,* 32, No. 3 (Summer 1963), 118-120, illus.
[Review.]

364 HODGENS, R. M. *Film Quarterly*, 16, No. 3 (Spring 1963), 60-61.
[Review.]

365 MANVELL, ROGER. *Films and Filming,* 9, No. 7 (April 1963), 28.
[Review.]

*366 PULLEINE, TIM. *Movie*, No. 11 (July-August 1963), p. 10.

367 SARRIS, ANDREW. *Movie*, No. 8 (April 1963), pp. 6-7, illus.
[Review.]

368 TOROK, JEAN-PAUL. "Cannes, 1963." *Positif,* Nos. 54-55 (July-August 1963), p. 89.
[Review.]

369 WEYERGANS, FRANCIS. "La Cabane de l'Enfance." *Cahiers du Cinema*, No. 145 (July 1963), pp. 57-58.
[Review.]

370 ANON. *Variety* (19 April 1967).

[Aldrich liquidates interest in *Baby Jane*; retains "What Ever Happened to..." title rights.]

371 SARRIS, ANDREW. *Confessions of A Cultist.* New York: Simon and Schuster, 1971, pp. 77-82.

See also: Aldrich, Robert, entry 865.

SODOM AND GOMORRAH

372 ANON. "Negative-Plus-Ballyhoo Outlay Raises Break-Even? Re 'Sodom & Gomorrah.'" *Variety* (24 May 1961), p. 3.
[Announces $4,000,000 promotional budget.]

373 ANON. *Daily Variety* (5 December 1962), pp. 3, 9.
[Review.]

374 ANON. *Monthly Film Bulletin*, No. 347 (December 1962), p. 174.
[Review.]

375 ANON. *Movie*, No. 4 (November 1962), p. 35.
[Review.]

376 BAKER, PETER. *Films and Filming*, 9, No. 3 (December 1962), 39-40, illus.

377 POWERS, JAMES. *Hollywood Reporter* (3 December 1962).
[Review.]

378 ANON. *Boxoffice* (28 January 1963).
[Review.]

379 ANON. *Cinema*, 1, No. 4 (June-July 1963), 43, illus.

380 ANON. *Cue* (26 January 1963).
[Review.]

381 ANON. *Filmfacts*, No. 2 (14 February 1963), 6-7, illus.
[Review.]

382 ANON. *Hollywood Reporter* (18 October 1963), p. 1.
[Estimate $12,500,000 gross.]

383 ANON. *Movie*, No. 6 (January 1963), p. 19.
[Interview with Aldrich concerning *Sodom and Gomorrah*.]

384 ANON. *New York Times* (24 January 1963).
[Review.]

385 ANON. *Time* (26 January 1963),
[Review.]

386 CROWTHER, BOSLEY. *New York Times* (6 February 1963).
[Review.]

*387 MEKAS, JONAS. *Village Voice*, 8, No. 16 (February 1963), 25.
[Review.]

FOUR FOR TEXAS

388 ANON. *Daily Variety* (20 December 1963), p. 3.
[Review.]

389 ANON. *New York Times* (26 December 1963).
[Review.]

390 LEVY, RAYMOND. *Motion Picture Herald* (25 December 1963).
[Review.]

391 SILKE, JAMES. "Three Directors In Danger: Robert Aldrich, Warlord on Warpath." *Cinema*, I, No. 6 (November-December 1963), 4-8.
[Report on location filming.]

392 ANON. *Filmfacts*, 6, No. 50 (16 January 1964), 316-318, illus.
[Credits, synopsis and excerpted reviews.]

393 ANON. *Monthly Film Bulletin*, No. 361 (February 1964).

394 BATES, DANIEL. *Film Quarterly*, 17, No. 3 (Spring 1964), 62.
[Review.]

395 BEAN, ROBIN. *Films and Filming*, 10, No. 5 (February 1964).
[Review.]

396 NARBONI, JEAN. *Cahiers du Cinema*, No. 156 (June 1964), pp. 53-56, illus.
[Review.]

397 SILKE, JAMES. *Cinema*, 2, No. 1 (February-March 1964), 46.
[Review.]

HUSH...HUSH SWEET CHARLOTTE

398 ANON. *Los Angeles Times* (3 October 1963).
[Henry Farrell replaces Lukas Heller as screenwriter.]

399 ANON. *Daily Variety* (29 May 1964), p. 4.
[Location filming begins in Baton Rouge, Louisiana.]

400 ANON. *Daily Variety* (20 October 1964), p. 8.
[Report on repeated location shutdowns.]

401 ANON. *Daily Variety* (17 December 1964), p. 3.
[Review.]

402 ANON. *Filmfacts*, 5, No. 41 (9 November 1964), 256-258, illus.
[Review.]

403 ANON. *Hollywood Reporter* (1 July 1964), p. 1.
[Filming suspended due to Joan Crawford's illness.]

404 ANON. *Hollywood Reporter* (25 August 1964).
[Olivia De Havilland replaces Joan Crawford.]

405 POWERS, JAMES. *Hollywood Reporter* (17 December 1964), p. 3.
[Review.]

406 ANON. *Daily Variety* (18 May 1965), p. 1.
[Henry Farrell sues for $200,000 over screen credit.]

407 ANON. *Hollywood Reporter* (16 March 1965).
[$1.5 million gross in five days in New York.]

408 ANON. *Monthly Film Bulletin*, No. 376 (May 1964), p. 70.
[Review.]

409 ANON. *Movie*, No. 13 (Summer 1965), p. 44.
[Review.]

410 ANON. *Time* (19 March 1965).
[Review.]

411 CROWTHER, BOSLEY. *New York Times* (21 March 1965).
[Review.]

412 DYER, PETER J. *Sight and Sound*, 34, No. 3 (Summer 1965), 150.
[Review.]

413 HODGENS, R. M. *Film Quarterly*, 18, No. 3 (Spring 1965), 60.
[Review.]

414 JOHNSON, IAN. *Films and Filming*, 11, No. 9 (June 1965), 33.
[Review.]

*415 SARRIS, ANDREW. *Village Voice,* 10, No. 37 (1 July 1965), 12, 14.
[Review.]

416 SILKE, JAMES. *Cinema*, 2, No. 4 (February-March, 1965).
[Review.]

*417 TOZZI, ROMANO. *Films in Review,* 16, No. 2 (February 1965), 112-114, illus.
[Review.]

418 FARBER, STEPHEN. *Film Quarterly*, 20, No. 1 (Fall 1966), 22-27, illus.
[Review.]

THE FLIGHT OF THE PHOENIX

419 ANON. *Hollywood Reporter* (19 October 1964), p. 1.
[Aldrich acquires novel rights.]

420 ANON. *Hollywood Reporter* (12 November 1964), p. 1.
[James Stewart signed to star.]

421 ANON. *Hollywood Reporter* (19 November 1964), p. 3.
[Lukas Heller signed to write screenplay.]

422 ANON. *Daily Variety* (14 December 1965), p. 3.
[Review.]

423 ANON. *Filmfacts,* 8, Nos. 8 & 9 (2 April 1965), 47-49, illus.
[Review.]

424 ANON. *Hollywood Reporter* (2 June 1965), p. 3.
[Aldrich suspends shooting for three days to direct promotion.]

425 ANON. *Newsweek* (12 June 1965).
[Report on location filming.]

426 ANON. *Variety* (5 May 1965).
[Aldrich and Stewart take ten percent interest instead of salary.]

427 POWERS, JAMES. *Hollywood Reporter* (14 December 1965), p. 3.
[Review.]

428 PRATLEY, GERALD. *Daily Variety* (21 July 1965).
[Report on location filming.]

429 WEBSTER, CAROL. *Cinema,* 3, No. 3 (December 1965), 48-49.
[Review.]

430 ANON. *Boxoffice* (10 January 1966), p. 299.
[Review.]

431 ANON. *Films and Filming,* 12, No. 5 (February 1966), 9, illus.

432 ANON. *Hollywood Reporter* (20 January 1966), p. 3.
[London premiere.]

433 ANON. *Monthly Film Bulletin*, No. 385 (February 1966), p. 14.
[Review.]

434 ANON. *New Yorker* (12 February 1966).
[Review.]

435 ANON. *Newsweek* (7 February 1966).
[Review.]

436 ANON. *Time* (4 February 1966).
[Review.]

437 CROWTHER, BOSLEY. *New York Times* (4 February 1966).
[Review.]

438 DELAHAYE, MICHAEL. *Cahiers du Cinema,* No. 180 (July 1966), 75.
[Review.]

439 DURGNAT, RAYMOND. *Films and Filming,* 12, No. 6 (March 1966), p. 18, illus.
[Review.]

440 FRENCH, PHILIP. *Sight and Sound*, 35, No. 2 (Spring 1966), 94-95.
[Review.]

441 HART, HENRY. *Films in Review,* 17, No. 3 (March 1966), 31.
[Review]

442 SARRIS, ANDREW. *Village Voice* (14 April 1966).
[Review.]

443 SCHICKEL, RICHARD. *Life* (18 January 1966).
[Review.]

444 WEAVER, WILLIAM R. *Motion Picture Herald* (5 January 1966), p. 443.
[Review.]

445 ANON. *Variety* (18 January 1967).
[C.A.B. rules death of stuntpilot Paul Mantz was due to intoxication.]

THE DIRTY DOZEN

446 ANON. *Daily Variety* (5 April 1965).
[Kenneth Hyman buys rights to E. M. Nathanson's novel.]

447 ANON. *Daily Variety* (22 June 1966), p. 2.
[Aldrich seeks locations in Spain.]

448 ANON. *Daily Variety* (16 June 1967), pp. 3, 6.
[Review.]

449 ANON. *Daily Variety* (8 July 1967), pp. 1, 4.
[*The Dirty Dozen* grosses $7.5 million in five weeks of U.S. release.]

450 ANON. *Filmfacts*, 10, No. 13 (1 August 1967), 155-157, illus.
[Review.]

451 ANON. *Monthly Film Bulletin*, No. 406 (November 1967), p. 167.
[Review.]

452 ANON. *Motion Picture Herald* (21 June 1967), p. 695.
[Review.]

453 ANON. *New Yorker* (22 July 1967).
[Review.]

454 ANON. *Time* (30 June 1967).
[Review.]

455 CROWTHER, BOSLEY. *New York Times* (16 January 1967).
[Review.]

456 DRUMMOND, GORDON. *Films in Review*, 18, No. 7 (August-September 1967), 445-446.
[Review.]

457 DURGNAT, RAYMOND. *Films and Filming*, 14, No. 1 (November 1967), 21-22.
[Review.]

458 EYLES, ALLEN. "The Private War of Robert Aldrich." *Films and Filming*, 13, No. 12 (September 1967), 4-9, illus.

[Based on an interview. Includes brief synopses of the careers of the major actors in the film.]

459 FARBER, STEPHEN. *Film Quarterly*, 21, No. 2 (Winter 1967-68), 36-41.
[Article.]

460 FRENCH, PHILIP. *Sight and Sound*, 36, No. 4 (Autumn 1967), 201-202.
[Review.]

461 HERBSTMAN, MANDEL. *Film Daily* (16 June 1967).
[Review.]

462 HUNT, DENNIS. *Film Quarterly*, 21, No. 1 (Fall 1967), 68.
[Review.]

463 KNIGHT, ARTHUR. *Saturday Review* (17 June 1967).
[Review.]

464 MAHONEY, JOHN. *Hollywood Reporter* (16 June 1967), p. 3.
[Review.]

465 MEDJUCK, JOE. *Take One*, 1, No. 6 (1967), 23-24.
[Review.]

466 SARRIS, ANDREW. *Village Voice* (29 June 1967).
[Review.]

467 SCHICKEL, RICHARD. *Life* (21 July 1967).
[Review.]

468 SETLOWE, RICK. "Bob Aldrich and Dick Lester Have Differing Views of War Films." *Daily Variety* (24 October 1967), p. 6.

469 STEEN, AL. *Greater Amusements* (July 1967).
[Picture of the Month.]

470 ZIMMERMAN, PAUL D. *Newsweek* (3 July 1967).
[Review.]

471 DEMEURE, JACQUES. *Positif*, No. 95 (May 1968), p. 56.
[Review.]

472 ROULET, JEAN. *Cahiers du Cinema*, No. 198 (February 1968), p. 76.
[Review.]

THE LEGEND OF LYLAH CLARE

473 ANON. *Daily Variety* (24 July 1968), pp. 3, 10.
[Review.]

474 ANON. *Filmfacts*, 11, No. 21 (1 December 1968), 344-346, illus.
[Review.]

475 ANON. *Los Angeles Times* (23 August 1968).
[Review.]

476 ANON. *New York Times* (29 September 1968).
[Review.]

477 ALPERT, HOLLIS. *Saturday Review* (31 August 1968).
[Review.]

478 CARROLL, HARRISON. *Los Angeles Herald Examiner* (3 September 1968).
[Review.]

479 FARBER, STEPHEN. *Film Quarterly* (Winter 1968-69), pp. 57-58.
[Review.]

480 GERTNER, RICHARD. *Motion Picture Herald* (21 August 1968).
[Review.]

481 GILLIATT, PENELOPE. *New Yorker* (5 August 1968).
[Review.]

482 HAMMER, GREGORY. *Films in Review,* 19, No. 8 (October 1968), 514-515.
[Review.]

483 HERBSTMAN, MANDEL. *Film Daily* (26 July 1968).
[Review.]

484 MAHONEY, JOHN. *Hollywood Reporter* (16 August 1968), p. 3.
[Review.]

485 MORGENSTERN, JOSEPH. *Newsweek* (9 September 1968).
[Review.]

486 SARRIS, ANDREW. *Village Voice* (3 October 1968).
[Review.]

487 SCHICKEL, RICHARD. *Life* (28 September 1968).
[Review.]

488 ADLER, RENATA. *A Year in the Dark.* New York: Random House, 1969, pp. 215-216.
[Review.]

489 COHN, BERNARD. "Le Demon des Femmes." *Positif,* No. 109 (October 1969), p. 65.
[Review.]

490 PIERRE, SYLVIE. *Cahiers du Cinema,* No. 212 (May 1969), p. 64.
[Review.]

THE KILLING OF SISTER GEORGE

491 ANON. *Hollywood Reporter* (17 April 1967), p. 1.
[Aldrich purchases film rights to Frank Marcus's play.]

492 ANON. *Los Angeles Herald Examiner* (20 May 1967).
[Bette Davis loses part of Sister George.]

493 ANON. *New York Times* (1 January 1967).
[Consideration of Bette Davis for lead in *Sister George.*]

494 ANON. *Boxoffice* (23 December 1968), p. 4167.
[Review.]

495 ANON. *Hollywood Reporter* (11 December 1968).
[*Sister George* is given an "X" rating.]

496 ANON. *Motion Picture Herald* (25 September 1968).
[Report on location work in London.]

497 ANON. *Time* (20 December 1968).
[Review.]

498 ARCHERD, ARMY. *Daily Variety* (11 December 1968), p. 2.
[Aldrich has difficulty with television and newspaper ads for *Sister George*. Announces intention to sue A.B.C. Also plans to add sound stage to Aldrich Studios.]

499 GERTNER, RICHARD. *Motion Picture Herald* (1 December 1968).

500 HERBSTMAN, MANDEL. *Film Daily* (17 December 1968), p. 7.
[Review.]

501 MAHONEY, JOHN. *Hollywood Reporter* (18 December 1968), p. 3.
[Review.]

502 ANON. *Daily Variety* (21 January 1969), pp. 1, 24.
[Aldrich self-applies "X" rating.]

503 ANON. *Daily Variety* (4 May 1969).
[Suit against Golden West Broadcasters is dismissed.]

504 ANON. *Filmfacts*, 11, No. 24 (15 January 1969), 481-482, illus.
[Review.]

505 ANON. *Hollywood Reporter* (12 March 1969), p. 14.
[Boston theater operator arrested for exhibiting *Sister George.*]

506 ANON. *Hollywood Reporter* (10 April 1969).
[MPAA refuses to support Aldrich's suit against advertising media.]

507 ANON. *Hollywood Reporter* (28 February 1969), p. 3.
[Los Angeles Times runs ads for *Sister George.*]

508 ADLER, RENATA. *A Year in the Dark.* New York: Random House, 1969, pp. 319-320.
[Review.]

509 ALPERT, HOLLIS. *Saturday Review* (11 January 1969).
[Review.]

510 DAWSON, JAN. *Monthly Film Bulletin*, No. 424 (May 1969), p. 92.
[Review.]

511 FARBER, STEPHEN. *Film Quarterly*, 22, No. 3 (Spring 1969), 61.
[Review.]

512 HULL, ROBERT. *Hollywood Reporter* (4 February 1969), p. 1.
[Interview with Aldrich.]

513 JONES, CHRIS. *Films and Filming,* 15, No. 9 (June 1969), 45-56.
[Review.]

514 MEISEL, MYRON. *Focus,* 5 (October 1969), 22-23.
[Review.]

515 MURPHY, A. D. *Daily Variety* (4 February 1969), pp. 1, 4.
[Aldrich sues the *Los Angeles Times* and Golden West Broadcasters for refusing to accept *Sister George* ads; problems with ABC Palomar over distribution.]

516 WHARTON, FLAVIA. *Films in Review,* 20, No. 1 (January 1969), 54.

517 WIDIM, ALLEN H. *Hollywood Reporter* (3 March 1969), p. 1.
[Suit filed against exhibitor in Boston.]

518 _____. *Hollywood Reporter* (27 March 1969), p. 44.
[Exhibition problems in Connecticut.]

*519 COHN, BERNARD. *Positif,* No. 126 (April 1971), p. 68.

520 SARRIS, ANDREW. *Confessions of a Cultist.* New York: Simon and Schuster, 1971, pp. 416-417.
[Review.]

See also: entries 114, 115; and BEAUPRE, LEE, entry 144.

THE GREATEST MOTHER OF 'EM ALL

521 GREENBERG, ABE. *Hollywood Citizen News* (25 July 1969).
[Report on filming.]

See also: entries 67, 115; and GREENBERG, ABE, entry 126.

TOO LATE THE HERO

522 ANON. *Daily Variety* (12 November 1968), p. 7.
[Production slated.]

523 ANON. *Motion Picture Herald* (16 July 1969), p. 8A.
[Location work.]

524 ANON. *Los Angeles Times* (20 May 1970).
[Review.]

525 ANON. *Motion Picture Exhibitor* (10 June 1970), p. 6.
[Review.]

526 ANON. *Time* (8 June 1970).
[Review.]

527 ANDREWS, NIGEL. *Monthly Film Bulletin,* No. 441 (October 1970), p. 203.
[Review.]

528 ARCHER, LEWIS. *Motion Picture Herald* (20 May 1970).
[Review.]

529 GOW, GORDON. *Films and Filming,* 17, No. 1 (October 1970), 44.
[Review.]

530 GREENSPUN, ROGER. *New York Times* (21 May 1970).
[Review.]

531 MAHONEY, JOHN. *Hollywood Reporter* (6 May 1970), p. 3.
[Review.]

532 MURPHY, A.D. *Daily Variety* (6 May 1970), p. 3.
[Review.]

533 SARRIS, ANDREW. *Village Voice,* 15, No. 24 (11 June 1970), 53, 58.
[Review.]

See also: entry 115; and BEAUPRE, LEE, entry 144.

THE GRISSOM GANG

534 ANON. *Daily Variety* (5 May 1970), p. 3.
[Tests for ABC.]

535 ANON. *Daily Variety* (3 July 1970), p. 1.
[Kim Darby signs for *The Grissom Gang* instead of *Red Sky At Morning.*]

536 ANON. *Hollywood Reporter* (13 April 1970), p. 3.
[Baum announces production.]

537 ANON. *Hollywood Reporter* (7 July 1970).
[Film assignments.]

538 ANON. Hollywood Reporter (20 August 1970), p. 15.
[Location work completed.]

539 ANON. *Variety* (22 April 1970), p. 22.
[Aldrich signed to direct.]

540 ANON. *Boxoffice* (21 June 1971).
[Review.]

541 ANON. *Cue* (29 May 1971).
[Review.]

542 ANON. *Filmfacts,* 14, No. 8 (August 1971), 166-168, illus.
[Review.]

543 ANON. *Monthly Film Bulletin,* No. 455 (December 1971), p. 239.
[Review.]

544 ANON. *New York* (14 June 1971).
[Review.]

545 ANON. *Variety* (26 May 1971), p. 13.
[Review.]

546 BACON, JAMES. *Los Angeles Herald Examiner* (20 September 1971).
[Popularity of *The Grissom Gang* in Italy.]

547 BONITZER, PASCAL. *Cahiers du Cinema*, No. 233 (November 1971), p. 57.
[Review.]

548 CANBY, VINCENT. *New York Times* (29 May 1971).
[Review.]

549 COHEN, LARRY. *Hollywood Reporter* (26 May 1971), p. 3.
[Review.]

550 CUSKELLY, RICHARD. *Los Angeles Herald Examiner* (28 May 1971).
[Review.]

*551 LEGRAND, GERARD. *Positif*, No. 133 (December 1971), p. 112.

552 MANNERS, DOROTHY. *Los Angeles Herald Examiner* (11 May 1971).
[Sneak previews in Houston and San Francisco.]

553 SARRIS, ANDREW. *Village Voice*, 16, No. 28 (15 July 1971), 49.
[Review.]

554 GOW, GORDON. *Films and Filming*, 18, No. 4 (January 1972), 52-53.
[Review.]

See also: entry 115; and BEAUPRE, LEE, entry 144.

ULZANA'S RAID

555 ANON. *Daily Variety* (20 October 1971), p. 1.
[Lancaster signed to star.]

556 ANON. *Daily Variety* (23 November 1971), p. 1.
[Aldrich signed to direct.]

557 ANON. *Hollywood Reporter* (20 October 1971), p. 1.
[Lancaster signed to direct.]

558 ANON. *Hollywood Reporter* (23 November 1971), p. 1.
[Aldrich signed to direct.]

559 ANON. *Los Angeles Herald Examiner* (30 November 1971).
[Aldrich signed to direct.]

560 ANON. *Boxoffice* (17 November 1972), p. 4540.
[Review.]

561 ANON. *Cue* (18 November 1972).
[Review.]

562 ANON. *Daily Variety* (17 August 1972), p. 2.
[American Humane Association charges cruelty.]

563 ANON. *Hollywood Reporter* (18 February 1972), p. 17.
[Film assignments.]

564 ANON. *Los Angeles Herald Examiner* (24 August 1972).
[American Humane Association charges cruelty.]

565 CANBY, VINCENT. *New York Times* (3 December 1972).
[Review.]

566 MURPHY, A.D. *Variety* (18 October 1972).
[Review.]

567 SHARP, ALAN. "White Man Unforks Tongue for Ulzana." *Los Angeles Times* (14 May 1972).

568 YANNI, NICHOLAS. *Hollywood Reporter* (16 October 1972), p. 3.
[Review.]

569 ANDREW, NIGEL. *Monthly Film Bulletin*, No. 470 (March 1973), pp. 60-61.
[Review.]

570 BOURGET, JEAN-LOUP. *Positif*, No. 154 (September 1973), p. 79.
[Review.]

571 STUART, ALEX. *Films and Filming*, 19, No. 7 (April 1973), 46-47, illus.
[Review.]

*572 AVRECH, R. "Lookback: Ulzana's Raid." *Millimeter* (June 1975), p. 41.
[Article.]

*573 SCHICKEL, RICHARD. "Why Indians Can't Be Villains Anymore." *New York Times* (9 February 1975).
[Article.]

*574 GROSS, L. "Alan Sharp, Screenwriter in a Strange Land." *Millimeter* (March 1976), pp. 22-25, illus.
[Interview.]

EMPEROR OF THE NORTH

575 ANON *Daily Variety* (6 July 1966), p. 4.
[Christopher Knopf signed by Arena Productions president Norman Felton to write original screenplay, *Emperor of the North Pole*.]

576 ANON. *Variety* (13 July 1966).
[Knopf script purchased by Felton.]

577 ANON. *Boxoffice* (24 May 1971).
[Kenneth Hyman slates first independent production of *Emperor of the North Pole*.]

578   ANON.   *Hollywood Reporter* (9 December 1971), p. 13.
[Speculation that Hyman is considering filming *Emperor* on location in the arctic.]

579   ANON.   *Daily Variety* (11 February 1972), p. 8.
[Hyman sets production.]

580   ANON.   *Daily Variety* (1 June 1972), p. 1.
[Aldrich signed to direct.]

581   ANON.   *Daily Variety* (11 July 1972), p. 1.
[Ernest Borgnine and Lee Marvin signed to costar.]

582   ANON.   *Daily Variety* (19 July 1972), p. 1.
[Film assignments.]

583   ANON.   *Daily Variety* (9 August 1972), p. 3.
[Aldrich using recording of F.D.R.'s voice.]

584   ANON.   *Hollywood Reporter* (13 January 1972).
[Hyman acquires project.]

585   ANON.   *Hollywood Reporter* (1 June 1972), p. 1.
[Aldrich signed to direct.]

586   ANON.   *Hollywood Reporter* (11 July 1972), p. 2.
[Borgnine set to star.]

587   BACON, JAMES.   "Another Chance with Lee Marvin." *Los Angeles Herald Examiner* (1 June 1972).

588   LEWIS, GROVER.   *Rolling Stone* (21 November 1972).
[Interview with Lee Marvin on location in Oregon.]

589   MANNERS, DOROTHY.   "Lee Marvin Plans Film on Hobos." *Los Angeles Herald Examiner* (7 June 1972).

590   ANON.   *Boxoffice* (4 June 1973), p. 4596.

591   ANON.   *Daily Variety* (21 May 1973), p. 8.
[*Emperor* will be shown out of competition at the Berlin Film Festival.]

592   ANON.   *Daily Variety* (23 May 1973), p. 2.
[Review.]

593   ANON.   *Daily Variety* (26 July 1973).
[Change of title to *Emperor of the North*.]

594   ANON.   *Entertainment Today* (29 June 1973).
[Review.]

595   ANON.   *Falling for Stars Newsletter,* 5, No. 21 (March-April 1973).
[Article on stunt men for *Emperor:* Jerry Gatlin for Borgnine, Walter Scott for Marvin, Jim Kingsley for Carradine.]

596   ANON.   *Hollywood Reporter* (13 April 1973), p. 3.
[Bill Medley will sing theme.]

597 ANON. *Rolling Stone* (19 July 1973), p. 19.
[Review.]

598 ANON. *Variety* (23 May 1973).
[Review.]

599 BEAUPRE, LEE. *Daily Variety* (21 July 1973).
["Aldrich philosophizes on Biz where 'You're only as good as you last pic.'"]

600 BOYUM, JAY GOULD. "Cult of Violence Much Overdone." *Wall Street Journal* (8 June 1973).

601 CALENDO, JOHN. *Interview* (July 1973).
[Review.]

602 CANBY, VINCENT. *New York Times* (3 June 1973).
[Review.]

603 COCKS, JAY. *Time* (11 June 1973).
[Review.]

604 COMBS, RICHARD. *Monthly Film Bulletin,* No. 476 (September 1973), pp. 190-191.
[Review.]

605 GARSAULT, ALAIN. *Positif,* No. 155 (October 1973), p. 65.
[Review.]

606 HOWARD, ALAN R. *Hollywood Reporter* (23 May 1973), p. 3.
[Review.]

607 KAEL, PAULINE. *New Yorker* (9 June 1973).
[Review.]

608 MAYERSON, DONALD. *Cue* (25 May 1973).
[Review.]

609 ZIMMERMAN, PAUL D. *Newsweek* (11 June 1973).
[Review.]

THE LONGEST YARD

610 ANON. "Braly 'Yard' Plotter." *Daily Variety* (13 November 1968), p. 4.
[Malcolm Braly signed by Al Ruddy to write screenplay.]

611 ANON. "Braly Screenplays Ruddy's Par 'Cold.'" *Hollywood Reporter* (13 November 1968), p. 3.
[Article mistakes Malcolm Braly's novel *It's Cold Out There* as basis for *The Longest Yard.*]

612 ANON. "Tracy Keenan Wynn Will Script 'Yard.'" *Hollywood Reporter* (15 June 1972), p. 1.

613 ARCHERD, ARMY. "Just for Variety." *Daily Variety* (4 May 1972), p. 2.

[Announces the separate productions of Coppola and Ruddy after *The Godfather*.]

614 ANON. "Atlanta 'Longest Yard' Casting Calls 700." *Boxoffice* (10 August 1973), p. 3.

615 ANON. "McAlester Prison Riots Stop 'The Longest Yard.'" *Boxoffice* (20 August 1973).

616 ANON. "Paramount will Film 'Longest Yard' in Georgia." *Boxoffice* (17 September 1973).

617 ANON. "Robert Aldrich Par's 'Longest Yard' Director." *Daily Variety* (18 August 1973).

618 ANON. *Daily Variety* (10 October 1973).
[Anitra Ford cast.]

619 ANON. "Par Rolls Three Today; Now Has Nine in Production." *Daily Variety* (15 October 1973).

620 ANON. *Daily Variety* (18 October 1973).
[Gene (Dino) Washington, formerly of Philadelphia Eagles, joins cast.]

621 ANON. "Aldrich Will Direct Par's '*Longest Yard.*'" *Hollywood Reporter* (10 August 1973), p. 3.

622 ANON. *Hollywood Reporter* (10 October 1973), p. 14.
[Eddie Albert cast.]

623 ANON. *Hollywood Reporter* (31 Octobr 1973), p. 10.
[Charles Tyner cast.]

624 ANON. *Hollywood Reporter* (23 November 1973), p. 2.
[Ji-Tu Cumbuka cast.]

625 ANON. "Touchdown." *New York Times* (29 April 1973).
[Announces plans for film.]

626 ANON. "Inside Stuff." *Variety* (24 January 1973).
[Announces film.]

627 ANON. "Cons Complicate Biz." *Variety* (8 August 1973).
[Production forced to find new location, as a riot breaks out at McAlester State Prison in Oklahoma.]

628 ANON. "'*Longest Yard*' Convict Pigskin Pic for Georgia." *Variety* (5 September 1973), p. 18.

629 ANON. "Gay Con Chorus for Jailyard Pic." *Variety* (19 December 1973), p. 16.
[Warden approves casting of homosexual convicts.]

630 ANON. "Making the Most News...." *Boxoffice* (7 October 1974).
[Discusses audience response in Atlanta, Georgia.]

*631 ANON. *Cinema Revue,* 54 (21 March 1974), 12-13, illus.
[Photo essay.]

*632   BAXTER, B.   *Films Illustrated,* 4 (December 1974), 126, 142-143.
[Review.]

*633   BUCKLEY, M.   *Films in Review,* 25 (October 1974), 505-506.
[Review.]

634   CANBY, VINCENT.   "Two Films About Men of Action." *New York Times* (15 September 1974).
[Review.]

635   CHAMPLIN, CHARLES.   "Cons Vs. Guards in 'Longest Yard.'"
Los Angeles Times (25 September 1974).
[Review.]

636   GERTNER, RICHARD.   *Motion Picture Product Digest* (4 September 1974).
[Review.]

637   GLAESSNER, VERINA.   *Monthly Film Bulletin,* 41, No. 491 (December 1974), 277-278.
[Review.]

638   JACOBSON, HARLAN.   "Chi Exhib Sues Par Over Pulling 'Longest Yard' From His Houses." *Daily Variety* (1 October 1974), p. 1.
[Oscar Brotman disputes Paramount's authority over method of exhibition. Paramount lost the suit.]

*639   JAMESON, R. T.   *Movietone,* 35, (September 1974), 29-30.

640   KAEL, PAULINE.   "The Current Cinema." *New Yorker,* 50   (14 October 1974), 174-176.
[Review.]

641   LOYND, RAY.   "'*Longest Yard*' Fired Up." *Los Angeles Herald Examiner* (25 September).
[Review.]

*642   McKEGNEY, M.   "The Big Game Pro and Con." *Village Voice,* 19 (12 September), 76.
[Review.]

643   MANNERS, DOROTHY.   *Los Angeles Herald-Examiner* (12 September).
[Review.]

644   MURPHY, ART.   *Daily Variety* (20 August), p. 3.
[Review.]

645   SCHICKEL, RICHARD.   "Dirty Eleven." *Time* (23 September).
[Review.]

646   ANON.   "In London." *Daily Variety* (7 February), p. 22.
[Announces London opening of film.]

*647 BEHAR, H. "Plein la Gueule." *Image et Son*, No. 295 (April), pp. 111-112.
[Review.]

*648 DEBURCHGRAVE, K. "The Mean Machine." *Film en Television*, No. 216 (May/June), p. 28.
[Credits, still.]

*649 ELIA, M. *Sequences*, 79 (January 1975), 38-40.
[Review.]

*650 GERVAIS, G. "Plein la Gueule." *Jeune Cinema*, 86 (April 1975), 42-43, illus.
[Review.]

651 GINNANE, A. "The Mean Machine." *Cinema Papers*, 2 (March-April 1975), 54-55, illus.
[Review.]

*652 GRISOLIA, M. "Plein la Gueule." *Cinema 75*, No. 197 (April 1975), p. 157.
[Review.]

*653 GROSSINI, G. "Quella Sporce Ultima Meta." *Cinema Nuovo*, 24 (September-December 1975), 434-436.

654 HENRY, MICHAEL. *Positif*, No. 169 (May 1975), p. 62.
[Review.]

*655 LACOMBE, A. "Plein la Gueule." *Ecran*, 36 (May 1975), 74-75.
[Review.]

656 McGILLIVRAY, DAVID. *Films & Filming*, 21, No. 5 (February 1975), 42-43.
[Stills from the film.]

657 —————. *Films & Filming*, 21, No. 8 (May 1975), 40-41.
[Review.]

*658 MAGNY, J. "Plein la Gueule." *Telecine*, No. 199 (May 1975), pp. 21-22.
[Review.]

*659 STJERNE, H. "Benknaeckargaenget." *Chaplin*, 17, No. 3 (1975), 113-114.

*660 ZIMMER, J. "Plein la Gueule." *Image et Son*, No. 299 (October 1975), p. 292.

See also: RINGEL, HARRY, entry 154.

HUSTLE

661 ANON. *Boxoffice* (4 November 1974).
[Announces Paramount's upcoming productions.]

662 ANON. *Daily Variety* (15 November 1974), p. 4.
[Paul Winfield cast.]

663 ANON. *Daily Variety* (21 November 1974), p. 2.
[Ben Johnson cast.]

664 ANON. "Reynolds, Aldrich Set to Produce 'Angels.'" *Hollywood Reporter* (31 May 1974), p. 23.
[RoBurt Productions.]

665 ANON. " 'Home Free' New Title for 'City of the Angels.'" *Hollywood Reporter* (5 September 1974), 3.

666 ANON. *Hollywood Reporter* (5 November 1974), p. 4.
[Catherine Deneuve cast.]

667 ANON. *Hollywood Reporter* (12 December 19074), p. 8.
[Jack Carter cast.]

668 ARCHERD, ARMY. "Just for Variety." *Daily Variety* (27 August 1974).
[Frank Yablans changes "City of Angels" title to "Home Free."]

669 ANON. *Boxoffice* (20 January 1975).
[Title changed from "Home Free" to "Hustle."]

670 ANON. " 'Hustle' Lensing Winds." *Daily Variety* (11 February 1975), p. 19.

*671 ANON. *Hollywood Reporter* (8 January 1975), p. 2.
[Title changed from "Home Free" to "Hustle."]

672 ANON. *"City of Angels* novel from Shagan Script Sparks Publishing Deals." *Hollywood Reporter* (14 February 1975), p. 21.
[Hardcover publisher, G. P. Putnam's Sons, sells paperback rights to Signet New American Library for publishing an edition to coincide with Film's release.]

673 ANON. "Aldrich in Hollywood After Europe 'Hustle.'" *Hollywood Reporter* (19 August 1975), p. 9.
[Meetings in Europe to discuss sale of *Hustle* and scout locations for *Twilight's Last Gleaming.*]

674 ANON. " 'Hustle' Coming Christmas Day." *Los Angeles Herald-Examiner* (22 December 1975).

675 ANON. "Movie Shootout." *Los Angeles Times* (9 January 1975).
[Series of six photographs of Burt Reynolds falling through glass door in film.]

676 ARCHERD, ARMY. "Just for Variety." *Daily Variety* (26 September 1975), p. 2.
[Sneak previews in Vancouver and Toronto.]

*677 BUCKLEY, M. *Films in Review,* 26, No. 564 (November 1975).
[Review.]

*678 COLEMAN, PAUL. *Film Information* (December 1975).
[Review.]

679 GERTNER, RICHARD. *Motion Picture Product Digest* (24 December 1975).
[Review.]

680 KIRSCH, ROBERT. *Los Angeles Times* (13 December 1975).
[Book review of *Hustle*.]

681 KNIGHT, ARTHUR. *Hollywood Reporter* (19 December 1975), p. 8.
[Review.]

682 MURPHY, A. D. *Daily Variety* (19 December 1975), p. 3.
[Review.]

683 TARG, WILLIAM. "So Why 'Home Free?' " *Variety* (15 January 1975).
[Letter to the editor from G. P. Putnam's Sons asking why title was changed to "Home Free" when *Books in Print* shows that there were three contemporary books with that same title.]

684 ANON. *Boxoffice* (12 January 1976), p. 4836.
[Review.]

685 ANON. *Film Review Digest*, 1, No. 3 (Spring 1976), 264.
[Credits and excerpted reviews from newspapers and magazines.]

*686 BARTHOLOMEW, D. *Film Bulletin*, 45 (January 1976), 24.
[Review.]

687 COCKS, JAY. *Time* (2 February 1976).
[Review.]

*688 COMUZIO, E. "Un Groco Estremamente Pericoloso." *Cinema Forum*, 152 (March 1976), 149-151.
[Review-Filmography.]

689 CRIST, JUDITH. *Saturday Review* (10 January 1976).
[Review.]

690 CUSKELLY, RICHARD. "An L.A. 'Hustle.' " *Los Angeles Herald-Examiner* (25 December 1976).

691 GOW, GORDON. *Films & Filming*, 22, No. 6 (March 1976), 32, 33.
[Review.]

692 KAEL, PAULINE. "Dirty Harry with Weltschmerz." *The New Yorker* (26 January 1976).
[Review.]

693 KROLL, JACK. "Macho Do About Nothing." *Newsweek* (12 January 1976).
[Review.]

694 MILNE, TOM. *Monthly Film Bulletin,* 43, No. 506 (March 1976), 53-54, illus.
[Review.]

*695 WILLIAMS, J. *Film Illustrated,* 5 (February 1976), 208.

*696 WILSON, R. A., JR. *Audience,* 8 (January 1976), 6-9, illus.

697 WOLF, WILLIAM. "Nihilism." *Cue* (10 January 1976).
[Review.]

TWILIGHT'S LAST GLEAMING

698 ANON. "Lorimar Buys 'Viper.' " *Daily Variety* (30 July 1971), p. 2.
[*Viper Three* novel by Walter Wager.]

699 ANON. "Sign 'Viper Three' writer." *Hollywood Reporter* (8 December 1971), 8.
[Tom Mankiewicz to write screenplay.]

700 ANON. "Lorimar Slates 9-Pix, Vid films for production." *Daily Variety* (11 April 1972), p. 6.
[Announces script *Viper Three* by Tom Mankiewicz to be directed by Jay Sandrich.]

701 ANON. "Lorimar-Bavaria Plans Nearly Set for 'Viper III' Pic." *Hollywood Reporter* (32 August 1972), p. 13.

702 ANON. *Boxoffice* (15 December 1975), p. 15.
[Aldrich signed to direct, title changed ot *Silo III,* production slated for location in Austria.]

703 MURPHY, MARY. *Los Angeles Times* (29 November 1975).
[Aldrich to direct Lorimar's *Silo III.*]

704 ANON. *Boxoffice* (15 March 1976).
[Joseph Cotten will costar with Burt Lancaster.]

705 ANON. "German Shelter Investor Behind Two International Films." *Daily Variety* (16 January 1976).
[*The Devil's Advocate* and *Silo III.*]

706 ANON. *Daily Variety* (24 February 1976).
[Joseph Biroc is replaced by Robert Hauser as director of photography. Biroc leaves due to family illness.]

707 ANON. *Daily Variety* (29 September 1976).
[Allied artists to distribute *Twilight's Last Gleaming* in the U.S. and Canada.]

708 ANON. "Aldrich's 'Gleaming' Will Start Monday." *Hollywood Reporter* (17 February 1976), p. 6.
[Announces seventy-five day shooting schedule.]

709 ANON. *Hollywood Reporter* (7 March 1976).
[Vera Miles and Leif Erickson signed; shooting began February 24.]

710 ANON. " 'Twilight' Winds Up Early, Principals in Cannes." *Hollywood Reporter* (24 May 1976), p. 5.

711 ANON. "Aldrich Expects Blast Over 'Gleaming' Film." *Hollywood Reporter* (26 May 1976), p. 22.
[Aldrich states he expects adverse critical reception.]

712 ANON. "Allied Artist Will Distribute 'Twilight.' " *Hollywood Reporter* (29 September 1976).

713 ANON. *Hollywood Reporter* (21 December 1976).
[Saul Bass and associates hired to create symbol, logo-type and advertising copy for *Twilight's Last Gleaming.*]

714 LEVIN, GERRY. "Aldrich to Munich for 'Twilight's Last.' " *Hollywood Reporter* (19 January 1976), p. 26.
[Bavaria Atelier handling the production and set design, Lorimar casting.]

715 _____ . "Lorimar Prods Sets $11.5 Mil for Two Pictures." *Hollywood Reporter* (29 March 1976).
[Interview with Lorimar producers Lee Rich and Merv Adelson.]

716 MILLS, BART. "Last Gleaming of Admiral X--Overlay of A Crackup." *Los Angeles Times Calendar* (6 June 1976), p. 36, illus.
[Based on interview with Aldrich; character of General Dell in *Twilight's Last Gleaming* is discussed.]

717 REISFELD, BERT. "Tax Breaks Lure U.S. Pix to Munich." *Daily Variety* (1 April 1976).
[Opportunities for filmmaking in Germany discussed, including *Twilight's Last Gleaming.*]

718 ANON. "Allied Pumping $3.5 Mil Into 'Gleaming' Hype." *Daily Variety* (20 January 1977), p. 34.
[Discusses advertising campaign.]

719 ANON. "Bob Aldrich Says 'Twilight's' Went Through Seven Scripts On Way to Final Version." *Daily Variety* (20 January 1977), p. 34.

720 ANON. "Aldrich Joins the Continuing 'Gleaming' Furor." *Daily Variety* (24 January 1977), p. 6.
[Aldrich replies to British exhibitor Alan Kean's statement that *Twilight's Last Gleaming* is "Anti-American."]

721 ANON. "Boston, Detroit Chains Sue Allied Over 'Twilight' Guarantee Advances." *Daily Variety* (6 May 1977).
[Boxoffice returns questioned by exhibitors.]

722 ANON. *Film Review Digest,* 2, No. 4 (Summer 1977), 436-438.
[Credits and excerpted reviews from newspapers and magazines.]

*723 ANON. *New York Times* (23 February 1977).
[Review.]

724 BARBOUR, JOHN. *Los Angeles* (March 1977).
[Review.]

725 BATCHELOR, RUTH. "A Glimmer of A Dilemma." *L.A. Free Press* (11-17 February 1977), p. 8.
[Review.]

726 CHAMPLIN, CHARLES. "America as Hostage in 'Last Gleaming.' " *Los Angeles Times* (10 February 1977).
[Review.]

727 _____. "Two Anti-Films Dabble in Politics." *Los Angeles Times Calendar* (13 February 1977).
[Comparison of *The Cassandra Crossing* and *Twilight's Last Gleaming*.]

728 CRIST, JUDITH. *Saturday Review* (19 March 1977).
[Review.]

729 CUSKELLY, RICHARD. "Bombs Away at Twilight." *Los Angeles Herald Examiner* (10 February 1977).
[Review.]

730 FARBER, STEPHEN. *New West* (28 February 1977).
[Review.]

731 GERTNER, RICHARD. " 'Twilight's Last Gleaming': Thriller with Political-Moral Axes to Grind." *Motion Picture Product Digest* (16 February 1977), 4, No. 18.
[Review.]

732 GRANT, LEE. "Oval Office." *Los Angeles Times* (12 February 1977).
[Brief quote of Aldrich claiming that President Stevens of *Twilight's Last Gleaming* is based on one of the "brightest guys" the director knows.]

733 MASLIN, JANET. "Bombs Away." *Newsweek* (21 February 1977).
[Review.]

734 MURPHY, A. D. "Twilight's Last Gleaming." *Variety* (2 February 1977), p. 22.
[Review.]

735 PENNINGTON, RON. "Twilight's Last Gleaming." *Hollywood Reporter* (28 January 1977), p. 3.
[Review.]

736 PYM, JOHN. "Twilight's Last Gleaming." *Monthly Film Bulletin*, No. 521 (June 1977), pp. 131-132, illus.
[Review and discussion of the 122 minute United Kingdom version distributed by Hemdale.]

*737 REILLY, CHARLES PHILLIPS. *Films in Review* (March 1977), p. 188.
[Review.]

*738 SARRIS, ANDREW. *Village Voice* (7 March 1977), p. 39.
[Review.]

739 SCHICKEL, RICHARD. "Bomb Bursting." *Time* (21 February 1977).
[Review.]

740 SIMON, JOHN. "The Star Spangled Boner." *New York* (14 February 1977), illus.
[Review of film and capsule summary of critics' evaluations of Aldrich's career.]

741 TUSHER, WILL. "Lorimar Emerges as a $6 Mil Film Org at La Costa." *Daily Variety* (19 January 1977), p. 1.
[Information regarding financial position of *Twilight's Last Gleaming* and future Aldrich Co. coproductions with Lorimar.]

742 _____. " 'Twilight's' And Controversy: They Wanted It and Got It." *Daily Variety* (20 January 1977), p. 1.
[Controversy over the political implications of the film voiced by foreign distributors.]

*743 WALL, JAMES M. *Film Information* (March 1977), p. 1.
[Review.]

*744 WOLF, WILLIAM. *Cue* (19 February 1977).
[Review.]

See also: BYRON, STUART, entry 187.

THE CHOIRBOYS

745 ANON. *Daily Variety* (11 November 1975).
[Lorimar acquires film rights to Wambaugh's novel, *The Choirboys*.]

746 ANON. "Robert Aldrich will Direct Wambaugh's 'The Choirboys.' " *Boxoffice* (23 February 1976), p. W-4.
[Lorimar signs Aldrich.]

747 ANON. "Aldrich will Direct Lorimar's 'Choirboys.' " *Hollywood Reporter* (12 February 1976), p. 2.

748 ANON. "Ex-cop Joe Wambaugh does First Screenplay; Fought Publisher Chill." *Variety* (26 May 1976).
[Details Wambaugh's coping with lack of publisher enthusiasm to produce a best seller and his authorship of the screenplay in nineteen days' time.]

749 LEVIN, GERRY. " 'Choirboys' unhurt by Bregni Abduction." *Hollywood Reporter* (6 August 1976), p. 1.

[Lorimar announces that the kidnapping in Rome of executive producer Mario Bregni will not affect production.]

750 McDONALD, KEVIN. " 'Boys' co-deal termed a First." *Hollywood Reporter* (20 July 1976), p. 1.
[Outlines the agreement between Italian-based P.A.C. Cinematografica and Lorimar.]

751 ANON. "Universal to Distribute Lorimar-P.A.C's 'Choirboys.' " *Boxoffice* (27 June 1977), p. C-8.
[U.S. and Canada distribution deal.]

752 ANON. "Production begins today." *Daily Variety* (28 March 1977), p. 7.
[Advertisement by Lorimar.]

753 ANON. *Daily Variety* (21 April 1977).
[Robert Webber cast.]

754 ANON. *Daily Variety* (22 April 1977).
[Joseph Perry cast.]

755 ANON. *Daily Variety* (29 April 1977), p. 2.
[Jeanie Bell cast.]

756 ANON. *Daily Variety* (3 May 1977).
[Michael Wills, Chris Forbes, Ta-Tanisha, Maile Souza, Linda Dano, Blair Brown, Morgan Paull cast.]

757 ANON. *Daily Variety* (17 May 1977).
[Cheryl Smith and Susan Batson cast.]

758 ANON. *Daily Variety* (18 May 1977).
[Phyllis Davis cast.]

759 ANON. "Wambaugh Sues Lorimar on 'Choirboys' Script." *Daily Variety* (24 June 1977), p. 6.
[Wambaugh files suit for $1 million and removal of his name from credits.]

760 ANON. "Wambaugh gets his named Axed from 'Choirboys.' " *Daily Variety* (7 October 1977), p. 1.
[Writers' Guild arbitration committee rules that Wambaugh's name should be removed from credits.]

761 ANON. "Three offer Reply to Wambaugh Statement." *Hollywood Reporter* (4 April 1977), p. 10.
[Aldrich, Adelson, and Rich reply to Wambaugh's assertion that his script has been distorted; they are quoted: "We are steadfast in our dedication to making the 'Choirboys' an outstanding motion picture and have the highest regard for the talents and great ability of Joseph Wambaugh."]

762 ANON. "Wambaugh Files $1 Million Suit against Lorimar." *Hollywood Reporter* (23 June 1977), p. 4.

[Suit in Los Angeles Superior Court alleges that Lorimar "drastically and crudely" altered Wambaugh's screenplay in breech of a promise made to him.]

763 ANON. *Hollywood Reporter* (27 June 1977), p. 5.
[Lorimar advertisement announcing completion of photography ahead of schedule and under budget.]

764 ANON. "Wambaugh wins fight to Relinquish 'Choirboys' credit." *Hollywood Reporter* (7 October 1977), p. 1.
[WGA rules for Wambaugh.]

765 ANON. *Los Angeles Herald Examiner* (16 June 1977).
[Aldrich named a pink poodle used in a sequence dealing with a homosexual "Anita Bryant."]

766 ARCHERD, ARMY. *Daily Variety* (1 April 1977), p. 28.
[Shooting continues despite the death of costar Walter McGinn in an auto accident on March 31.]

767 _____ . *Daily Variety* (5 April 1977).
[Charles Haid replaces Walter McGinn as Yanov.]

768 BYRNE, BRIDGET. "L.A.'s Finest, 'The Choirboys,' Let Go after Midnight Hours." *Los Angeles Herald Examiner* (19 June 1977).
[Article on the filming.]

769 CHAMPLIN, CHARLES. "Aldrich: He spreads the Credits around." *Los Angeles Times* Calendar (26 June 1977), pp. 1, 13, 45.
[Article on the filming.]

770 DICENZO, GEORGE. *Hollywood Reporter* (21 July 1977), p. 7.
[Paid advertisement of an open letter to Wambaugh asking him to "take a peek at some of the film before you jump all over Bob Aldrich."]

771 GRANT, LEE. " 'Choir' Boy." *Los Angeles Times* (12 February 1977).
[Article on the casting of Charles Durning.]

772 _____ . *Los Angeles Times* (18 May 1977).
[Interview with Randy Quaid on the filming and his character.]

773 _____ . "Songs of Discord from 'The Choirboys.' " *Los Angeles Times* (7 December 1977).
[Details of Wambaugh's complaints--the upbeat ending; not iden-tifying the Los Angeles Police Department by name; use of MacArthur Park; a sadomasochistic scene--and Aldrich's comments at a post-Preview press conference, during which he described several scenes excised to reduce running time from four hours, legal problems with the L.A.P.D., and shooting concurrently a television version with softer language.]

774 KAMINSKY, RALPH. "Press Luncheon gives Opportunity to See Realism of 'Choirboys' set." *Box Office* (13 June 1977), p. 18.

[On the dimensions and physical detail of the "MacArthur Park" set.]

775 KILDAY, GREGG. "Police Story." *Los Angeles Times* (28 March 1977).
[Article on Wambaugh and the theme of the film.]

776 _____. "Rough Going." *Los Angeles Times* (6 April 1977).
[Problems with the filming including Wambaugh's dissatisfaction and the death of actor Walter McGinn.]

777 KNIGHT, ARTHUR. *Hollywood Reporter* (21 December 1977), p. 3, 22.
[Review.]

778 LEVIN, GERRY. *Hollywood Reporter* (22 December 1977), pp. 5, 16.
[Universal's plans to promote the film.]

779 McBRIDE, JOSEPH. " 'Choirboys' shooting largely on soundstages." *Daily Variety* (4 April 1977), p. 2.
[Article on filming.]

780 _____. " 'Choirboys': Laffs over Credo." *Variety* (6 April 1977), p. 6.
[Reprint of 779.]

781 MURPHY, A. D. *Daily Variety* (21 December 1977), pp. 3, 4.
[Review.]

782 PULITZER, RAMELLE C. "Aldrich on Steady Course with 'The Choirboys.' " *Hollywood Reporter* (25 May 1977), p. 11.
[Article on filming.]

783 THOMAS, KEVIN. *Los Angeles Times* (23 December 1977), p. 18.
[Review.]

784 WAMBAUGH, JOSEPH. *Daily Variety* (1 April 1977), p. 13.
[Paid advertisement containing an open letter from Wambaugh denouncing Lorimar's attempt to conceal changes made in his script and distortion of his material and concluding with both an apology to all policemen and his readers and a promise to sue Lorimar.]

785 ANON. *Daily Variety* (9 January 1978).
[The film is condemned by the Legion of Decency.]

786 ANON. *Daily Variety* (25 January 1978).
[Wambaugh settles his suit against Lorimar out of court.]

787 ANON. *Los Angeles Herald Examiner* (26 January 1978).
[Wambaugh's lawyer reports that almost all his demands were met in an out-of-court settlement.]

788 ANSEN, DAVID. *Newsweek* (2 January 1978), p. 59.
[Review.]

789 GERTNER, RICHARD. *Motion Picture Production Digest* (4 January 1978) , pp. 61, 62, 64.
[Review.]

790 SCHICKEL, RICHARD. *Time* (16 January 1978), p. 76.
[Review.]

791 WOLF, WILLIAM. *Cue* (7 January 1978), p. 24.
[Review.]

THE RIDE BACK

792 ANON. "Tony Quinn to Star in 'The Ride Back.' " *Daily Variety* (9 April 1956), p. 10.

793 CROWTHER, BOSLEY. *New York Times* (30 April 1957).
[Review.]

794 GILBERT, S. *Daily Variety* (17 April 1957), p. 3.
[Review.]

795 McCARTEN, JOHN. *New Yorker* (11 May 1957).
[Review.]

796 POWERS, JAMES. *Hollywood Reporter* (17 April 1957), p. 3.
[Review.]

797 CUTTS, JOHN. *Films and Filming*, 4, No. 6 (March 1958), 27.
[Review.]

See also: entry 51.

WHAT EVER HAPPENED TO AUNT ALICE?

798 ANON. *Daily Variety* (12 June 1967).
[William Inge contracted by Aldrich to write screenplay for film. No further information found concerning this agreement.]

799 ANON. *Hollywood Reporter* (13 September 1967), p. 1.
[Aldrich purchases *The Forbidden Garden* by Ursula Curtiss to become basis of film.]

800 ANON. "Aldrich's Company to Produce Four Films for Palomar." *Hollywood Reporter* (3 October 1967), p. 1.
[Announces *The Killing of Sister George, Too Late the Hero, The Greatest Mother of 'Em All, What Ever Happened to Aunt Alice*.]

801 ANON. " 'Aunt Alice' Role for Ruth Gordon." *Daily Variety* (15 August 1968).

802 ANON. "Girard Out After Tiff; Katzin Directs 'Alice.' " *Daily Variety* (25 November 1968), p. 2.
[Girard replaced.]

803 ANON. "This Old House Was Made For Filmin'." *Hollywood Citizen News* (12 December 1968), illus.
[Article about the Los Angeles Victorian-style mansion used as a location for the production.]

804 ANON. *Hollywood Reporter* (9 July 1968),p. 1.
[Geraldine Page cast.]

805 ANON. "Aldrich Signs Gerard [sic] for 'Alice.'" *Hollywood Reporter* (27 August 1968), p. 1.
[Bernard Girard engaged as director.]

806 ANON. *Hollywood Reporter* (17 September 1968).
[Mildred Dunnock and Robert Fuller to costar in film.]

807 ANON. "It's Pleasant Work, But Not Very Steady." *Hollywood Reporter* (8 November 1968), p. 10.
[Kuth-Lee Geronimo, seventy-two year old grandson of the famous Indian leader, cast in film.]

808 ANON. "Aldrich's 'Aunt Alice' Shoots Out of Three Compact Trucks." *Hollywood Reporter* (20 November 1968), p. 3.
[Article on the production process.]

809 ANON. "Girard Quits as Director 'Alice.'" *Hollywood Reporter* (25 November 1968), p. 1.
[Bernard Girard resigns as director.]

810 ANON. "Katzin Helming 'Alice' Launched." *Hollywood Reporter* (27 November 1968), p. 8.
[Lee Katzin replaces Girard as director.]

811 ANON. "What Ever Happened to Aunt Alice?" *Boxoffice* (28 July 1969), p. 4219.
[Review.]

812 ANON. "What Ever Happened to Aunt Alice?" *Cue* (26 July 1969).
[Review.]

813 ANON. *Daily Variety* (17 June 1969), p. 6.
[Four French songs, music by Gerald Fried and sung by Lilyan Chauvin, are added to soundtrack.]

814 ANON. "What Ever Happened to Aunt Alice?" *Filmfacts,* 12, no. 16 (1969), 390-392, illus.
[Filmography, synopsis, excerpted reviews.]

815 ANON. "Aldrich Plans 3rd '*Happened*' Pic; Nelson Producing." *Hollywood Reporter* (9 October 1969), p. 1.
[Announcing "Whatever Happened to Dear Elva?"]

816 ANON. "What Ever Happened to Aunt Alice?...It May Impolitely Scare You to Death!" *Motion Picture Herald* (16 July 1969), p. 3A, illus.

[Short article with filmographic data, may have been a paid advertisement.]

817 ANON. "Whatever Happened to Aunt Alice?" *Motion Picture Herald* (30 July 1969).
[Review.]

818 CANBY, VINCENT. "What Ever Happened to Aunt Alice?" *New York Times* (24 July 1969).
[Review.]

819 COMBS, RICHARD. "What Ever Happened to Aunt Alice." *Monthly Film Bulletin,* 36, no. 430 (November 1969), 238.
[Review.]

820 GOW, GORDON. *Films and Filming,* 16, no. 2 (November 1969), 53.
[Review.]

821 HERBSTMAN, MANDEL. *Film and Television Daily* (23 July 1969).
[Review.]

822 KNIGHT, ARTHUR. "Little Lulus." *Saturday Review* (9 August 1969), p. 22.
[Review.]

823 MAHONEY, JOHN. *Hollywood Reporter* (21 July 1969), p. 3.
[Review.]

824 TONE, A. *Daily Variety* (21 July 1969), p. 3.
[Review.]

See also: entry 115; and BEAUPRE, LEE, entry 144.

Film-Related Activities

A. Feature Films as Second Assistant Director for RKO Studios

1942

825 JOAN OF PARIS
Director: Robert Stevenson

826 THE FALCON TAKES OVER
Director: Irving Reis

1943

827 BOMBARDIER
Director: Richard Wallace

828 BEHIND THE RISING SUN
Director: Edward Dmytryk

829 A LADY TAKES A CHANCE
Director: William A. Seiter

830 ADVENTURES OF A ROOKIE
Director: Leslie Goodwins

1944

831 ROOKIES IN BURMA
Director: Leslie Goodwins

832 GANGWAY FOR TOMORROW
Director: John Auer

[There may have been over a dozen more films, but neither Aldrich nor The Directors Guild of America has a record of them.]

B. Short Films as First Assistant Director for RKO Studios

833 Between 1942 and 1945, Aldrich graduated to first assistant director status while working on two-reel comedies. He worked on unspecified titles of the Edgar Kennedy series, originally titled the "Mr. Average Man" series, and also on unspecified titles of the Leon Errol series.

C. Feature Films as First Assistant Director

1945

834 **THE SOUTHERNER** (United Artists)
Director: Jean Renoir

1946

835 **THE STORY OF G.I. JOE** (United Artists)
Director: William Wellman

836 **PARDON MY PAST** (Columbia)
Director: Leslie Fenton

837 **THE STRANGE LOVE OF MARTHA IVERS** (Paramount)
Director: Lewis Milestone
Note: Aldrich replaced Richard McWhorter as assistant after three-fourths of the filming had been completed.

1947

838 **THE PRIVATE AFFAIRS OF BEL AMI** (United Artists)
Director: Albert Lewin

839 **BODY AND SOUL** (United Artists)
Director: Robert Rossen

1948

840 **ARCH OF TRIUMPH** (United Artists)
Director: Lewis Milestone

841 **SO THIS IS NEW YORK** (United Artists)
Director: Richard Fleischer

842 **NO MINOR VICES** (M.G.M.)
Director: Lewis Milestone

1949

843 **FORCE OF EVIL** (M.G.M.)
Director: Abraham Polonsky

844 **THE RED PONY** (Republic)
Director: Lewis Milestone

845 **A KISS FOR CORLISS** (United Artists)
Director: Richard Wallace

1950

846 **THE WHITE TOWER** (R.K.O.)
Director: Ted Tetzlaff

1951

847 **THE PROWLER** (Universal)
Director: Joseph Losey

848 **M** (Columbia)
Director: Joseph Losey

849 **OF MEN AND MUSIC** (20th Century-Fox)
Director: Irving Reis
[Aldrich and Joseph Boyle First Assistant Directors.]

850 **NEW MEXICO** (United Artists)
Director: Irving Reis

1952

851 **ABBOTT AND COSTELLO MEET CAPTAIN KIDD** (Warner Brothers)
Director: Charles Lamont

852 **LIMELIGHT** (United Artists)
Director: Charles Chaplin

D. Feature Films as Production Supervisor

1951

853 **WHEN I GROW UP** (United Artists)
Director: Michael Kanin
Producer: S. P. Eagle

E. Feature Films as Assistant to the Producer

1951

854 **TEN TALL MEN** (Columbia)
Director: Willis Goldbeck
Producer: Harold Hecht

1952

855 **THE FIRST TIME** (Columbia)
Director: Frank Tashlin
Producer: Harold Hecht

856 *F. Feature Films as Screenwriter*

1956

THE GAMMA PEOPLE [Uncredited]
(Columbia-Warwick Films, produced in U.K.)

Director: John Gilling
Producer: John Gossage

1959

TEN SECONDS TO HELL
[Screenplay written with Teddi Sherman.]
See entry 11.

1963

FOUR FOR TEXAS
[Screenplay written with Teddi Sherman.]
See entry 15.

1970

TOO LATE THE HERO
[Story written with Robert Sherman; screenplay written with Lukas Heller.]
See entry 22.

857   G.   *Feature Films as Producer*

Each film was directed by Robert Aldrich unless otherwise noted.

1954

WORLD FOR RANSOM
[Coproducer with Bernard Tabakin; Plaza Production] *See* entry 2.

1955

KISS ME DEADLY
[Parklane Productions] *See* entry 5.

THE BIG KNIFE
[Associates and Aldrich]

1956

ATTACK!
[Associates and Aldrich]

1957

THE RIDE BACK
[Aldrich was Executive Producer, Associates and Aldrich]
Directors: Allen H. Miner, Oscar Rudolph

1962

WHAT EVER HAPPENED TO BABY JANE
[Associates and Aldrich — Seven Arts]

1963

FOUR FOR TEXAS
[The S.A.M. Company, Essex Productions, Claude Productions, and Associates and Aldrich]

1964

HUSH...HUSH, SWEET CHARLOTTE
[Associates and Aldrich]

1966

THE FLIGHT OF THE PHOENIX
[Associates and Aldrich]

1968

THE LEGEND OF LYLAH CLARE
[Associates and Aldrich]

THE KILLING OF SISTER GEORGE
[Associates and Aldrich]

1969

WHAT EVER HAPPENED TO AUNT ALICE
[Associates and Aldrich — ABC Palomar]
Directors: Lee H. Katzin and Bernard Girard

1970

TOO LATE THE HERO
[Associates and Aldrich — ABC Palomar]

1971

THE GRISSOM GANG
[Associates and Aldrich — ABC Pictures]

1975

HUSTLE
[RoBurt Productions — Paramount in association with Churchill Service Company]

858   *H.   Television Work*

1952-1953

"The Doctor" (NBC)
[Aldrich directed seventeen episodes, three from his own scripts.]

"China Smith" (ABC)
[Aldrich directed four episodes.]

"Four Star Theater" (CBS)
[Aldrich directed an unspecified number of episodes.]

1959

"Adventures in Paradise" (ABC)
[The pilot episode for this series was directed by Aldrich.]

"The Sundance Kid" (CBS)
[Aldrich directed the pilot for this proposed series but the name of the series was changed to "Hotel de Paree" [sic] for broadcasting.]

859 *I. Periodical Articles by Aldrich*

High Price of Independence." *Films and Filming,* 4, No., 9 (June 1958), 7, 35.
  [On the difficulties of studio work in the U.S. and free-lance work overseas.]

"Mes Deboires en Europe." *Cahiers du Cinema,* No. 107 (May 1960), pp. 2-6,
  [On problems with European production. Translated by Gene Moskowitz and Louis Marcorelles.]

"Learning from my Mistakes." *Films and Filming ,* 6, No. 9 (June 1960), 9, 33, illus.
  [On problems with *Ten Seconds To Hell* and *The Angry Hills.*]

"The Care and Feeding of Baby Jane." *New York Times* (4 November 1962).
  [On preproduction and shooting problems with *What Ever Happened To Baby Jane.]*

"Hollywood...Still an Empty Tomb." *Cinema ,* 1, No. 3 (May-June 1963), 4-6, 28, illus.
  [Discussion of the "Hollywood" movie and the emphasis on commercial success.]

"American Report." *Cahiers du Cinema,* Nos. 150-151 (December-January 1964), pp. 24-25, illus.
  [Aldrich's responses to six questions from *Cahiers* about current projects and working problems.]

"What Ever Happened to American Movies?" *Sight and Sound,* 33, No. 1 (Winter 1963-64), 21-22.
  [On plans to cross-collateralize commercial ventures with less popular, "art" films.]

"Director's Formula for a Happy Cast." *Los Angeles Times* (7 February 1966).
  [On *The Dirty Dozen* and working with actors.]

"Filmmaking in an Era of New Liberality." *Los Angeles Times* (15 December 1968).
  [On *Killing Of Sister George.*]

"Why I Bought My Own Studio." *Action*, 4, No. 1 (January-February 1969), 7-10.
[Economic reasons for buying his own facility.]

"Impressions of Russia." *Action*, 6, No. 4 (July-August, 1971), 11, illus.
[Aldrich's visit to Russia through an exchange program organized by the Directors Guild.]

Bertolucci, Bernardo. "Dialogue." *Action*, 9, No. 2 (March-April 1974), 23-25, illus.
[Transcript of a conversation of Aldrich and Bertolucci on censorship.]

"Sex and Violence Justified." *America*, 92 (n.d.).
[Discussion of current trends in American production.]

"The New Audience."
[Unpublished; on the change in what an audience expects from a film-maker.]

"What Ever Happened to the Majors?"
[Unpublished; on the loss of viability of the studio system because of high overhead and wasteful methods]

860 *J. Film Performances*

1951

The Big Night (United Artists)
Director: Joseph Losey
Producer: Philip A. Waxman

Robert Aldrich played a small uncredited role as a ringside fight fan.

861 *K. Projects*

1954

"My Gun Is Quick," second adaptation of a Spillane novel produced by Victor Saville (Parklane Production) originally to be filmed by Aldrich. Ultimately filmed in 1956, directed by George White.

1955

"Kinderspiel," original project concerning student revolts in England to be produced by Columbia and directed by Aldrich. Shelved after the dispute with the studio over *The Garment Jungle*.

"Candidate for President," screenplay by Ted Sherman from a story by Don Weis. Shelved.

"Machine for Chuparosa," romantic adventure of a man and his daughter who plan to purchase a fantastic machine in Mexico City. Shelved.

"Potluck for Pomeroy," a British comedy by Herbert Baker about the rivalry between a British and an American General who are vying to hire a top-notch cook. Shelved.

"Tyranny," original screenplay by A.I. Bezzerides about the problems of the Mexican majority in Texas during the time it was an independent country. Shelved.

1957-58

"The Undefeated," based on a novel by I.A.R. Wylie. Sold by Aldrich to Hammer Films because he considered it to be anti-French.

"3:10 to Yuma," project given up by Aldrich after his dispute with Columbia Studios over the *The Garment Jungle*. Subsequently directed by Delmer Daves.

1960

"Taras Bulba," sold by Aldrich after his work overseas. Eventually purchased by Harold Hecht. Directed by J. Lee Thompson and released by United Artists in 1962.

1963

"The Tsar's Bride," a Sixteenth Century adventure romance written by Aldrich about Dmitri, the Polish Pretender to the Russian throne. Project was abandoned by Aldrich because he found it unfeasible to produce it in the Soviet Union and yet felt that it was impossible to film in a different local.

[A film on a similar theme, *The Tempest* produced by Dino DiLaurentis and directed by Alberto Lattuada and starring Van Heflin as Peter III, pretender to the throne of Tsarina Catherine, was released in the U. S. in April 1959. The Rimsky-Korsakov opera, "Tsarskaya Nevesta," was filmed in 1965 by the Riga film studio in the U.S.S.R. and featured the Bolshoi Opera company. This film, which relates the story of Ivan the Terrible's fiancee who is accidentally poisoned by the Tsar's bodyguard was released in the U.S. in 1965 by Artkino under the title *The Tsar's Bride*.]

"Brouhaha" or "Sheik of Araby" [new working title, 1964]. British comedy play by George Tabori to star Peter Sellers as a bungling Sultan. Aldrich invested $50,000 in script development. After postponement because of production overrun on *Hush...Hush Sweet Charlotte* and loss of acting committment from Vittorio Gassman the project was shelved.

"Cross of Iron," script by Lukas Heller about a German submarine captain in a prison camp after sinking his vessel. Shelved. *Note: Cross Of Iron* (1977), directed by Sam Peckinpah, was based on different material

"The Sheltering Sky," script adapted from Paul Bowles novel. Aldrich was signed to direct this story about North Africa for 20th Century-Fox by Richard Zanuck. Project abandoned.

"Vengeance is Mine," script by Aldrich and A.I. Bezzerides concerning a deported gangster in Italy during World War II. Abandoned after litigation with Italian producers.

1964

"Paper Eagle," announced after Aldrich optioned a novel in progress by Tony Ellis. Shelved.

"Mister Man," television series, planned to star Victor Buono and be produced by Aldrich. Shelved by network.

"There Really Was A Gold Mine," planned as a semi-sequel to *Vera Cruz* to be produced by Aldrich. Shelved.

"Now We Know," from a story by John O'Hara; "Pursuit of Happiness," and "The Strong are Lonely." Materials optioned by Aldrich. Shelved in development stage.

1965

"Genghis Khan's Bicycle," based on a Turkish play by Refik Enduran about emigres in Istanbul. Shelved after the release of *America, America* and several adventure films shot in Turkey because Aldrich believed the market for films set in that locale had been saturated.

"Monte Walsh" or "Sunset Trail" [new working title in 1966] script by Lukas Heller from a novel by Jack Schaeffer. Originally scheduled to be shot for 20th Century-Fox after *The Dirty Dozen*. Shelved when MGM agreed to finance *The Legend Of Lylah Clare*. Schaeffer's novel was subsequently purchased by National General and an adaptation was directed by William Fraker in 1969.

"Nightmare," a one-hour television series of suspense dramas developed by Larry Cohen to be produced by Aldrich. Shelved by network.

1968

"Coffee, Tea or Me," comic novel about airline stewardesses optioned by Aldrich. Scripted by Ben Starr in 1969. Shelved after the termination of Aldrich's contract with ABC Palomar in 1971.

"Rebellion," script by Theodore Apstein, based on the life of rebel general and later president of Mexico Victoriano Huertra, to be filmed in 1968 starring Ernest Borgnine and George Kennedy on a budget of $7,000,000. Shelved after ABC Palomar refused to finance the film for that amount. [*See* Appendix.]

1969

"Angry Odyssey," script by Lukas Heller from a story by Aldrich and Robert Sherman about a gangster's deportation from the United States. Scheduled to be filmed in Greece in 1969 for MGM but shelved after Aldrich secured financing for *Too Late The Hero*.

"The Crowded Bed," script by Theodore J. Flicker, to be produced by ABC Palomar. Shelved after termination of Aldrich's contract in 1971.

"What Ever Happened to Dear Elva," script by Theodore Apstein based on the novel *Goodbye, Dear Elva* by Elizabeth Fenwich. Shelved.

1970

"Rage of Honor," screenplay by Denne Bart Petitclerc from his novel about Northern California in 1929. Rights sold December 1971.

"Billy Two Hats," sold to Norman Jewison, to be filmed by Ted Kotcheff.

1973

"The Yakuza," screenplay by Paul Schrader and Robert Towne. Aldrich was engaged by Warner Brothers to direct this film but was replaced by Sidney Pollock, who subsequently directed the motion picture. Aldrich believes that he was replaced because of Robert Mitchum's objections.

"Kill the Dutchman," script by Leon Griffiths based on a novel by Paul Sann. To have been produced and directed by Aldrich for MCA-Universal. Shelved.

1975

"Seven Day Soldiers," adaptation by Lukas Heller from Tony Kendrick's novel. To have been produced and directed by Aldrich for First Artists. Postponed indefinitely.

1977

"Memoirs of Hecate County," screenplay by Wendell Mayes based on the novel by Edmund Wilson. Aldrich planned to direct this for his revitalized "Aldrich Co."

"The Day That I Die," screenplay by Abraham Polonsky adapted from the novel by P.F. Kluge about Micronesia during World War II. Aldrich will produce and direct. Charles Russell announced as associated producer. Two "Aldrich Co." productions announced in 1977.

"Someone Is Killing the Great Chefs of Europe," screenplay by Peter Stone from the comic mystery novel written by Nan and Ivan Lyons. Produced by William Aldrich (Robert's son) and directed by Ted Kotcheff in a coproduction agreement between the Aldrich Co. and Lorimar Productions. Adell Aldrich (Robert's daughter) planned to direct "Bruno Bonelli" for the Aldrich Co. from an original screenplay by Frank Perelli.

1979

"Sudden Death," project to be produced by Mace Wenfeld for Warner Brothers/Orion. Tentatively scheduled for late in year.

862. *L.   Awards and Nominations*

1955

THE BIG KNIFE [6] Golden Lion Award for Best Direction at the Venice Film Festival (August 25-September 8).

1956

AUTUMN LEAVES [7] Silver Bear Award for Best Direction at the Berlin Film Festival (June 22-July 3).

ATTACK! [8] Selected for screening at the Venice Film Festival (August 28-September 8).

1962

WHAT EVER HAPPENED TO BABY JANE [13] Academy Award for Best Costume Design, black and white (Norma Koch). Four Academy Award nominations: Best Actress (Bette Davis); Best Supporting Actor (Victor Buono); Best Cinematography (Ernest Haller); Best Achievement in Sound (Jack Solomon).

1963

HUSH...HUSH, SWEET CHARLOTTE [16] Seven Academy Award nominations: Best Supporting Actress (Agnes Moorehead); Best Cinematography (Joseph Biroc); Best Art Direction and Set Decoration, black and white (William Glasgow and Raphael Bretton); Best Costume Design, black and white (Norma Koch); Best Film Editing (Michael Luciano); Best Music Score (Frank De Vol); Best Song ("Hush...Hush, Sweet Charlotte," music by Frank De Vol, lyrics by Mack David).

1965

THE FLIGHT OF THE PHOENIX [17] Two Academy Award nominations: Best Supporting Actor (Ian Bannen); Best Editing (Michael Luciano).

1967

THE DIRTY DOZEN [18] Director of the Year Award from the National Association of Theater Owners. Academy Award for Best Sound Effects (John Poyner). Three Academy Award nominations: Best Supporting Actor (John Cassavetes); Best Editing (Michael Luciano); Best Sound (MGM Studio Sound Department).

1967

A Retrospective of Aldrich's work was held at the San Francisco Film Festival (week of October 21, 1967).

1973

Silver medal awarded by the Cinematheque Francaise in conjunction with a retrospective of Aldrich's films.

1978

Retrospective of Aldrich's films by the British Film Institute at National Film Theater, London.

863 *M. Citations*

1958

American representative on the Judge's Panel at the Brussels Film Festival.

1959

American representative and chairman of the Judge's Panel at the Berlin Film Festival.

1975

Elected President of the Directors Guild of America.

Film Distributors (16 mm)

864 Film Distributors (16 mm)
Argosy Film Service
1939 Central St.
Evanston, IL 60201
(312) 491-9090

     What Ever Happened To Baby Jane [13]

865 Cine-Craft Co.
1720 W. Marshall
Portland, OR 97209
(503) 228-7484

     Ulzana's Raid [24]
     What Ever Happened To Baby Jane [13]

866 Charard Motion Pictures
2110 E. 24th St.
Brooklyn, NY 11229
(212) 891-4339

     What Ever Happened To Baby Jane [13]
     Four For Texas [15]

867 The Film Center
915 Twelfth St. NW
Washington D.C. 20005
(202) 393-1205

     What Ever Happened To Baby Jane [13]
     Four For Texas [15]

868 Films Incorporated
5625 Hollywood Blvd.
Los Angeles, CA 90026
(213) 466-5481
        -and-

4420 Oakton St.
Skokie, IL 60076
(312) 676-1088

>*The Angry Hills* [10]
>*The Big Leaguer* [1]
>*The Dirty Dozen* [18]
>*The Emperor Of The North* [25]
>*The Flight Of The Phoenix* [17]
>*The Grissom Gang* [23]
>*Hush...Hush, Sweet Charlotte* [16]
>*Hustle* [27]
>*The Killing Of Sister George* [20]
>*The Legend Of Lylah Clare* [19]
>*The Longest Yard* [26]
>*What Ever Happened To Aunt Alice* [31]
>*Too Late The Hero* [22]

869 Institutional Cinema Service
915 Broadway
New York, NY 10010
(212) 673-3990

>*Four For Texas* [15]

870 Ivy Films/16
165 W. 46th St.
New York, NY 10036
(212) 765-3940

>*World For Ransom* [2]

871 Macmillan Films
34 MacQuesten Pkwy, S.
Mount Vernon, NY 10550
(914) 664-5051

>*What Ever Happened To Baby Jane* [13]
>*Four For Texas* [15]

872 Media International
30 E. Johnson St.
Madison, WI 53703
(608) 255-7221

>*What Ever Happened To Baby Jane* [13]

873 The Movie Center
57 Baldwin St.

Charlestown, MA 02129
(617) 242-3456

The Last Sunset [12]
What Ever Happened To Baby Jane [13]

874   Modern Sound Pictures
1402 Howard St.
Omaha, NB 68102
(402) 341-8476

What Ever Happened To Baby Jane [13]
Four For Texas [15]

875   Mottas Films
1318 Ohio Ave. NE
Canton, OH 44705
(216) 454-8821

What Ever Happened To Baby Jane [13]

876   National Film Service
14 Glenwood Ave.
Raleigh, NC 27602
(919) 832-3901

What Ever Happened To Baby Jane [13]

877   Roa's Films
1696 N. Astor St.
Milwaukee, WI 53202
(414) 271-0861

What Ever Happened To Baby Jane [13]

878   Select Film Library
115 W. 31st St.
New York, NY 10001
(212) 594-4500

What Ever Happened To Baby Jane [13]
Four For Texas [15]

879   Swank Motion Pictures
201 S. Jefferson Ave.
St. Louis, MO 63166
(314) 534-6300

What Ever Happened To Baby Jane [13]
Four For Texas [15]

880 Twyman Films
329 Salem Ave.
Dayton, OH 45401
(513) 222-4014

What Ever Happened To Baby Jane [13]

881 United Artists 16
729 Seventh Ave.
New York, NY 10019
(212) 575-3000

Attack! [8]
The Big Knife [6]
Kiss Me Deadly [5]
The Ride Back [30]
Ten Seconds To Hell [11]
Vera Cruz [4]

882 United Films
1425 S. Main St.
Tulsa, OK 74119
(918) 583-2681

What Ever Happened To Baby Jane [13]
Four For Texas [15]

883 Universal 16
445 Park Ave.
New York, NY 10022
(212) 759-7500

The Last Sunset [12]
Ulzana's Raid [24]

884 Warner Brothers
Non-Theatrical Division
4000 Warner Blvd
Burbank, CA 91503
(213) 843-6000

What Ever Happened To Baby Jane [13] [for lease]

885 Westcoast Films
25 Lusk St.
San Francisco, CA 94107
(415) 362-4700

What Ever Happened To Baby Jane [13]
Four For Texas [15]

886 Wholesome Film Center
20 Melrose St.
Boston, MA 02116
(617) 426-0155

> *What Ever Happened To Baby Jane* [13]
> *Four For Texas* [15]

887 Willoughby-Peerless
110 W. 32nd St.
New York, NY 10001
(212) 564-1600 or 687-1000

> *What Ever Happened To Baby Jane* [13]
> *Four For Texas* [15]

Appendix:
Interview With Robert Aldrich

INTERVIEW HISTORY

The following interview was commissioned by *Film Comment* Magazine in November, 1970, and recorded on the afternoon of December 21, 1970, in Robert Aldrich's office at the Aldrich Studios, 201 North Occidental Boulevard, Los Angeles, California. Aldrich was then in the process of supervising editing of *The Grissom Gang*. Also present during the interview was Jerry Pam, Aldrich's press agent.

This text was edited from a transcription of approximately one hour and forty-five minutes of recorded time and includes a substantial amount of material which was deleted from the published version (*Film Comment*, Spring, 1972). Also incorporated here are some remarks and observations made by Aldrich during an informal half-hour conversation after the tape recorder was turned off.

INTERVIEW

SILVER: I want to ask about your tie, which you drape around your neck the same way Barney Sheean does in *The Legend of Lylah Clare*.
ALDRICH: That's a dull joke actually. When I first came out here I used to be reasonably athletic, enough to stay in shape. Then came a time in the fifties that I put on forty pounds, and I just didn't have the time or the money to get a brand new wardrobe. So it became expeditious not to button my shirt, simply because I couldn't. By the time I had enough money to buy new shirts, it had become a habit. I don't know why they fascinate, but you hang on to those idiosyncrasies. So I gave it to Ernie Borgnine--Barney Sheehan was a poor man's Harry Cohn.
SILVER: No tape decks arrayed behind the desk?

ALDRICH: We thought about it, but it doesn't work. It only worked with Cohn.

SILVER: I was originally planning to start with the standard line about your early career as production clerk and assistant director or "How to build a small studio empire in thirty years...."

ALDRICH: Well, thanks for the small empire. But if I were starting out today, I'd marry some producer's daughter or illegitimate cousin--the only way to start in this business is at the top.

SILVER: Well, then, how *did* you get that first job directing a feature [*The Big Leaguer* for MGM]?

ALDRICH: Mayer before his decline, before he was overthrown by Dore Schary, had wanted to put the sons of the guys who helped him form Metro into production work; and they had this thing called the "sons of the pioneers," that was really the name of it. Matt Rapf was one of them. Arthur Loew was one. Three or four guys whose father had been helpful in first forming Metro. Under Schary they made seven or eight pictures.

I had been at Enterprise [Studios], and Herbert Baker, who had written one of the pictures for Kramer [*So This Is New York*], was doing a baseball picture with Matt Rapf. And Herbie told him, "There's a very bright guy in town who's done a lot of productions; he's doing television now in New York. You should get this guy--he's a very good athlete, he knows athletes." Well, there was nobody there who really had any production experience. So they were looking for "bright young guys" who'd been on the firing line for a while, someone they thought they could give an opportunity to and who knew what he was doing because they didn't. So we made that picture with Eddie Robinson in what is now Cape Kennedy in sixteen, seventeen days, out of nowhere. The world wasn't waiting for that picture. It was a picture about the New York Giants and Metro had the foresight to open it in Brooklyn, so you can't have expected it to do very well. Nothing much came out of it, and I did some more television and *World For Ransom*. Hecht and Lancaster saw *World for Ransom* and liked it; and out of that, not out of *The Big Leaguer,* came *Apache.* I had wanted to buy the [Paul I.] Wellman novel myself but couldn't afford it. Of course, United Artists and Hecht became apprehensive of that so-called downbeat ending. I had worked for Hecht-Lancaster before, under a different relationship. I was associate producer or assistant to the producer or something; but we had had a pretty good relationship.

SILVER: Did your background in economics relate in any way to those early jobs, to breaking in?

ALDRICH: It had some bearing. I broke in when they were making filmed television in New York. They really didn't know how to make filmed television there; they just didn't have a clue. All they were paying directors was scale. Who the hell wanted to go live in New York and work for scale? Only guys who had never directed or couldn't get a shot. Walter Blake, who is now associate producer on most of my pictures, convinced these people who were doing the Camay soap shows that I was a genius waiting behind a rock out here. I had been assistant director on a Chaplin picture [*Limelight*], so he told them that I had directed Chaplin. Nobody directs Chaplin except Chaplin, but these guys didn't know the difference. So I went back to New York and did, I don't know, thirty or forty shows.

SILVER: It was kind of flukish then....

ALDRICH: *Luck*, luck....

SILVER: Those few months in New York, not all the assistantships to Losey or Milestone....

ALDRICH: Not a thing. They couldn't care less. That opened the door enough for the first step inside. But otherwise it's no different than if any sergeant in the world tells a captain, "I can do the lieutenant's job"-- nobody's going to believe you.

All those years they don't mean as much as you might think they mean. They mean that much in terms of personal gratification. But your experience or knowledge doesn't really have much to do with that "trial period." And waiting out that period is always tough. Someone once said that lasting power is the most important power. Especially in this business, staying at the plate or staying at the table, staying *in* the game, is the essential. You can't allow yourself to get passed over or pushed aside. Very, very talented people got pushed aside and remained unused. That's the problem: staying at the table.

SILVER: You seem to have a fair share of luck "at the table."

ALDRICH: An old joke. Because there are so many of those talented people, if you must make a choice between luck and talent, you have to opt for luck. It's nice to have some of both, or a lot of both; but if you can't, luck is the answer. Nowhere else more so than in this business. The right place, the right time, the right script, all the right auspices--they made the difference to directors, writers, actors....

SILVER: Is it really necessary nowadays to act as your own producer in order to *remain* a director?

ALDRICH: Well, yes, you lessen the enemy. Then you only have the distributor to fight. One discovers during any kind of growth in this industry that [that's the case]. Growth is a pompous word; but we do shut our eyes to thievery--at what level do we participate? Do we endorse it? Probably we're all guilty of that, at some time.

SILVER: But has money or unwillingness to "shut your eyes" ever really hampered you?

ALDRICH: I think I made three very good movies: *The Big Knife, Attack!*, and *Kiss Me Deadly*. I worked almost for nothing, economically, on those movies. They got caught up in the system and were not profitable pictures. Things that you hoped would explode out of good movies didn't quite happen. And I came back to this country, after having made some dogs in Europe, to cash in on what I thought would see me through another period of trial, namely my considerable ownership in these former projects. They cost so little that I thought they had to have a large equity; T.V. sales, at least. I found that I had almost no equity, or at best nominal. I think my fifty percent in those three pictures was $35,000, not each but altogether, of which I had to pay a large part to my producer representative who watched the store. So you end up with $20,000 for half of three pictures; and you begin to understand, you have a graphic lesson in what the ground rules are. And they are:

you don't get yours, they get theirs. You have to divide up, between you and them or [between] you and you. You become cynical in terms of what preference to give survival and what preference to give material that might make a fine film which nobody or very few would go to see. That was the break. I realized that if you're careful in choosing projects and settling costs, your taste and knowledge will, out of every six or seven pictures, produce one that makes a good deal of profitable return for everybody. I also realized that for all the critical acclaim, *Big Knife* and *Attack!* and *Kiss Me Deadly* could not keep me in the ball game. I added a few disasters of my own after that.

SILVER: *Kiss Me Deadly* wasn't always one of your favorites?

ALDRICH: People have always said that. Because *Kiss Me Deadly*, at its depth, had to do with the McCarthy Era and the end justifying the means and the kind of materialistic society that paid off in choice rewards, sometimes money, sometimes girls, sometimes other things. But it wasn't as profound as many of the French thought it was. I did like it; it did everything I hoped it would do and more.

SILVER: You call *Kiss Me Deadly* an anti-McCarthy picture. Yet the McCarthy figure--although Stanley Hoff is basically Cohn, whom we've already mentioned, and Mayer--seems more physically present in *The Big Knife*. When Danziger raises his arm in a kind of neo-Fascist salute, "Hail, Columbia," both meanings are there.

ALDRICH: Well, of course, he [Hoff] is McCarthy. But I'm terribly ambivalent about the Hoff character. When we made *The Big Knife,* Harry Cohn and Jack Warner were still in full flower, and Mayer was only recently fallen. Nobody had seen the abyss. We'd had twenty years of petty dictators running the industry, during which time everybody worked and everybody got paid, maybe not enough, but they weren't on relief. Seventeen years later you wonder if the industry is really more healthy in terms of creativity. Are we making more or better pictures without that central control? But when everybody worked under those guys, they hated them. So we took the drumroll from Nuremburg and put it under the Hoff character's entrances and exits. It was too subtle. But, you know, Cohn took a while to realize that I did *The Big Knife.* Halfway through the "honeymoon" period when I was signed with Columbia, he asked me, "Did you do *The Big Knife?*" I said, "Yes." "You son of a bitch. If I'd known that you never would have been here." The Hoff crying came from Mayer, who is reported to have been able to cry at the drop of an option. But the big rebuff that Odets suffered was at the hands of Columbia, so there was more of Cohn in the original play than there was of Mayer.

SILVER: Why did you use long takes in *World for Ransom, Kiss Me Deadly,* and *The Big Knife?*

ALDRICH: It has a direct relation to economy and personnel. Ernie Laszlo is a very good cameraman, but his trademark isn't speed. That was a problem. *The Big Knife* was made in sixteen days, and *Kiss Me Deadly* was made in twenty-two days. If you elect to go with a cameraman that's not very, very fast, you have to, up front, make the decision that you are not going to get the kind of cutting coverage you'd normally like to have. You have to sacrifice setups and hope the performances are good enough, because they're cast in concrete. On *Attack!*, made in the same period, I wanted Joe Biroc, who is almost twice as fast. That gives you an opportunity to work with a one-camera system (which I used until the time I came back from Italy) and still get twice as much coverage. So the election of the cameraman sets a good deal of the style of the picture. You have a five or six page sequence which needs to be lighted once, and it'll take three to five times longer to light it for six or seven close-ups or cutaways--so you did it in a master.

SILVER: You have some recurring framing concepts. For example, you will place characters in close-shot foreground, say frame left, and frame right will be another figure with good definition, depth of focus, medium shot, background, and with perhaps a lamp or some other object further restricting the space. You do that in both *Big Knife* and *The Angry Hills*, just to name two. Now those are several years apart, different cameramen in different countries, and yet striking similar in visual conception. So I wondered how much time and detail you put into planning your shots, how precisely you know what you want in advance of shooting?

ALDRICH: You have--I think "style" is a pompous word--but you have a certain way of doing things. Ordinarily, when you block out the scenes, you have in mind the kind of composition that would lend itself to what you want to say in that sequence. With quick lenses, you can stage in depth, you can pose something in the foreground and build up enough to hold something else in the background. I never use Panavision lenses because the staging will fall off to such a degree that you'll have to let somebody go, either keep the guy in front sharp and forget the guy in back or dial back and forth, which is always disconcerting. When we block the scenes, we have those four ugly faces in South Dakota: the modified Rushmore, the medium Rushmore, and the Big Rushmore. A big Rushmore puts a guy right up in the foreground with somebody back there. They're just trade names, that I use with Biroc mostly because we've been together so long.

Some scenes lend themselves to that kind of framing: but you'll find with a certain kind of dialogue scene, it's not always there. And you can't bend a scene to fit the camera; it just doesn't work that way.

SILVER: Why do you use all that foreground clutter?

ALDRICH: Well, Milestone used to tell young hopefuls that there wasn't enough real interest in any frame to justify attention any longer than necessary. If you could find something to block off the concentration of the audience towards the point in the frame that interests you, if you could throw garbage in front of the camera to block off the rest of the apartment or the rest of the desert, [you might] possibly enhance the shot. You'll see Losey do it, and Dassin do it, in terms of trying to limit the area of concentration. A lot of framing is done for that reason. That isn't always the motivating [factor], but it really is better than over-the-shoulder when you want to get rid of the rest of the room and just concentrate on what somebody is answering.

SILVER: Are those the kind of shots that you block out in your mind ahead of time?

ALDRICH: When you're through blocking a scene, at the end of a rehearsal, you know pretty much where the master angle's going to be, what kind of coverage you're going to have, and, in most cases, where the camera's going to be. Now, what you don't know and what the bane of your existence is are the little things that you're going to add. When you're through with rehearsal, in theory, the script clerk should be able to give you a pretty close timing; yet it's always off by an hour. An hour because, when you actually do the scene, you add a second here or a second there, an extra bit of business here, two extra lines there. By the end of the picture you've put on sixty minutes. Now perhaps those sixty minutes will prove better or more important than sixty minutes that were in the picture originally. Probably not, but let's say twenty of those will stay and another forty will go. So, yes, you know pretty well where the camera's going to be when the time comes, but you may frequently alter or append your original conception.

SILVER: Do you actually change lines or add lines, before or during shooting, to any great extent?

ALDRICH: Well, I don't think the script is holy. We change lines all the time to make it work. I like to work very closely with the writer in the first place. I wrote the original on the Sinatra picture [*Four For Texas*]; you could change that over and over and it was still a disaster. I did the original on *Too Late the Hero*, and Lukas Heller made it a much better script. There is no frozen reverence towards what's written. That's not to say that the writer didn't conceive of a proper line in the first place. He just wasn't privy to the pressures of the moment that might bring out a better line. I say to the actors, "Look, if you're uncomfortable with the line, come up with one that you are comfortable with that says the same thing." We try it once or twice. If it works, we keep it. If it doesn't, we throw it out. It's as simple as that.

SILVER: You said once that you had a weakness for "flowery dialogue."

ALDRICH: Well, look at *The Big Knife*. At the time, I thought that kind of theatrical flavoring was extraordinary. I'm afraid neither Jim Poe nor I were tough enough in editing some of Odets' phrases as we should have been. But when Poe did *Attack!* right after that, we tried to keep the exaggerated, larger-than-life kind of attitude, in terms of speech pattern, out of it. I did two or three pictures with Hugo Butler, and he'd just go...wild.

SILVER: "Take a chance, Mr. Callahan. Love is a white bird, yet you cannot buy her."

ALDRICH: *World for Ransom*. That's Butler, He wrote that script. Funny thing. There are optimists in this society, not many left, who thought that some day those guys would get post-mortem credits for their work. So he wrote *World for Ransom,* and I put my name on it to try and get him the credit. And it went into arbitration with the Writer's Guild, and another guy [Lindsay Hardy] got total screen credit on it. It was a joke. He no more wrote that script than walked on water. Butler made that total screenplay.

SILVER: Did you have any trouble with the Marian Carr character, the overtones of perversion?

ALDRICH: We had more trouble with Madie Comfort handling the mike in *Kiss Me Deadly* than we did with that. We thought we would get in trouble with half the things in *World for Ransom*. Nobody ever questioned them; nobody seemed aware of it.... We made that picture in ten days, ten and a half days. We ran out of money and went back to do some Eversharp commercials to get enough to finish it.

SILVER: Was it envisioned as a kind of spin-off, to capitalize on the popularity of *China Smith*?

ALDRICH: We had a break in the *China Smith's*--I did quite a few of them. We had about four weeks off, and we told [Bernard] Tabakin, who was producing the series, that if he could come up with a script, we would all donate our services. I guess that's literally what we did.

SILVER: And you called Butler an optimist. How was it that you could be associated with him, Joe Losey, Chaplin, Jules Dassin, Abraham Polonsky--a large number of blacklistees--and come out unscathed?

ALDRICH: Well, you know, that's not a new question. I always answer that I was either too dumb or too young to be a Communist. If I had worked with Ring Lardner or Losey or Rossen or Polonsky or Butler or Trumbo or any of those guys, who were five or ten years older than I was, earlier, a kind of hero worship might have made it necessary for me to be a member of the Party. But by the time I got into close contact with them, the heat was already on. They were already in trouble or about to be; the handwriting was on the wall. They weren't looking for recruits. It wasn't as much a matter of converting anybody anymore as a matter of personal survival...who was going to Mexico, who was going to Paris, who was going to England. When I was assistant for a lot of them, they were on the verge of making *Music Master* shorts for Piatagorsky and Rubenstein and Hiefitz, just to get enough money to skip the country. I got served but nobody ever picked up the subpeona, and I was never called to testify. Just fortunate.

SILVER: What was the cause of your difficulties with Columbia? And *The Garment Jungle?*

ALDRICH: Very simple. Harry Kleiner had written a very, very good script. Tough as nails. I had an across-the-room relationship with Cohn; we wanted me to come there, I didn't want to come there; he had certain projects, I didn't like them. But he offered me this script, and I said fine and went to New York to start shooting.... A strange thing happened at the start. A girl I had known in New York, just a friend of a friend, called my wife to go out to lunch; and she told her, "I don't think Bob should make *Garment Jungle* until he gets it cleared." "What do you mean cleared?" She said, "Bob'll know what I mean. I can set dinner with *a guy*." My wife told me this story, and I couldn't believe it, because this "guy" was Frank Costello's right hand man. So I called Cohn and said, "That's bull-shit. We've got this cleared and there's no problem." But when I went to dinner the next night with this guy, who was very proper, very polite, terribly solicitous, he told me again, "Bob, don't make this picture. It hasn't been cleared. We'd like you to make it, no reason you shouldn't, but Mr. Cohn knows this has to be cleared." So I left for California the morning after, and I reported this to Cohn. Finally, after some hectic calls to Las Vegas, they discovered [that] a copy of the script had never been sent to be cleared. They ironed it out. But Cohn's little oversight could have caused trouble.

As time went on, Cohn became more and more apprehensive about the project. And Lee Cobb was impossible. He had just come off a big triumph in [*Death of a*]*Salesman*; he didn't want to be a rough father. He didn't want to have people dislike him. And it was necessary for him to be a tough, miserable son-of-a-bitch, not a good guy. So every day someone or other would want me to soften the script. Then I got very sick on a Thursday night, I had the flu. Five o'clock Friday afternoon, Ingo Preminger came up to see me and announced, "I don't know how to tell you this, but you're fired." I said, "You've got to be kidding." But I called up Briskin, and he wouldn't talk to me. I called up Cohn, and *he* wouldn't talk to me, so I figured I was fired.

SILVER: What was your contractual arrangement with them that caused you to be out of work for some time?

ALDRICH: Nothing. I didn't breach the contract,so they had to pay it out. They paid me, and I sat home; and I couldn't get a job. Now that year was over, and I couldn't get a job. It goes back to staying at the table. Anybody that stays away for a while, voluntarily or involuntarily, risks never coming back. Then somebody brought me *The Phoenix (Ten Seconds to Hell)*. I figured I might as well get out of town, so I rewrote it much to its detriment and went to Germany.

I stayed to make *The Angry Hills* for Raymond Stross. He understood that Metro was buying film by the yard then, and Mitchum was reasonably hot. So they thought that as long as it was an hour and a half with Mitchum and some Greek scenery, it would work. Obviously, it didn't.

SILVER: It was cut to around that length after you left, wasn't it?

ALDRICH: Yeah. That's when they really do the old-fashioned thing. You asked me about producers. Well, the Stross's of this world just hang back there and let you work your ass off, till you're all through, and then say, "Fine. Good-bye. Thank you, very much." Despite whatever promises about length or final cut they made to you, they take it back then and do what they were going to do in the first place.

SILVER: It makes that end title rather ironic: "Finis. A Raymond Stross Production." That whole question of final cut brings to mind a scene from *Lylah Clare,* the Sheean/Zarkan negotiation at the Brown Derby. I suppose part of the irony of that scene is that, for all the past problems with producers, you have come to fill both roles, Sheean's and Zarkan's, producer and director.

ALDRICH: The irony, it seems to me, is that the system, at best, just doesn't work. Sure a producer has to be judicious about handing one or three or five million dollars to someone; but once it's been done he should have enough confidence in himself, in his own choice, to back that guy. You don't have to make him a full partner, but at least support his decisions or don't go into it. In any case, are they qualified by being close enough to that material to make a judgement about cutting, six months, a year, or a year and a half later?

It's not a new moan and groan. I can tell you twenty pictures, mine included, that would be helped enormously if they were cut. But to whom are you going to entrust that task? We are in that position now with a picture that we're making for ABC. Marty Baum, who up until a year ago was an agent, runs ABC. Has he in that year learned all there is to know about cutting? And yet I know that the distributor, when I turn the picture in, will make changes. That doesn't make my life happy or worry free--because it's like having a professional who's designed a car discover that somebody's gardener is going to come along and want to change the front wheel.

SILVER: Are you satisfied with *The Legend of Lylah Clare?*

ALDRICH: I think it has a number of flaws. I was about to bum-rap Kim Novak, when we were talking about this the other day, and I realized that would be pretty unfair. Because people forget that Novak can act. I really didn't do her justice. But there are some stars whose motion picture image is so large, so firmly and deeply rooted in the public mind, that an audience comes to a movie with a preconception about that person. And that preconception makes "reality" or any kind of myth that's contrary to that preconceived reality impossible. To make this picture work, to make Lylah work, you had to be carried along into that myth. And we didn't accomplish that. Now, you know, you can blame it on a lot of things; but I'm the producer and I'm the director. I'm responsible for not communicating to that audience; *I* just didn't do it.

SILVER: Perhaps the reason I'm singling *Legend of Lylah Clare* out is that I've always had the feeling it was particularly close to you as a project. You are sitting there now with a painting of Lylah Clare hanging on the wall behind you.

ALDRICH: Yes, I always thought that picture would work. With the exception of a change of leading ladies, I'd make the same picture, tomorrow, again. Of course, it still wouldn't make money.

SILVER: Is your disappointment in it mainly financial then?

ALDRICH: No. My disappointment with it is believability. I think Kim did a very good job, but she's very angry with me. I used a German voice for her during the German period, because nobody can speak with that kind of accent, they really can't. So I brought over a German actress of some repute and worked for a long time to get it done well. Of course, she was furious because, quite properly, her ego tells her that she does a good German accent. It may be good, but it's not good enough. Things like that make the difference. So audiences never believed that picture, and that's why it didn't work. You'll find people who like bits of it--Peter Finch or the Italian women or Borgnine--and then you'll find some who took the whole concept as an affront....

SILVER: You can't help but see in it, I think, a reflection of that vulgarization which Hollywood has subjected people to. That freeze-frame at the end-- the bared fangs--is genuinely savage. More savage it seems than the whole of *The Big Knife* and perhaps more "antisocial" or "anti-establishment" in its implications than anything in *The Dirty Dozen* for all its controversy.

ALDRICH: *That* was pretty good. But you can't get too many people to agree with that. I'd agree with you...but. With *The Dozen*, two things happened. One, Heller and I stumbled onto the dissatisfaction, particularly on the part of the younger public, with the establishment. I'd like to say we anticipated that kind of success, but we didn't really. If you read the book, however, that kind of anti-authoritarian attitude, that point of view, isn't there; and Heller did an excellent screenplay. So we got on a wave that we never knew was coming; not a wave, a tidal wave. But we didn't see it forming.

SILVER: And you made a lot of money.

ALDRICH: Oh, Christ. One of the sad rewards of this business is that when money comes in that fast, some of it has to stick. Somebody has to pay you.

SILVER: What about the problems with *The Killing of Sister George*? Did you see them coming? Would that even be a problem, an "X," if you made it today?

ALDRICH: Well, I'd have to suggest that you rephrase your question. "Is that an 'X' today?" depends on who you make it for. If you made it for Metro, Mr. Valenti and his hatchet men would go and say that it was a family picture--you'd probably get a "G" for it. If you made it as an independent, it would probably still be an "X." They might consider it for an "R" or "GP," for a minute.

SILVER: Is it just that you had the bad fortune of being one of the first to arrive at the ratings board--after all that prepublicity before they realized that if all the pictures like *Sister George* were "X's" they would end up with too many on their hands?

ALDRICH: A number of things happened. You know that we tried to get ABC to join us in a suit against the [Los Angeles] *Times*, in a suit against KMPC [A Los Angeles radio station]; but they wouldn't. So we went ahead and sued the *Times* anyway, by ourselves; and we asked the Federal Communications Commission to revoke the license of KMPC, which they didn't do. Two years have gone by, and you find Valenti battling the press up in San Francisco and paraphrasing word for word our indictment about censorship of movies, which is a little ludicrous. But the big problem was that the majors never believed they could make profitable "X" pictures. They jumped to the conclusion that "X" was a dirty letter. Once *Midnight Cowboy* came out and was very profitable and won awards, they wanted to take the "dirty" label off. So they drew up a whole new bill of particulars. Everything that was made by a major studio for a cost of at least X amount of dollars suddenly had some redeeming, "artful" feature and became an "R." I guess we're the only business in the world that has retroactive legislation of that sort. But we had finished production on *Sister George* before those abc's of the "X's" were out. People think that Preminger changed the Code. That's bull shit. The Code was changed on narcotics when Fox bought *Hatful of Rain*. It was changed on profanity when Warners made *Virginia Woolf* and didn't care. It was changed on sex when Metro won that rerating on *Ryan's Daughter*. The majors, the fellows in the club, they pay the dues and they prescribe the rules. Eventually, ABC behaved a lot better over *Sister George's* rating than they did about economic issues.

SILVER: In that economic context, how did the old projects such as *Too Late The Hero* or *Lylah Clare*, the former of which you've said had been lying around in a drawer for a decade, and which quite a few people had probably pegged--correctly as it turned out--as losers, still come to be made?

ALDRICH: When you've had a big, big, success, people who should know better lose their perspective about your infallibility. Right away it's "Let's make another one!" Let's go back and buy the first novel of some guy who, ten novels later, wrote a hit. That's ludicrous. You may have better projects, but you can't sell better projects, you really can't. ABC wanted another *Dirty Dozen.* The only other "Dirty Dozen" I had in the drawer was one I wrote in 1959 with Bob Sherman. So we pulled out *Too Late The Hero,* and they thought it was sensational. So did Metro. But at Metro they wanted a budget of nine million seven [hundred thousand] to make it, which was too high. Well, we'd had *Lylah Clare* in the store for a couple of years, and Metro was in a buying mood, so I said, "What about something like *The Big Knife?*" And we made *Lylah Clare.* Now, I think we have some extraordinarily good, fresh projects. But *Hero* was less than successful, so now all our properties are scrutinized at a whole other level. It can get terribly sad, but it's true that your opinion is only as good as your last picture.

SILVER: What ever happened to *The Greatest Mother of 'Em All?*

ALDRICH: We made that mini-movie with Peter Finch, Alexandra Hay, and Ann Southern just at the time that everybody was getting very sanctimonious about sex pictures. It's a half-hour movie, like a long trailer, and I think it's pretty good. But nobody wanted this thing about a broken-down Hollywood director who found a sixteen year old girl and shacked up with her and had a heart attack, etc. We spent $90,000 getting it mounted to show people what it was all about, which I thought was an ingenious piece of showmanship, but nobody else agreed with me. I also think that it was very stupid timing. If I had been bright enough, I would have realized that the cycle had passed. Whereas a year before that picture would have sold like hot-cakes. So no more war pictures and no more "Hollywood" pictures for a while. I'm a sucker for them. I can't find any and I'm trying not to look.

SILVER: You've got *The Grissom Gang* roughly assembled now. Are you satisfied with it at this stage?

ALDRICH: I think it's a good picture. It's a personal story; but, yes, it has quite a bit of violence. Still, I think it's quite sentimental.

SILVER: How did you come to pick Scott Wilson for the picture?

ALDRICH: It was like a play-off in the National League. The system is that we had a nomination, then ABC had one, then we had one, then they had one until we had exhausted a series of three each. We had a notion of who they wanted and who they didn't. I'd seen Scott Wilson in several pictures and liked him, and of all those that ABC would be likely to nominate, he was the least objectionable. So we played the game: we nominated someone that we knew they did not like to knock off someone that they really wanted. And Again it was really luck. He is much better than the actor we originally wanted for the picture. But if ABC had put him out of sequence, nominated him in another position, we'd have ended up with somebody else, *he* would have been knocked off.

The Grissom Gang may or may not make money. It's not a commercially oriented picture. It won't make money for us because it's cross-collateralized back against our lawsuit with ABC.

We had a big western called *Rebellion*. It was at the very heart of our lawsuit with them. It was *Vera Cruz* with balls, energy, and real sex. They approved the project, they had a major commitment; and we came up with a budget of seven million dollars. Now, I don't blame them for not wanting to make the picture for seven million. I do blame them for not honoring their contract, for not trying to find a way out, a compromise solution. We spent a lot of time preparing that picture. Seven million was too big a risk for them to take on that material, from their position. And yet I think just as many people will go broke trying to make *Easy Rider* sequels, for a little money, as went broke trying to follow up *Sound of Music*. That's studio management. As with *Greatest Mother* or *Too Late The Hero*, you have to be terribly careful about not making a picture that will be affected by a change in the audience's framework of acceptance between the time you start and the time you finish. That's an enormous problem. Whatever you say today risks strongly going out of date in the fifteen month time-lag between the start of shooting and release.

SILVER: So you make *The Grissom Gang*, a thirties picture.

ALDRICH: That has something to do with it. Yes.

Indices

Author Index

[Note: References in indices are to entry rather than page numbers.]

Film Title Index

[Note: Completed features are in Italics; television programs, announced projects, and scripts are in quotation marks. References are to entry numbers. Numbers after the semicolon refer to 16mm film distributors.]